The Golden Era Cubs 1876-1940

*by Eddie Gold
and Art Ahrens*

BONUS BOOKS *Chicago, 1985*

89   88   87   86   85   5   4   3   2   1

Text photos: Supplied by Art Ahrens from his personal collection
Book Design: Productotemp, Inc./Newton Jacobson
Endpaper photo: West Side Park, 1906

Library of Congress Catalog Card Number:
85-60184

International Standard Book Number:
0-931028-66-3

Bonus Books, Inc.
160 East Illinois Street
Chicago, Illinois 60611

Printed in the United States of America

Table of Contents

Acknowledgments

The authors wish to express their heartfelt gratitude to the following: Dr. Steve Boren, L. Robert Davids, Bill Loughman, Emil Rothe, Jim Rowe, John C. Tattersall, Richard Topp, all the members of SABR, and the Chicago Public Library, where we loitered for eons looking at roll after roll of microfilm.

Foreword

For a lot of years, I've made a good living telling people about the Cubs, the White Sox, the Bears and assorted other sports organizations. I've always prided myself on doing my homework. I make it my business to know my subjects.

After reading this book, I found I don't know what homework is. Eddie Gold and Art Ahrens make me (and some of my colleagues) realize what an incomplete job we've done. They have done their homework. And how.

What fun it is to have those Cub heroes parade past us once again. What a pleasure to supplement the memories and anecdotes we knew about them with even more interesting stories we've never known before. For example, I knew the Cubs had a Hack Miller in the early '20s. I didn't know he was perhaps the strongest man in baseball history — lifted cars, bent iron bars, drove spikes with his hands, etc. And played some outstanding outfield. Because of their powerful builds, both he and the more famous Hack (Wilson) were nicknamed Hack after the famous wrestling champion, Hackenschmidt. Speaking of Wilson, what a fight that would have been had he gone through with the bout with Art "Whattaman" Shires of the White Sox. But I now learned that Judge Landis said "no".

I talked to Charlie Root who threw that famous "called shot" home run pitch to Babe Ruth in the 1932 World Series. Yet in reading this version I learned a few things he didn't tell me.

As well as I knew Cub Hall of Famer Kiki Cuyler, I didn't know till now he was a champion dancer and won several cups for waltzing.

I thought I knew Rogers Hornsby — a personal friend. Yet

I just learned that when he joined the Cubs as their new superstar his stature was such that he could demand a "perfect roommate." This meant "a man who doesn't talk in his sleep or snore; or doesn't get up early or come in late; or doesn't whistle while he's shaving — and above all doesn't keep gin in the room." Thanks to traveling secretary Bob Lewis, Hornsby got his perfect roommate. And a great double-play partner too. But I'm going to be ornery here. You'll have to read on in this book to learn his name.

Gabby Hartnett was the gabbiest catcher in the league. Ask any umpire. Yet that was not the reason for his nickname. As a rookie leaving for camp, his mother told him not to talk too much. On the train he sat next to Dean Sullivan, the Chicago sportswriter, who tried several times to start a conversation with no luck. Finally he said to young Hartnett, "you're certainly a gabby guy." And a nickname was born. Did you know that? I didn't.

Incidentally, regarding that famous "Darkness Homer" in 1938. I personally interviewed Pirate pitcher Mace Brown, catcher Al Todd and Gabby himself about that pitch. It made a good story, but the in-depth story in this book is much better.

What a hysterically funny memory came rushing back with the story of Charlie Grimm and Bobby Lewis teaming up as Hitler and Goering at the baseball writers' dinner in 1945. I was there. The skit was a last minute improvisation worthy of Second City's best. But read how it happened in Grimm's own words.

You don't have to go far to get hooked on this book. Right at the start you find yourself reading the dramatic story of Cub President William Hulbert's founding of the National League, and you wonder how they can possibly omit him from the Hall of Fame. And so it goes.

There's an old saying — if you steal from one person it's plagarism, but if you steal from enough, it's research. As a sports broadcaster for years, I've been an ardent "researcher". After all, when you have a play-by-play assignment that can use up from two to eight hours you have to utter a lot of words. As one fellow figured it, a full length novel just about every day. And you won't hold your audience by saying, "ball three . . . strike one" and "there's a routine ground ball to second" all afternoon. No, the audience wants more and by more I don't mean only statistics. They want the so-called human interest items — the athlete's background, family, hobbies, outside talents, interests, adventures, etc. — a lot of information you don't get from the press guides. There's no easy way to get it. You dig and dig and dig. After a while you wind up with a list of "research" sources you can usually count on for reliable and accurate (let me emphasize these two words) items.

When I was asked to write this foreword I had two reactions. One, I was flattered. Two, how the heck could I refuse if I wanted to? I've "researched" Eddie Gold's material for years. With the total lack of shame characteristic of broadcasters, I've called him for information and answers and never been turned down. How often that one-liner, dropped in at the right moment, has given the play or the turn at bat that little added something to spice up the narration.

Eddie Gold and Art Ahrens, the Chicago Cub historian, are listed as members of the Society for American Baseball Research. As far as I'm concerned they *are* the society. When you read this book I'm sure you'll agree.

I suppose this might be the right time to admit that Eddie, without knowing it, has gotten even with me for all that free "research" I've lifted. Eddie, that blankety-blank trivia quiz you run every Sunday in the *Sun-Times* drives me crazy! Even with multi-choice answers, if I get a passing grade (7 out of 10), I feel like buying a drink for the house. Here I am, a so-called successful big league sports broadcaster who should know the answers. Do you know what it's like to have to explain to my wife that the reason I used that kind of language (on Sunday yet!) was because I only got four out of ten and one of those was a lucky guess! What an ego-buster! Of course, once in a while I get lucky. Like solving your recent trivia question, the answer to which was "the mid-40s; University of Illinois Whiz Kids."

Well, old pal, I got that one for a good reason. I'm the one who named them the Whiz Kids. It was a play on words relating to the popular network show in those days called the Quiz Kids. I hung it on them on my WGN nightly sports show and it stuck. Later, you may remember, the same name was applied to the 1950 National League Champion Philadelphia Phillies. Oops. Here I go playing trivia with the masters. Forget it, Brickhouse!

Just do like the rest of the folks fortunate enough to read

this book. Savor the work of a couple of top pros making life more enjoyable for all of us.

Eddie and Art take us back, back, back — hey, hey, it's out of here. They've hit a home run of a book.

Jack Brickhouse
February, 1985

In 1876 the United States had 38 states, Grant was president, Custer met his end at Little Big Horn, and the Cubs were Chicago's first "White Sox" team.

First, some backtracking. After the Cincinnati Red Stockings astounded the baseball world in 1869 by declaring themselves professional, other teams followed. Since the Chicago team, founded in 1870, wore white hose, it was appropriately dubbed the White Stockings. When the first professional league, the National Association, was formed in 1871, the White Stockings contended for the championship until the Chicago Fire destroyed their lakefront ballpark. Forced to play their last three games on the road, they lost all three and finished second.

During the next two seasons, the team lapsed into semipro status. Upon reentering the National Association in 1874, the White Stockings were strictly of second division status. All the select players had been signed by Eastern clubs.

In June 1875 a local businessman, William Hulbert, purchased the team. After secretly signing star players from the East, including Boston pitcher Albert Spalding and Philadelphia infielder Adrian "Cap" Anson, Hulbert succeeded in reorganizing the association as the National League in February 1876. Thanks to Spalding, Anson, and such other key men as Ross Barnes, Paul Hines, and Cal McVey, the White Stockings won the first National League pennant.

Spalding soon retired from play to devote his time to the sporting goods firm which still bears his name. In 1879 Anson was appointed manager. Under his leadership, the White Stockings became the majors' first dynasty, reeling off pennants in 1880, '81, and '82. The lineup included such fabled names as outfielders Abner Dalrymple and George Gore, catcher-outfielder Mike "King" Kelly, infielders Tommy Burns and Ed Williamson, and pitchers Larry Corcoran and Fred Goldsmith.

Following a two year hiatus, Chicago put together two more pennants in 1885 and '86. By then, the pitching was done by John Clarkson and Jim McCormick, while superstar second baseman

The Chicago Baseball Club, 1886

Fred Pfeffer and outfield great Jimmy Ryan had been added to the team.

But Chicago's star had set. Spalding's ill-advised dealings of such standouts as Kelly, Gore, McCormick, and Clarkson left the White Stockings greatly weakened. With the old-timers being replaced by a crowd of youngsters, papers began calling them the Colts, which really caught in 1890, when most of the veterans jumped to the Players' League.

Although there were no more pennants after 1886, Chicago remained in contention for five more years, finishing second three times and third twice. In 1892, however, a serious decline set in. The club's newly appointed president, James Hart, considered Anson a relic of the past. Anson countered that Hart was unwilling to spend money and encouraged rebellion among the players. Consequently, the remainder of the century was marked more by individual achievement than by team effort.

Anson and Ryan continued to play stellar ball throughout the 1890s. They were joined by Walt Wilmot, Bill Dahlen, Clark Griffith, Bill Lange, Bill Everett and Jimmy Callahan, all of whose performances shone brightly. By 1895 unprecedented crowds of more than 20,000 began showing up at West Side Grounds, where the club had relocated two years earlier.

In 1898 Anson was fired, and for the next several years people called the team the Orphans. His successor, Tommy Burns, led the team to a strong fourth in '98, but the resurge did not last. They again sank below .500 as the 19th century drew to a close and the team approached its 25th anniversary.

Baseball's biggest blunder is the omission of William Ambrose Hulbert from its Hall of Fame. The wavy-haired, silver-tongued executive not only founded the National League, but the Chicago Cubs as well.

In 1875 the old National Association was reeking with corruption and falling apart. The presidency of the weak Chicago franchise was offered to Hulbert, a local businessman and junior executive of the club.

Before accepting, Hulbert sought out Albert Spalding, an Illinois resident who was the star pitcher of the Boston club of the National Association. Spalding agreed to play the next season for Hulbert and convinced teammates Ross Barnes, Cal McVey, and Deacon White to join. Cap Anson was another big name who joined that group.

Word spread throughout the National Association before the 1875 season ended, and there was talk of expelling those who had agreed to go with Hulbert. But Ambrose had other ideas.

He was disgusted with baseball's rampant evils. Gambling was widespread, players were frequently intoxicated, and the game was becoming demoralized. With the help of a St. Louis judge, Hulbert and Spalding drew up a formal league constitution. They also drafted a standard player contract, which was designed to do away with jumping from one club to another.

Next Hulbert invited representatives from St. Louis, New York, Hartford, Cincinnati, Boston, Philadelphia, and Louisville to tell of his plans for a new league. Hulbert represented the Chicago franchise.

The group met on a wintry February day in New York's Grand Central Hotel. Hulbert fished from his coat pocket the constitution for a new National League of Professional Baseball Clubs.

Hulbert's constitution listed the following objectives:
1. To encourage, foster, and elevate the game of baseball
2. To enact and enforce proper rules for the exhibition and conduct of the game
3. To make baseball playing respectable and honorable

The club owners wanted Hulbert to head the new league, but he urged Morgan G. Bulkeley to assume the presidency. He figured the Bulkeley name, prominent in banking and politics, would lend a touch of respectability to the game. Thus, on Feb. 2, 1876, the National League was born.

The infant circuit was off to a rocky start. The fans did not flock to the ballparks as expected, probably because Hulbert's Chicago White Stockings (forerunners to the Cubs) ran away with the pennant.

The New York and Philadelphia clubs, expecting to lose money, refused to make their final western road trips. Then it was disclosed that four Louisville players were involved in throwing games.

The situation was too much for Bulkeley. He copped out after the inaugural season. Bulkeley later became governor, then senator of the state of Connecticut.

Hulbert was immediately installed as league president, turning

WILLIAM HULBERT

HULBERT, WILLIAM AMBROSE
B. Oct. 23, 1832, Burlington Flats, N.Y.
D. April 10, 1882, Chicago, Ill.

3

over the Cubs to Spalding. He expelled the New York and Philadelphia clubs and banished the Louisville culprits for life. Louisville dropped out of the league, but Hulbert rounded up other teams and had the loop back to eight teams in 1879.

Unfortunately, the strong man of baseball became ill and died in the spring of 1882 at the age of 49. Upon his death, Hulbert was lauded in newspaper editorials. The National League passed a resolution "that to him alone is due the credit of having founded the National League, and to his able leadership, sound judgment, and impartial management is the success of the league chiefly due."

The irony of the Hulbert story is that when the pioneering executives were first elected to the Hall of Fame in 1937, in went Bulkeley, whose association with the game terminated nine months after it began. In addition, Byron Bancroft Johnson, who founded the American League in 1901, was enshrined along with Bulkeley in the second year of the balloting.

Today a Cooperstown visitor can look in awe at the bronze plaque of Bulkeley, bearing the following inscription: "First president of the National League and a leader in its organization in 1876 which laid the foundation of the national game for posterity." But he was only a front.

When will this injustice to Hulbert be rectified? Only when serious attention is focused on the origin of the National League.

Enshrinement would be like a homecoming for Hulbert, for he was born in Otsego County only a few miles from Cooperstown. Although he once said, "I'd rather be a lamppost in Chicago than a millionaire in any other city," he certainly wouldn't mind if a plaque were erected a few miles from where he was born.

The irony doesn't end in Cooperstown. Hulbert is buried in Chicago's Graceland Cemetery, only two blocks from Wrigley Field. The Cubs, beginning a new tradition, have started their own Hall of Fame. Plaques, containing a likeness of the inductee and detailing his career accomplishments, are being mounted along the Wrigley Field concourse. Who's among the missing? William Ambrose Hulbert.

ALBERT SPALDING

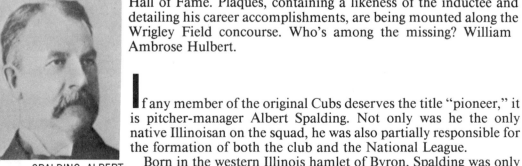

SPALDING, ALBERT
GOODWILL
B. Sept. 2, 1850,
Byron, Ill.
D. Sept. 9, 1915,
Point Loma, Calif.
BR TR 6'1" 170 lb.

If any member of the original Cubs deserves the title "pioneer," it is pitcher-manager Albert Spalding. Not only was he the only native Illinoisan on the squad, he was also partially responsible for the formation of both the club and the National League.

Born in the western Illinois hamlet of Byron, Spalding was only 15 when he began his baseball career with the semiprofessional Forest City team of Rockford. Although Spalding was officially a grocery clerk by occupation, he was actually paid to pitch. By the time he was 17, he was earning $40 a week. Over the next several years, he gained a reputation for his straight-armed, underhand fastball and his statuesque delivery.

By 1870 full-fledged professionalism was taking hold, spurred on by the example of the Cincinnati Red Stockings the year before. Quickly following suit, the Rockford club declared itself professional, as did numerous others. During a trip westward to Marshalltown, Iowa, Spalding first made the acquaintance of Adrian Anson, who would play an important part in Spalding's future.

When the National Association was formed in 1871, Spalding signed with the Boston club, which was also called the Red Stockings. Although the National Association is not today regarded as a true major league, it made Spalding the Sandy Koufax of the 1870s. Between 1872 and '75, he pitched Boston to four straight championships. The beanball and the balk (when it was still legal) were among his specialties. He won 20 games in 1871, 37 in '72, 41 in '73, 52 in '74, and 57 in '75.

In Chicago, William Hulbert purchased controlling interest of the local franchise, the White Stockings, in June 1875. Determined to build a winner, Hulbert secretly signed Spalding to pitch for Chicago the following year. Spalding, in turn, recruited Ross Barnes, Deacon White, and Cal McVey from Boston, and Cap Anson from Philadelphia. When the news hit the press, the association threatened all five with expulsion. Hulbert reassured them, however, that they were more important than the league itself.

To be certain, the association had fallen on hard times. Scheduling was piecemeal, contract jumping rampant, betting was openly flaunted at the ballparks, fans were getting increasingly rowdy, and game throwing was an everyday occurrence. Largely through Hulbert's efforts, the National Association was dissolved in favor of the National League on Feb. 2, 1876.

On the White Stocking team, Spalding was given the dual task of pitching for and managing the team. Opening day came at Louisville, April 25, 1876. Considered the first game in Cub history, Albert shut out the locals 4-0, aiding his own cause with three hits.

Deacon White was credited with the first Cub RBI when he singled home a run in the fourth inning on April 25, 1876, at Louisville. The Cubs won 4-0.

Following a successful road trip, the Cubs played their home opener May 10. As a crowd of between five and six thousand shoehorned its way into a tiny wooden enclosure at 23rd and State Streets, Spalding blanked the Reds 6-0. For the next 30 years, whenever a team was shut out, it was "Chicagoed."

Spalding pitched nearly every game for the team that fledgling season, amassing 529 innings with 46 victories and only 12 losses, whitewashing the opposition 8 times. Even with a pitching distance of only 45 feet, it was a splendid accomplishment. To add two layers of frosting on the cake, he batted .312 and the Cubs won the National League's first pennant. During his "rest" days, Spalding switched positions with first baseman Cal McVey.

Unfortunately, Al's arm went lame over the winter, forcing him to play the infield and outfield the following year. He batted only .256 that year. In 1878, with Bob Ferguson as the new manager, Spalding played only one game, going two-for-four. With that, his playing career came to an end.

Business pursuits were now Spalding's main concern. With his brother and a brother-in-law, he had already begun the sporting goods firm that still bears his name. Through his name and influence, he made sure his brand obtained exclusive use as the official National League baseball. He bought out his toughest competitor, Alfred Reach, in 1883, and the Reach label has been produced by the Spalding house ever since.

Another feature was the annual *Spalding Guide,* which sold for 10 cents and contained a thorough review of the previous baseball season, replete with commentary and statistics. In the 1890s photographs were added so that fans could view the icons of their heroes. These yearly tomes remained with the Spalding company until 1942, when *The Sporting News* assumed their publication.

Upon William Hulbert's death in 1882, Spalding assumed ownership and presidency of the Cubs. Under his regime, numerous innovations came into practice. He employed a new-fangled device—the telephone—to establish a hot line between the front office and the clubhouse, and he made refreshment vendors a regular sight at the park. Under the advice of Cap Anson, Spalding arranged baseball's first spring training for the Cubs at Hot Springs, Ark., in 1886. During the winter of 1888-89, Spalding took the Cubs and a selection of "All-Americans" on baseball's first world tour, introducing the national pastime to such far-away places as Rome, Paris, Ceylon, and Honolulu. In Egypt the players were photographed atop the Sphinx with one of the great pyramids as a backdrop.

In 1892 Spalding appointed James Hart to the club presidency, gradually withdrawing from the team's operations. This also marked the kiss of death for Anson, whose relations with Hart were mutually antagonistic from day one. Forced to choose between the two, Spalding ultimately went with Hart, announcing on Feb. 1, 1898, that Anson's contract would not be renewed. Spalding afterward sent Anson a letter purporting to offer him the club for $150,000. Anson felt that this option was not made in good faith,

West Side Grounds,
Chicago—1908

and even if it were, he would not have been able to raise the funds. Later, in what might have been an attempt to mollify his conscience, Spalding announced a public monetary tribute, which Anson refused, saying, "I am not a pauper and do not wish to be treated like one." Another proposal, to start a baseball school under Anson's tutelage, was also declined. The proud Anson, in fact, expressed his opinion that it was nothing more than a scheme to unload some unwanted real estate. After 22 years of friendship, the two parted in bitterness.

In 1902 Spalding sold out his final interests in the club to Hart and retired to Point Loma, Calif. Several years later, the *Spalding Guide* perpetrated one of the all-time myths of history when it announced that baseball had been invented in Cooperstown, N.Y., by Abner Doubleday in 1839. The "evidence," such as it was, was largely based on the testimony of one elderly man, Abner Graves, who must have been quite a storyteller. For Doubleday to have been at that place and time, he would have had to have been AWOL from West Point, where he was studying. Furthermore, Doubleday, who gained fame as a general in the Civil War, never even mentioned baseball in his memoirs, much less claimed to have invented it. Yet because of Spalding's prestige, the legend was accepted as gospel truth for nearly two generations.

Spalding's semi-autobiographical volume, *America's National Game,* published in 1911, contained a treasury of fact and folklore about the sport's embryonic days. When he died of a heart attack four years later, an era passed along with him.

Historians are divided in their evaluations of Spalding. To some, he was a Horatio Alger-type character whose straightforward honesty restored integrity to the game at a time when it was desperately needed. To others, he was simply a crafty wheeler-dealer who was out for himself, not above exploiting other people to suit his own ends. Whatever the truth, he left an indelible imprint on baseball and was enshrined in the Hall of Fame in 1946.

ROSS BARNES

BARNES, ROSCOE CONKLING
B. May 8, 1850, Mt. Morris, N.Y.
D. Feb. 8, 1915, Chicago, Ill.
BR TR 5'8½" 145 lb.

Ross Barnes was the second baseman of the original Cubs, becoming their first batting champion with a .404 average. His 138 hits, 126 runs scored, 21 doubles, and 14 triples were also tops in the league. In fact, under today's rules Barnes would have been a .429 hitter, but that season a base on balls was charged as a time at bat without a hit. On May 2 he hit the first home run in National League history, an inside-the-park smash off Bill Cherokee in Cincinnati as the Cubs crushed the Reds 15-9. His greatest day came July 27, when he went six-for-six, with a double, a triple, and three runs scored as the Cubs beat the Reds again 17-3.

Barnes's stock-in-trade was the "fair-foul" single, which was a legal safety only for that season. Any ball which bounced in fair territory when first hit, even though it might roll foul while going down the baseline, was called a "fair-foul" safety as long as the batter made it to first. Even the partisan Chicago press regarded some of Barnes's hits as "questionable" and the "fair-foul" hit was reduced to an ordinary foul the following year. Deprived of his hitting livlihood, Barnes dropped to .272 in 1877 and never again crossed the .300 level. After playing for the Reds in 1879 and the Braves in '81, Barnes retired from the game.

CAP ANSON

ANSON, ADRIAN CONSTANTINE
B. April 17, 1852, Marshalltown, Iowa
D. April 14, 1922, Chicago, Ill.
BR TR 6'1" 220 lb.

Adrian "Cap" Anson was the 19th century equivalent of "Mister Cub." With the possible exception of Ernie Banks, no other player has had such a profound influence on Cub history.

Born in a log cabin in a town founded by his father, Henry Anson, the young Adrian played with his father and his brother, Sturgis, on the Marshalltown team that defeated all comers. In 1869 he went to Notre Dame, where he organized that school's first baseball team.

Anson's academic career was short-lived. By the following year he was back in Marshalltown playing ball. In 1871 he made his professional debut with Rockford of the National Association. When the club disbanded after that season, he signed with Philadelphia, where he stayed for the next four years. In the City of Brotherly Love, Anson developed the batting skills that pitchers would grow to hate, and he met the woman he would later marry.

As we have noted, Anson came to Chicago at the urging of Albert Spalding when William Hulbert took control of the local team, the White Stockings.

The White Stockings won the new league's first pennant in 1876. Anson, stationed at third base, contributed a .343 batting average. During the off season, Anson married Virginia Fiegel and resettled in Chicago permanently.

For the next two years, Anson continued to play solid ball, but the team foundered. The turning point came in 1879, when Anson was appointed manager and switched to first base, which remained his lifelong position. At this time he was also nicknamed "Cap," an abbreviation of captain, which was synonymous with manager.

Together, Anson and Spalding assembled a squad that would soon dominate the league. In 1879 Ed Williamson, George Gore, Abner Dalrymple, and Silver Flint were added to the roster. They were joined the following year by Larry Corcoran, Fred Goldsmith, Mike Kelly, and Tommy Burns. All became first-rate performers under Anson's tutelage. Chicago clicked off three straight pennants in 1880, '81, and '82. The 1880 team won 21 consecutive games, which remained the standard until the Giants captured 26 in a row in 1916. Two more pennants were added in 1885 and '86, as the Cubs became baseball's first dynasty with five flags in seven years. By then, such outstanding performers as John Clarkson, Fred Pfeffer, and Jimmy Ryan had supplanted those who had faded earlier.

Anson paced the Cub attack with his torrid bat, winning batting championships with marks of .396 in 1879, .399 in '81, .421 in '87, and .344 in '88 (the 1887 figure was inflated by the fact that bases on balls were counted as hits that season). On July 3, 1883, Anson stroked four doubles in one game during a 31-7 romp over Buffalo. Perhaps his greatest day at the plate was Aug. 24, 1886, when he slashed five hits, including two home runs, and crossed the plate six times, as the Cubs made beans out of Boston 18-6. Generally batting in the clean-up position, Cap drove in more than 100 runs seven times in eight years between 1884 and '91, and scored 100 or more runs for six straight years (1884-89).

Cap was an outstanding place hitter who could knock the horsehide wherever he wanted to. With his cold, gray eyes and stern countenance, he intimidated many a pitcher simply by staring him down. Thanks to his pinpoint vision, Anson never struck out more than 30 times in one season. Although a slow baserunner, his reflexes were so quick that he supposedly was never hit by a pitch during his entire 22-year tenure with the Cubs.

Off the field, Anson was second to none at three cushion billiards, an expert bowler and golfer, and a crack shot with both pistol and rifle. Refusing to allow himself one iota of fat, he scrupulously avoided fried foods, starches, and rich desserts. While a heavy drinker in his early days, Anson gave up the bottle when he became serious about marriage, and remained a teetotaler thereafter. Unlike many of his teammates, he kept a celibate bed on road trips. Spalding wrote of Anson years later, "He was a man whose word was as good as his bond."

As player-manager of the Cubs for 19 years, Cap Anson was innovative in many ways but backward in others. He was the first manager to use two pitchers on a regular basis instead of one, alternating Larry Corcoran and Fred Goldsmith as early as 1880. In March 1886 he initiated the practice of spring training when he took the Cubs to Hot Springs, Ark., to "boil out their fat." Within a few years, the preseason warm-up jaunt southward was part of every team's repertoire. Some historians credit Anson with being the first to play his position away from the bag rather than with his foot glued to first base, as was the previous practice. Others, however, say that Charles Comiskey of the St. Louis Browns (American Association) was the originator of this custom.

On the negative side, Anson refused to employ the sacrifice bunt, even though it was fast becoming accepted strategy by the 1890s. He ran his team with an iron hand, imposing strict curfews and heavy fines. He was not reluctant to use fisticuffs to mete out discipline. In fairness, Anson never demanded anything that he was unwilling to do himself. Among his teammates, he had both admirers and detractors, but none could accuse him of hypocrisy. As an umpire baiter, Cap made Leo Durocher look like a Boy Scout.

A white supremacist, Anson was directly responsible for blacks being barred from major league ball. There were numerous Negroes on minor league rosters during the early 1880s, and in 1884 the Walker brothers, Moses and Welday, made it to the big time with Toledo of the American Association. The Cubs were in Toledo that year for an exhibition game. When Anson learned about the presence of blacks on the team, he threatened to take his players off the diamond, unless the blacks were removed. The Toledo management refused and Anson let it go at that. However, a similar incident took place three years later between the Cubs and Newark of the International Association, which had a star black pitcher, George Stovey. When Anson saw Stovey warming up, he protested, and the hurler left the field voluntarily.

That was the beginning of the end of baseball's first experiment at integration. A few blacks continued to reach the minors in the 1890s, but by 1900 professional ball at all levels was rigidly segregated and remained so for nearly half a century.

After winning his fifth pennant, Anson's success as a manager was limited. Nevertheless, the team stayed in contention for several more seasons, finishing third in 1887, second in '88, third in '89, and second again in 1890 and '91. All the while, the years were slowly catching up to the captain. With his hair growing thinner and his 40th birthday drawing near, fans began calling him "Pop" as well as Cap. For the first time in his career he was batting less than .300, and critics began hinting that he was too old to play and should retire.

On Sept. 4, 1891, Anson came to the plate wearing a false gray wig and whiskers, keeping them on for the rest of the game, in mockery of his detractors. Although Cap went zero-for-three, he scored once as the Cubs beat visiting Boston 5-3.

But such triumphs were fleeting as Anson's final playing years—1892 through '97—were largely unhappy. The primary reason was Albert Spalding's appointment of James A. Hart to the club presidency in 1892. Never on good terms, Hart and Anson grew increasingly hostile toward each other as time went on. Anson called Hart a tightwad, who vetoed potentially good trades, and a usurper, who undermined Anson's authority by encouraging rebellion among the players. Whoever was right or wrong, the team suffered, finishing seventh in 1892, ninth the following year, and eighth the year after that.

By 1895, with writers again suggesting that he retire, the aging hero announced, in typical Ansonian fashion, "I will play first base this year or die in the attempt." That he was still alive and well was proven by his .335 batting average. Furthermore, the team finished a surprising fourth, spurred on by such developing stars as Bill Lange, Bill Dahlen, Clark Griffith, and Bill Everett.

After another strong showing the next season, Anson felt confident that he could capture another championship in 1897. Such was not to be. Injuries to key players and dissension within the ranks toppled the Cubs back to ninth place.

Even so, the season was not without its moments. Since Anson had already announced that it would be his last year as a player, a generation of fans who had grown up with him decided to pay him tribute. The home opener, May 4, 1897, was Cap Anson Day at Chicago's West Side Grounds. The warm, sunny weather attracted a near-capacity crowd of 14,968 to the park. Among those in attendance were comedian Eddie Foy, actor Maurice Barrymore and his daughter Ethel, and Alderman John Maynard Harlan, whose son became a U.S. Supreme Court justice.

An hour before game time, the Cubs and their St. Louis opponents stood at attention along the baselines as a brass band played John Phillip Sousa's "El Capitan" in Anson's honor. Cap was then presented with a silver dining service and numerous testimonials. Anson gave simple but deep thanks to everyone, calling it "the proudest moment of my life," He saluted the Chicago fans as "friends who have never lost faith in us in our darkest hour."

Once the game was under way, Anson was given a standing ovation as he came to bat. According to newspaper accounts, the applause was so thunderous that it blotted out every other sound for two minutes. Inspired by his fans' enthusiasm, Anson singled, and to make the day more complete, the Cubs beat St. Louis 5-2.

Another personal milestone came July 18, when Anson collected the 3,000th hit of his career, a fourth inning single in a 6-3 victory over Baltimore. Finally, on Oct. 3, he became the oldest player in major league history to hit a home run, connecting twice in a 10-9 loss to the Cardinals. Finishing with a .302 batting average for the year, Anson was also the oldest player to bat .300 for a full season.

His 22-year playing career having drawn to a close, Anson retired with a .333 lifetime batting average; 3,041 hits; 532 doubles; 124 triples; and 97 home runs. He scored 1,719 runs while driving home 1,879. He is still the all-time Cub leader in hits, doubles, runs scored, and RBI. As Cub manager, he won 1,288 games while losing 944, a .577 percentage.

Following his release as Cub manager on Feb. 1, 1898, Anson briefly served as field boss of the New York Giants, but this did not last. Returning to Chicago, he published his autobiography in 1900 and devoted his time to various interests, including his downtown billiard hall. Elected City Clerk on the Democratic ticket in 1905, he was defeated in a reelection bid two years later. He then formed his own semipro team, Anson's Colts. He was still playing first base as late as 1911, when he was 59. Anson maintained an active interest in baseball to the end of his life. He was elected to baseball's Hall of Fame in 1939.

BOB FERGUSON

FERGUSON, ROBERT
B. 1845
Brooklyn, N.Y.
D. May 3, 1894,
Brooklyn, N.Y.
BB TR 5'9½"
149 lb.

Bob Ferguson was the Cub shortstop and manager in 1878. He batted .351 and piloted the team to a 30-30 mark and a fourth place finish during his only season in Chicago.

In his nine-year stay in the majors, Bob was a .271 lifetime batter. A well-traveled player, Ferguson also served—both as player and field boss—for Hartford, Brooklyn, Troy, Philadelphia, and Pittsburgh, the last mentioned being in the American Association rather than the National League.

Ferguson boasted the most unusual nickname in baseball. Because of his ability to snag line drives, he was known as "Death to Flying Things."

ABNER DALRYMPLE

DALRYMPLE, ABNER
FRANK
B. Sept. 9, 1857,
Warren, Ill.
D. Jan. 25, 1939,
Warren, Ill.
BL TR 5'10½" 175 lb.

Abner Dalrymple was the Cubs' regular left fielder for Cap Anson's greatest teams. Breaking in with Milwaukee in 1878, he batted .354 his rookie season. But the franchise folded after one season, and Abner's contract was grabbed by the Cubs.

In his first year with Chicago, Dalrymple batted .291. The next season, 1880, was his best as a Cub. He batted .330 while leading the league in hits (126) and runs scored (91). For an encore, he hit .323 the following year. Dalrymple generally batted in the lead-off spot, topping the league in times at bat on four occasions. In 1884 he became the first player in major league history to come to bat 500 times in a season, with a total of 521 official at bats. Unfortunately, he was a poor fielder also, leading the league three times in outfield errors.

Although primarily a singles hitter, Abner could also belt the long ball. When the Cubs smashed a record 14 doubles en route to a 31-7 drubbing of Buffalo on July 3, 1883, Dalrymple was at the top of the list with four, and added a single for good measure. On Sept. 27, 1884, on his way to another five-hit outing, he collected two safeties—including a homer—in a 10-run first inning as the Cubs outslugged Providence 15-10. With Cap Anson and Jimmy Ryan, "Dal" was one of three Cubs to homer in the third inning during a 20-4 walloping of St. Louis on July 20, 1886. This was the first time the Cubs hit three homers in one inning—and the last until 1929, with a far livelier ball. During the previous season, Abner's 11 homers were good enough to top the league.

Not all of Dalrymple's contributions were toward the winning of ball games, however. Anson recorded that in Abner's early days with the Cubs, he was the stingiest player on the team. He would borrow the daily newspaper from teammates rather than spend a penny for his own. Once he finally opened up, however, he became the number one spend-thrift on the team, blowing money as if it were going out of style. Dalrymple could be a tough character, also, once punching a hoodlum through a streetcar window for giving him a hard time.

In 1886 Dalrymple's batting average dipped to .233, and he was sold to the newly formed Pittsburgh franchise that winter. After two poor seasons with the Pirates (when they were known as the Alleghenies), Abner drifted out of the majors for awhile, then reemerged with the Cincinnati-Milwaukee team of the American Association in 1891. After batting .311 in 32 contests as a reserve outfielder, Dalrymple left the big time for keeps. His lifetime batting average was .288, with 1,202 hits. Living to the age of 81, he was the last of the 1886 Cub champions to pass on.

Back in the days when pitching staffs were a one-man operation (at a distance of 45 feet), Frank "Terry" Larkin performed most of the duties for the Cubs in 1878 and '79. He put together a 29-26 record the first year and a 30-23 mark the second, with innings-pitched totals of 506 and 513.

FRANK LARKIN

LARKIN, FRANK
B. Brooklyn, N.Y.
D. Sept. 12, 1894, Brooklyn, N.Y.
BR TR

Unfortunately, a tragic accident brought Larkin's career—and eventually his life—to an early end. During a practice session late in 1879, a drive off Cap Anson's bat struck Larkin on the head. He became mentally deranged as a result of the mishap. After failing in attempts to make a pitching comeback with Troy (National League) in 1880 and Richmond (American Association) in '84, Larkin spent the rest of his life in and out of insane asylums.

Larkin attempted suicide several times and finally succeeded by slashing his throat with a razor in a Brooklyn mental hospital.

His lifetime record was 89-80.

When baseball fans of the 19th century spoke of rough-hewn, hard-nosed catchers, the first name to come to mind was Frank Flint, the bulldog-faced Cub backstop of the 1880s.

FRANK FLINT

FLINT, FRANK
SYLVESTER
B. Aug. 3, 1855, Philadelphia, Pa.
D. Jan. 14, 1892, Chicago, Ill.
BR TR 5'10" 170 lb.

Flint began his career with the Indianapolis (National League) team in 1878. When the franchise folded after that season, the Cubs snatched him up, and he became a mainstay for 11 years. He was nicknamed "Old Silver," but the reasons for this moniker are unclear.

In spite of a .284 batting average in 1879 and a .310 mark two years later, Flint was not a good batsman. In fact, during his 743 major league games, Frank batted only .239. Nevertheless, he earned the admiration of friend and foe alike with his gutsy style behind the plate and his slingshot pegs to second base.

During his heyday with the Cubs, Flint caught some of the hardest-throwing pitchers in the league—Larry Corcoran, Fred

Goldsmith, and, later, John Clarkson. Often credited with being the first catcher to position himself right behind the batter, "Old Silver" snatched their pitches on the throw while others were still catching on the bounce. Refusing to wear a glove, which he considered an insult to his masculinity, Flint caught blazing fastballs, hot foul tips, and towering pop-ups with his bare hands. He went into the lineup with raw palms, stiff fingers, torn fingernails, swollen knuckles, and cracked bones; yet he never complained. Despite all this abuse, he led the league in assists in 1878, fielding average in '80, and putouts and fielding average in '85. Frank was also known to imbibe in whiskey after a hard day's work.

Perhaps the best description of the kind of character Flint was can be found in Cap Anson's memoir, *A Ballplayer's Career:*

> A pluckier man never stood behind a bat, there never coming a ball his way that was too hard for him to handle, or at least to attempt to. In "Old Silver's" day the catcher's glove had not come into use, and all of his work was done with hands that were unprotected. Those hands of his were a sight to behold, and if there is a worse pair today in the U.S., or a pair just as bad, I should certainly like to have a look at them. His fingers were bent and twisted out of all shape and looked more like the knotted and gnarled branches of a scrub oak than anything else I can think of.
>
> Long before the gloves now used by catchers were invented I had a buckskin mitt made at Spalding's that I thought would fill a long felt want, and this I finally persuaded "Old Silver" to try.
>
> He tried it for about half of an inning, then threw it down, declaring it was no good, and went on in the old way.

After 1885 Flint played less frequently because his hands were simply worn out. When he retired in 1889, he said that every joint in every one of his fingers had been broken at least once, his nose broken many times, and his teeth smashed once. Not long after leaving baseball, Flint developed tuberculosis, then incurable. He was dead within three years. His devoted wife, who nursed him through his final illness, contracted it herself and died shortly afterward.

GEORGE GORE

GORE, GEORGE F.
B. May 3, 1852,
Saccarappa, Me.
D. Sept. 16, 1933,
Utica, N.Y.
BL TR 5'11" 195 lb.

George Gore was a star Cub outfielder of the 1880s whose exploits have been forgotten thanks to the passage of a century. Breaking in with the team in 1879, Gore batted only .263 his rookie year, but player-manager Cap Anson stuck with him. The following year his batting average soared to a league-leading .360 as the Cubs coasted to an easy pennant. On May 7, 1880, George collected six hits in six at bats—all of them singles—in a 20-7 Cub win over the Providence Grays.

Gore, who generally appeared in centerfield, was known as "Piano Legs." He was a demon on the basepaths. On June 25, 1881, he set a major league record by stealing seven bases in one game.

In an unduplicated performance, Gore stole second base five times and third twice as the Cubs beat Providence 12-8. Unfortunately, stolen bases were not recorded on a daily basis at that time, so his career total will probably never be known.

The mustachioed Gore also possessed a keen batting eye and rarely struck out. He waited out his pitches, topping the league three times in bases on balls. A consistent .300 hitter, he led the club again with a .334 average in 1883 and .313 two years later. He was one of seven Cubs to collect four hits apiece in a 35-4 drubbing of Cleveland on July 24, 1882.

Finally, George etched his name into the record books again on July 9, 1885. This record—stroking five extra base hits in one game—has been tied several times. Gore amassed three doubles and two triples as the Cubs took Providence 8-5.

During the off-hours, George was a nighttime reveler. Anson noted that "wine and women were his downfall." After the Cubs lost the 1886 World Series to the St. Louis Browns (American Association), club president Albert Spalding, angered by their drinking habits, began dismantling the team. Among the first to go was Gore, who was sold to the Giants that winter.

George still had some good seasons left in him, as proven by a .305 average for the pennant-winning Giants of 1889. After jumping to the New York (Players' League) team the following year, Gore returned to the Giants in 1891. He finished up with St. Louis the year after that. In his 14-year jaunt in the majors, Gore was a .301 batter with 1,612 hits. He scored more than 100 runs seven times in his career, twice leading the league during his Cub days.

ED WILLIAMSON

Thanks to a freakish ground rule, Cub third baseman Ed Williamson held the major league record for most home runs in one season until George Herman Ruth came along. The year was 1884, when the Cubs played at Lakefront Park, situated at Michigan and Randolph in downtown Chicago. Like most enclosures of that era, the ballpark was a tiny, wooden bandbox, with the right field fence only 230 feet from home plate.

Prior to 1884, a ball hit over the right field fence was an automatic double. The Cubs used this to their advantage, topping the league in doubles for five straight years beginning in 1879. In 1883 Williamson's 49 doubles set a record which lasted several years. This included four in one game during a 31-7 drubbing of Buffalo on July 3.

In 1884 the ground rule was changed to give the batter a home run. Then the fun began. In the second game of a Memorial Day twinbill, Williamson signaled the shape of things to come when he smashed three "home runs" off Detroit in a 12-2 Cub win. It was the first time in history that a player hit three homers in a game. The feat was duplicated later in the year by Cub first baseman Cap

WILLIAMSON, EDWARD NAGLE
B. Oct. 24, 1857, Philadelphia, Pa.
D. May 3, 1894, Hot Springs, Ark.
BR TR 5'11" 170 lb.

Anson, also on the home grounds. By the end of the season, Ed had racked up 27 home runs, all but two of them at Lakefront Park. The team, meanwhile, hit 142 homers, of which only 11 came on the road. For the rest of the Cub squad, Fred Pfeffer hit 25 homers; Abner Dalrymple, 22; Anson, 21; and Mike Kelly, 13.

For decades Williamson's dubious home run record stuck out in the books like a sore thumb. Williamson's 27 was not surpassed until 1919, when Babe Ruth of the Red Sox hit 29. The Cubs' total remained the standard until it was broken by the 1927 Yankees— also led by Babe Ruth—with 158. Before the alteration of the ground rules, Williamson had never hit more than three home runs in a season, and during one year—1880—he had none at all.

In 1885 the Cubs moved to West Side Park at Congress and Loomis. Their home run total dipped to 55, but it was still good enough to lead the league. Williamson's homer output plummeted to three, after which the best he could deliver was nine in 1887. His lifetime count was a mere 63. Among Ed's teammates, the only one who came even close to his 1884 figure was Fred Pfeffer, who enjoyed 16 homers in 1887.

Unfortunately, the phoniness of Williamson's home run record has led historians to forget that which he deserves to be remembered for. Namely, Ed was one of the greatest infielders of his day, first at third base and later at short.

Williamson, who was also called "Ned," began his career with Indianapolis in 1878. He signed with the Cubs when the Hoosier team folded after that season. From 1879 through '88, Ed topped the league at his position seven times in assists, five times in double plays, four times in fielding average, twice in putouts, and twice in total chances per game. He was especially renowned for his swift and powerful throwing arm. Switched to shortstop in 1886, he made the transition gracefully despite the fact that he was gaining weight. In his early days, Ed was a good batter also, hitting .294 in 1879 and .282 in '82.

Ed was no sissy off the field either. The gang was playing poker on an off day when Anson bid with four queens. But Williamson, who had four aces, won a $95 pot. Words were exchanged and Williamson grabbed a water pitcher, threatening to test Anson's skull. The squabble was broken up before violence erupted, but perhaps the pitcher had contained something other than water.

During the winter of 1888-89, Ed accompanied his Cub teammates on baseball's first world tour. During a game in Paris on March 6, 1889, he tore his kneecap sliding into second base. Williamson did not return to the lineup until August, and he was never the same afterward, batting only .237 in 47 contests. Following another poor showing with the Chicago team of the Players' League in 1890, Ed retired with 1,159 hits and a .255 lifetime batting average.

Shortly after leaving baseball, Williamson developed dropsy. He moved to Hot Springs for his health and tended bar to earn a living. Four years later, at age 37, he died of the disease.

Tommy Burns was part of the Cubs' famous "stonewall infield" of the 1880s, first at shortstop and later at third base. Burns entered professional ball with Hornell of the National Association in 1878. He moved to Albany of the same circuit a year later. Although his minor league statistics were nothing special, the Cubs signed him to play shortstop in 1880. He responded with a strong .309 average as a rookie.

Although his batting marks fluctuated greatly over the next several years, Burns established himself as a solid performer, more through hustling and determination than through natural talent. Unlike most of his teammates, Tommy did not drink or smoke, which made him a favorite of manager Cap Anson. Meanwhile, his frequent head first dives into base made him a favorite with the fans.

Then came a day never to be forgotten—Sept. 6, 1883. On that afternoon long ago the Cubs bludgeoned visiting Detroit in the worst one-inning carnage of all time, crossing the plate 18 times in the bottom of the seventh. By the time the massacre had ceased, Tommy found himself in possession of six major league records, several of which were set concurrently by teammates Fred Pfeffer, Fred Goldsmith, Billy Sunday, and Ed Williamson. The breakdown was as follows:

- Most hits, inning-3 (also by Pfeffer, Williamson, and Gene Stephens of the Red Sox on June 18, 1953)
- Most runs, inning-3 (also by Sammy White of the Red Sox on June 18, 1953)
- Most times facing pitcher, inning-3 (also by Pfeffer, Williamson, Goldsmith, Sunday, and many others)
- Most extra base hits, inning-3 (two doubles and a home run. This one Tommy holds by himself)
- Most total bases, inning-8 (also by many others)
- Most doubles, inning-2 (also by Goldsmith and many others)

Needless to say, the Cubs won 26-6. Burns collected four hits in six at bats and scored four runs. It was also a good season for Burns, as he hit .294 with 37 doubles.

In 1886 Burns switched positions with third baseman Ed Williamson, and the hot corner turned out to be his proper niche. During the ensuing years he topped the league twice in putouts, twice in assists, and once in double plays. In 1889, Tommy was number one in all three departments.

The following year nearly the entire team deserted the Cubs in favor of the short-lived Players' League. The exceptions were Burns, Anson, and pitcher Bill Hutchison. Another historic inning came on August 16, 1890. In the fifth frame, Burns and Malachi Kittredge became the only players to hit grand slams in the same inning. The Cubs, meanwhile, exploded for a baker's dozen on the scoreboard, en route to an 18-5 scuttling of the Pirates.

The 1890 campaign turned out to be Tommy's last hurrah with his bat. His .277 average was his highest in seven years. He also

TOMMY BURNS

BURNS, THOMAS EVERETT
B. March 30, 1857, Honesdale, Pa.
D. March 19, 1902, Jersey City, N.J.
BL TR 5'9" 165 lb.

Tommy Burns and Milachi Kittredge hit grand-slam homers in the same inning for the Cubs in 1890.

reached career highs by knocking home 86 runs and scoring the same number. The next season Burns dropped to .226 in 59 games, drawing his release.

Burns signed with the Pirates as player-manager for the 1892 season, but he ran into contract problems and was fired 55 games into the schedule. He left the majors a .264 batter with 1,299 hits.

Tommy then embarked on a lengthy managerial career, serving as field boss of the Springfield club in the Eastern League from 1893 through '97. When Cap Anson was dismissed in February 1898, Burns was hired to manage the Cubs. It started off well, with the team finishing a strong fourth in 1898, but when they dropped to eighth the next season, Tommy was given the heave-ho. His record as Cub manager was 160-138.

After a one year hiatus, Burns managed Buffalo of the Eastern League for part of the 1901 season. He was under contract to manage the Jersey City team (Eastern League) when he died unexpectedly from a heart attack.

LARRY CORCORAN

CORCORAN, LAWRENCE J.
B. Aug. 10, 1859, Brooklyn, N.Y.
D. Oct. 14, 1891, Newark, N.J.
TR

Larry Corcoran was the ace of the Cubs' pitching staff during the first half of the 1880s. Joining the team a few months before his 21st birthday, Corcoran burned through the league with one of the most amazing rookie seasons of all time. Displaying a fast submarine ball (all pitching was underhand until 1884), Corcoran won an incredible 43 games while dropping only 14. He finished 57 of his 60 starts, and his 268 strikeouts led the league. Even considering that the pitching distance was only 45 feet then, it was still a remarkable achievement. Cap Anson wrote that Corcoran "had the endurance of an Indian pony."

From the very start, Larry was destined to make history. On July 8, 1880, he was the winning pitcher as the Cubs edged Providence 5-4 for their 21st straight victory, a club record. Barely a month later, he became the first Cub pitcher to hurl a no-hit game, blanking Boston 6-0 at Chicago's Lakefront Park. Finally, he won the pennant clincher Sept. 15 with a 5-2 win over the Reds at Cincinnati, helping his own cause with a clutch double.

After a season like that, it was difficult to make any kind of encore, but Corcoran did not let his fans down. He won 31 games in 1881 and 27 the next year, including a pair of 10-game winning streaks. He was a fair batsman as pitchers go and often contributed to his wins with his stick. This was especially true on June 20, 1882, when he smashed two singles, a double, and the first grand slam in Cub history during a 13-3 romp over Worcester.

That July 4, in the longest game played in Chicago up to that time, the Cubs took Troy 9-5 in 14 innings. The winning pitcher? You guessed it: Larry Corcoran. On Sept. 20 he etched his name into the books again with his second no-hitter, a 5-0 job on Worcester at Chicago.

After a 34-20 season in 1883, Corcoran pulled the no-hit trick once more on June 27, 1884, this time whitewashing Providence 6-0 at Chicago. To this date, more than a century later, Larry remains the only Cub pitcher with three no-hitters to his credit.

Meanwhile, Corcoran had induced manager Cap Anson to try his kid brother Michael. After one appearance in the pitcher's box, during which Mike yielded 16 hits, 7 walks, and 5 wild pitches during a 14-0 drubbing from Detroit, Anson decided he had seen enough. Thus the younger Corcoran's major league debut was also his finale—and not a very grand one at that. Fortunately, Larry more than compensated for it with a 35-win season.

At this point, Corcoran appeared to have the pitching world by the tail. But after winning five of seven decisions in 1885, Corcoran strained the shoulder muscles of his pitching arm, and the arm went lame. Released by the Cubs, Corcoran was signed by the Giants and later drifted to Indianapolis (then a National League franchise), making only occasional appearances. By 1887 his career was over. During his eight years in the majors, Corcoran won 177 games and lost but 90 for a winning percentage of .663, seventh highest in history. All but two of his wins came in a Cub uniform.

Like most of his teammates, Corcoran was a heavy drinker, and it put him in an early grave. He was only 32 when he died of Bright's disease in 1891.

FRED GOLDSMITH

GOLDSMITH, FRED ERNEST
B. May 15, 1852, New Haven, Conn.
D. March 28, 1939, Berkely, Mich.
BR TR 6'1" 195 lb.

In 1870, Fred Goldsmith was just an 18-year-old kid when he announced to an equally youthful baseball world that a ball could curve when thrown properly. Many thought his claim impossible; at best, they said, it could only be an optical illusion.

To convince the skeptics, Fred arranged for a public demonstration of his novel pitch. The scene was Brooklyn and the date was Aug. 16, 1870. A huge throng of fans and curiosity seekers gathered.

A chalk line was drawn along the ground for a distance of 45 feet, and three poles were staked in a straight line. Goldsmith was at one end and the catcher at the other as Fred fired his first pitch. It snaked to the right of the first pole, left of the second pole, and right of the third. He repeated it to the awe-struck crowd again and again, convincing the critics that his curve ball was no fake. In an account written by Henry Chadwick, the *Brooklyn Eagle* reported that "what had been an optical illusion is now established fact."

Goldsmith's fame spread as he pitched for semipro teams in Bridgeport and New Haven; Springfield, Mass.; and London, Ontario. In 1879 he entered the National League with Troy, but he made only a few appearances before joining the Cubs in 1880. Fred won 21 games that year and lost only 3 for a league-leading percentage of .875—the highest in Cub history, until Rick Sutcliffe broke it with a 16-1 mark (.947) in 1984.

Pitching was strictly an underhand art in those days and Goldsmith had the best underhand curve in the game, winning 24 games in 1881, 28 in '82, and 25 in '83. Thanks in no small part to Fred, the Cubs won three straight pennants, and the curve ball has since become part of nearly every hurler's repertoire.

Fred was also a fair batsman as pitchers go. On Sept. 6, 1883, he stroked two doubles in the seventh inning as the Cubs scored a record 18 runs en route to a 26-6 victory against Detroit. He became the first Cub pitcher to hit two home runs in a game, connecting in a 14-6 victory over Buffalo on May 27, 1884. The Cubs released Goldsmith late that season, after which he pitched briefly for Balitmore of the American Association before retiring. Lifetime, he was 112-68 with a 2.73 ERA.

Throughout the 19th century, Fred was universally recognized as the inventor of the curve ball, but an article in *Collier's* magazine later claimed that Arthur "Candy" Cummings originated it. Cummings was heralded and Goldsmith was forgotten, even though his claim was the more credible since he had made the first recorded public demonstration. Fred was nearing 87 when he died a forgotten man, embittered at what he regarded as a gross injustice. As legend has it, a faded newspaper clipping of his Brooklyn demonstration was found clutched in his hand when he passed away. *The Sporting News* credits Goldsmith and Cummings as having been co-inventors of the curve ball.

KELLY, MICHAEL JOSEPH
B. Dec. 31, 1857, Troy, N.Y.
D. Nov. 8, 1894, Boston, Mass.
BR TR 5'10" 180 lb.

KING KELLY

Possibly the most colorful performer to step on a diamond in the 19th century, Mike Kelly began his career with the Reds in 1878 but gained his fame as a Cub, where he spent seven lucky seasons from 1880 through '86.

Upon coming to Chicago, Kelly earned the love of the fans with his cocky, no-holds-barred style of play that drove the opposition to distraction. Soon he was the most popular man on the team with the possible exception of Cap Anson. Primarily an outfielder and catcher, Mike also appeared at all the other infield positions at one time or another. He even took a couple of turns in the pitcher's box. Nicknamed "King," he was just that in the eyes of his fans. His picture poster adorned many a saloon, pool hall, and barber shop, while cigar makers and clothiers begged for his endorsement. With his genial Irish wit, Kelly was an instant hit with men, women, and children alike.

A first-class batsman and, when sober, a good fielder as well, Kelly won the batting crown with a .354 mark in 1884 and again with a sizzling .388 in '86. He topped the league in doubles in 1882, '83, and '89 and in runs scored in 1884, '85, and '86. Kelly's 155 runs scored in 1886 was the Cub standard until Rogers Hornsby broke it, by one run only, in 1929.

One of the high points of Kelly's career was July 24, 1882, when he was one of seven Cubs to collect four hits apiece in a 35-4 romp over Cleveland. On July 3, 1883, Mike garnished five hits as the Cubs trounced Buffalo 31-7. In addition, his daring baserunning inspired "Slide, Kelly, Slide," a popular baseball song of that era.

Kelly possessed a nimble, innovative mind, devising many tricks that are today taken for granted. It was he who developed the ploy of dropping his mask in front of home plate to scare a runner considering a slide. In right field, he was the first to demonstrate that it was possible to catch a ball on the bounce and still throw the runner out at first. In the catcher's box, he taught his pitchers the value and necessity of signalling.

He employed his cleverness in devious ways, also. It was the bottom of the 12th, so the story goes, with the game tied, and the sun rapidly sinking. Once the inning was over, the game would be called because of darkness, but the enemy had the bags loaded with two out. Then the batter smashed one so deep into right field that it could not be seen in the twilight. Mike leaped, clasped his hands, and headed to the clubhouse as the umpire signalled the third out. All his teammates were smiling, but Mike was smiling even more. "That ball was a mile over me head," he grinned. Although probably legendary, this incident typified the Kelly brand of baseball.

Kelly's off-the-field antics were extraordinary, too. Although one of the best paid stars of his day, he squandered it recklessly on food, alcohol, women, friends (including the "fair weather" variety), and tailor-made suits. Whenever the gang went out drinking or womanizing, Mike was usually at the head of the pack.

By 1885 club president Albert Spalding, having heard scores of unflattering but unverified reports concerning the nighttime proclivities of Kelly and crew, hired a Pinkerton detective to check up on them. He shadowed the team for a week, following them in and out of nearly every saloon, barrelhouse, and bordello on North Clark Street.

Finally, the players were summoned into Spalding's office. On his desk was a file a couple of inches thick. Explaining that he had a report on their behavior, Spalding said, "Now, boys, what shall I do with it?"

"Read it," said one.

"Read it," echoed the rest.

Spalding had one of the players read the findings, which held the undivided attention of them all. As expected, Anson, Billy Sunday, and a couple of others were given a clean bill of health. Not so with the rest of the team. Finally, Kelly broke the silence, "I have to offer only one amendment. In that place where the detective reports me as taking a lemonade at 3 a.m., he's off. It was straight whiskey. I never drank a lemonade at that hour in my life."

Another time, while with Cincinnati, Kelly was drinking at a German beer garden in the Queen City, feeling no pain. Suddenly he stripped to his underwear, jumped into the Ohio River, and swam across into Kentucky—all on the spur of the moment. Cap Anson recorded that "the last time I ever saw him, . . . he threw in enough whiskey to throw an ordinary player under the table."

Spalding finally wearied of Kelly's clowning and on Feb. 14, 1887, sold him to Boston for the unprecedented sum of $10,000. After three productive seasons with the Braves, Kelly jumped to the Boston (Players' League) team in 1890. The new league folded after one season, and the following year Kelly found himself the player-manager of an American Association team, which came to be known as "Kelly's Killers." The fly-by-night franchise began in Cincinnati, but switched to Milwaukee in midseason, shortly after which Mike was axed. After a few games with the Boston (American Association) team, he went back to the Braves, where he finished the season. His skills were now on the wane. After one more year at Boston, he finished with the Giants in 1893. Lifetime, he was a .307 hitter with 1,820 hits.

Kelly's habits soon caught up with him. Having spent all his baseball money, he began making theatrical appearances to keep afloat. On a cold November day in 1894, Mike gave his last overcoat to a beggar before boarding a New York to Boston train in a semidrunken state. He fell ill on the trip, and upon arrival, was carried in a stretcher to Boston Emergency Hospital. A few days later, he was dead from pneumonia, shortly before turning 37. But in 1945 he attained immortality when he was named to baseball's Hall of Fame.

FRED PFEFFER

PFEFFER, NATHANIEL FREDERICK
B. March 17, 1860, Louisville, Ky.
D. April 10, 1932, Chicago, Ill.
BR TR 5' 10½" 168 lb.

Second baseman Fred Pfeffer was the cement that held together the Cubs' famed "stonewall infield" of the 1880s. Born and reared by German parents in Louisville, he became known as "the greatest Dutchman ever born on Saint Patrick's Day." That he spoke fluent German in his adult life makes it likely that his parents were immigrants.

Pfeffer began his baseball career with a hometown semipro team called the Eclipses in 1879. Three years later he made his major league debut with Troy (National League), but when the Trojans disbanded, Fred was temporarily out of work. In October, 1882, the Cubs recruited him to play shortstop for a nine-game exhibition series. Manager-first baseman Cap Anson liked what he saw, and Fred was given a contract. Since Chicago already had a large German population, Pfeffer became known as "Unser Fritz." He was probably the first Cub player of German descent.

In the following years, the quick, slender Pfeffer earned a reputation as the best pivot man in the game. Anson, who was often at odds with Fred, still said that Fred was "as good a second baseman as there was in the profession," "a brilliant player," and "a hard worker and always to be relied upon." Cub contemporary Mike Kelly said, "Fred Pfeffer was the greatest second baseman of them all. . . . He could lay on his stomach and throw a hundred yards." Charles Comiskey ranked Fred with Nap Lajoie and Eddie Collins as the greatest second basemen he had ever seen.

Fred was equally deft at moving to his left and his right. He probably covered more ground than any other infielder of his day, making diving stabs that nobody else would even attempt. From 1884 through '91 Fred topped his league (including one season in the Players' League) in putouts eight consecutive times, a mark exceeded only by Nellie Fox of the White Sox, who led nine straight times (1952-60). During the same stretch, Pfeffer led in total chances per game seven times, double plays seven times, and assists four times. He once won a gold medal for throwing a baseball 400 feet. Amazingly, he accomplished most of this without the aid of a glove. Not until 1896—near the end of his career—did he adopt the protective handgear.

Although Fred's highest batting average as a Cub was .289 in 1884, he was as dangerous as any in the clutch. On Sept. 30, 1885, Fred's seventh-inning homer provided the margin as the Cubs edged the Giants 2-1 in the pennant clincher. In the World Series against the St. Louis Browns that fall, he collected 11 hits in 27 trips for a .407 average. Another great day was June 22, 1888, when the Cubs rallied for 11 runs in the sixth inning to overcome a 6-1 deficit and defeat the visiting Pirates, 12-6. Pfeffer drove in four of the runs with a single and an inside-the-park home run. Fred also made a handful of pitching appearances, winning two out of three decisions.

Pfeffer's frequent rifts with Cub management, both on the field and in the front office, led him to join John M. Ward's Brotherhood of Professional Baseball Players, where he became Ward's right hand man in the movement. When the Brotherhood bolted in 1890 to form its own circuit, the Players' League, Fred raised $20,000 in a half hour for the effort. More significantly, almost the entire Cub team defected with him. Most of the gang joined Fred on the Chicago team of the Players' League, the Onions, while the rest signed with other clubs in the new league. Pfeffer also recruited Charles Comiskey from the St. Louis Browns to manage the new Chicago franchise.

However, the Players' League was a financial disaster and went defunct after one season—with Pfeffer losing $10,000 on the deal. Fred's contract was resumed by the Cubs, and in 1891 he was back on the scene. But Fred's relations with management had become colder than ever, for obvious reasons, and the following April 4 he was traded to the Louisville Colonels for second baseman James Canavan and cash. In Louisville Fred batted .308 in 1894 for the high mark of his career. He also managed briefly in the 1892 season, although without much success.

After four years with Louisville and an extremely short period with the Giants, Fred rejoined the Cubs on June 1, 1896, settling his former differences with Anson. By then he was slowing down, however, and was released June 30, 1897.

In his 16 big league seasons, Fred was a lifetime .255 hitter averaging a hit per game—1,671 in 1,670 contests. It is for his fielding accomplishments that he is remembered.

Fred coached baseball at the University of Wisconsin for awhile, later ran a semipro team and baseball school on Chicago's South Side, then managed Decatur of the Three-I League in 1902 before quitting the game.

In 1911 Fred opened a saloon in back of McVickers Theatre in downtown Chicago. It became a popular watering hole, and Fred had a thriving business for several years. Unfortunately, the advent of Prohibition in 1920 forced him out of business, and he became head press box custodian of the area race tracks during the summer months. This was his occupation when he died in 1932, the last of the "stonewall infield" to pass on. He is buried in All Saints Catholic Cemetery in Des Plaines, Ill., a northwest suburb of Chicago.

JOHN CLARKSON

CLARKSON, JOHN GIBSON

B. July 1, 1861, Cambridge, Mass.

D. Feb. 4, 1909, Cambridge, Mass.

BR TR 5' 10" 150 lb.

A winner of 327 major league games (ninth highest on the all-time list), John Clarkson spent a little more than three years with the Cubs, but he emerged as one of the team's greatest pitchers. In a Cub uniform he was 137-57.

After a brief trial with Worcester in 1882, Clarkson drifted to Saginaw of the Northwestern League. Cap Anson spotted him and did not want to pass him up, signing him to a contract in September 1884. On Sept. 30, Clarkson showed the baseball world what he was made of by fanning seven consecutive batters in the second, third, and fourth innings as the Cubs cut the Giants down to size 17-2 at Chicago. For the game John struck out 13, and for the season he was 10-3 with 102 whiffs in just 118 innings.

As a pitcher, Clarkson relied on a drop curve, a change-up, and an overhand fastball. (At that time many still threw underhanded.) On his pitching hand, his wrists and fingers were so well coordinated that he could spin a billiard ball around in a complete circle. Anson regarded Clarkson as the best pitcher he ever had.

Anson also discovered that Clarkson had an extremely high-strung, moody temperament. When criticized, Clarkson would refuse to pitch, but when his work was praised, John would take to the box day after day and love it. He did just that in 1885, assembling one of the most remarkable seasons ever enjoyed by a pitcher.

The Cubs began the year with two pitchers, Clarkson and Larry Corcoran, but Corcoran's arm went dead in May. John found himself pitching nearly every game until Jim McCormick was acquired late in July. In the meantime, Clarkson was piling up victory after victory.

June 6 was the Cubs' first home game of the year after more than five weeks on the road. It was also the inauguration of West Side Park at Congress and Loomis. To celebrate the christening, John went the route to beat St. Louis 7-2. By June 24, Clarkson had won his 13th consecutive game and the team its 18th as he mastered the Phillies 12-2. The following day the Phillies won, however, ending both streaks.

Clarkson's greatest game came July 27, as he held the Providence Grays hitless on their own grounds, beating them 4-0. On Sept. 19 he won his 50th game of the season by scalping the Braves 10-3 at Chicago. To top it off, John won the pennant clincher 11 days later, a 2-1 duel over Tim Keefe of the hated New York Giants. Even in 1885, the rivalry between the two teams was bitter.

For the season John won 53 games and lost only 16, fanning a league-leading 318 batters in 623 innings. He completed an incredible 68 of his 70 starts, and had an ERA of approximately 1.85. Clarkson's 10 shutouts set an all-time Cub record. His 53 wins are second in history only to Charlie Radbourn, who won 60 for Providence the previous year. Even considering that the pitching distance then was only 50 feet, it was a breath-taking achievement.

The following season Clarkson had Jim McCormick and rookie John Flynn helping him tend the pitcher's box all year, so he won "only" 36 games and dropped 17. On Aug. 18, 1886, he set a Cub record by striking out 16 batters in a 7-2 win over Kansas City. His 340 whiffs for the year also set a club high. In 1887 John was again in rare form with a 38-21 mark, which included an 11-game winning streak from June 11 through July 9.

But Cub owner Albert Spalding could not resist tempting offers for John's services. Against Anson's advice, he sold Clarkson to Boston in the spring of 1888 for $10,000. He had sold catcher Mike Kelly to the same club for an identical sum a year earlier, so the pair became known as the "$20,000 battery." John had many fine seasons ahead of him in Beantown, the best of which was a 49-19 log in 1889. In midseason 1892 he was traded to the Cleveland Spiders, where he wound up his career two years later.

Away from baseball, Clarkson became morose and embittered at life. Sulking led to despair, and he died in an insane asylum. More than half a century later, he attained baseball's equivalent of sainthood as he was enshrined in the Hall of Fame in 1963.

BILLY SUNDAY

"**C**hicago was that toddlin' town that Billy Sunday could not shut down." That song helped immortalize Sunday, who was already famous as an evangelist. But before he hit the "sawdust trail" preaching against demon rum, William Ashley Sunday ran like a demon as a ballplayer.

Billy Sunday was born in a log cabin in Ames, Iowa, on Nov. 19, 1862. He never saw his father, who died of pneumonia while serving as a soldier in the Union Army. Billy's mother, unable to support her three children, sent Billy to an orphan asylum.

Sunday's first job was with an undertaker in Marshalltown, Iowa, the hometown of Cub manager Cap Anson. Young Billy embarked on his baseball career as an outfielder on the Marshalltown team, which won two state championships.

Anson plucked Sunday off the sandlots after scouting him on the

SUNDAY,
WILLIAM ASHLEY
B. Nov. 19, 1862,
Ames, Iowa
D. Nov. 6, 1935,
Chicago, Ill.
BL TR 5' 10" 160 lb.

recommendation of his aunt. Sunday made his debut with the Chicago White Stockings on May 22, 1883. He faced Boston's Spider Jim Whitney four times and fanned four times.

Although he wasn't much of a hitter, Sunday was a brilliant outfielder and a daring baserunner. However, he didn't get on base often enough to set basestealing records. In his five seasons as a spare Cub outfielder, Sunday batted .241, .222, .256, .243, and .291.

Sunday was not a hard drinker, but he would take a little beer and wine now and then. He was converted when the hymns of a revival meeting caught his ear while he was in a saloon with teammates King Kelly and Ed Williamson. The music was emanating from the Pacific Garden Mission, which still stands today on South State Street. Sunday was so impressed as he listened to the message delivered by another evangelist that he injected prayer into his play.

The Cubs were playing Detroit for the National League pennant in 1886. It was the ninth inning and Detroit had two men on base with two out. Charlie Bennett was at bat.

"The count on Bennett was full," recalled Sunday. "Benches had been placed on the field for the overflow crowd. As the ball sailed through my territory, I realized I was going over the crowd, and I yelled, 'Get out of the way.' The crowd opened, and as I ran and leaped those benches, I said one of the swiftest prayers ever offered.

" 'Lord, if you ever helped a mortal man, help me get that ball.' I threw out my hand and the ball struck and stuck. The game was ours. I am sure the Lord helped me catch that ball. It was my first great lesson in prayer."

Sunday got his first chance to play regularly when he was sent to Pittsburgh in 1888. He actually got into 120 contests, but batted only .236. He wound up his career with the Phillies in 1890, closing with a .248 career batting average and a dozen homers.

He forsook his monthly baseball check of $400 to organize the religious activities at a Chicago YMCA at $83 per month. Sunday held that position until 1893 and then launched into evangelism on his own.

Sunday never presented anything new to his audiences, but the manner in which he delivered his sermons made him take like wildfire wherever he appeared.

On a platform, under a big revival tent, he would strip down to his shirt, with sleeves rolled up and collar off. Then he would prance, slide, run, and jump during his slam-bang fire-eating sermons as if he were body-wrestling with the devil.

To Sunday, a saloonkeeper was not just a saloonkeeper, but a "red-nosed, buttermilk-eyed, beetle-browed, peanut-brained, stall-fed, old saloonkeeper."

Reluctant foes who refused to obey his edict to "Get right with God" were "pusillanimous mutts with small brains and a large bump of conceit."

Once, in a Chicago crusade, he had his moments with young

hecklers. He blasted them as "swaggering, tough sports, with high-water pants and fingers yellow with cigarettes, and as frizzle-headed Jane kind of girls, who can't turn a flapjack without spattering the wall with batter, who are not the kind who do the world's work."

Sunday set the country ablaze with his fervent eloquence. He was also a shrewd businessman, averaging $40,000 a year while drawing his heavy fire on "rum and the devil." He always insisted that tin plates be used as contribution boxes, because a pants button won't ring like a silver dollar on a tin plate.

During his 39-year career as an evangelist, it was estimated he drew more than 85 million people. In comparison, another Billy (Graham) has faced an estimated 42 million during his crusades.

Sunday took satisfaction that many towns voted dry in the wake of his appearances. He then set about to save the sinning city of Chicago.

A huge wooden tabernacle was erected for him in 1918 at Chicago Avenue and the lakefront for a 10-week crusade. Sunday drew 1.2 million people, but at the conclusion, he admitted defeat.

"God, I can look the whole city of Chicago in the face and tell you I'm clean of the blood of every sinner, because I brought them their chance of salvation, and they wouldn't heed," sighed Sunday.

Sunday, who was thrice married and twice divorced, was saddened in his final years by the sudden death of his daughter, the suicide plunge of his son from a San Francisco hotel room, and the repeal of Prohibition.

On Nov. 6, 1935, Sunday sat in his favorite rocker in his brother-in-law's home. At 8 p.m. he put down his good book, turned to his wife, Helen (Ma) Sunday, and in a dazed look said, "Oh, I feel so dizzy." They were his last words. He was dead within minutes. Sunday was two weeks shy of his 73rd birthday.

It was said he died of nervous exhaustion. He was ill, but remained hard at work, trying to make all of his base hits home runs.

JIM McCORMICK

MCCORMICK, JAMES
B. 1856,
Paterson, N.J.
D. March 10, 1918,
Paterson, N.J.
BR TR 5' 10½" 226 lb.

Jim McCormick, who had his best seasons with the Cleveland team of the National League, pitched for the pennant-winning Cubs of 1885 and '86, posting a 20-4 record the former season and 29-11 the latter. Unbeatable when he was hot, the bulky, heavy-drinking McCormick won 14 straight in 1885 and 16 in a row the following year.

In his 10-year career, McCormick also pitched for Indianapolis, Pittsburgh, and Cincinnati (Union Association), showing a lifetime 262-215 record.

JOCKO
FLYNN

FLYNN, JOHN A.
B. June 30, 1864,
Lawrence, Mass
D. Dec. 30, 1907,
Lawrence, Mass
5' 6½" 143 lb.

As a Cub rookie in 1886, pitcher John "Jocko" Flynn helped the team to the pennant with a 24-6 record for a league-leading win-loss percentage of .800. On June 14 he fanned 13 batters en route to a 6-1 win over Kansas City, then a National League franchise.

Arm trouble felled him the following year, and after one brief appearance in the box, he dropped out of baseball, never to return.

JIMMY
RYAN

RYAN, JAMES E.
B. Feb. 11, 1863,
Clinton, Mass.
D. Oct. 28, 1923,
Chicago, Ill.
BR TL 5' 9" 162 lb.

Possibly the greatest outfielder the Cubs ever had, Jimmy Ryan is, sadly, among their most forgotten heroes. In his 18 years in the majors, Ryan collected 2,531 hits (2,102 as a Cub) and batted .310, scoring 1,640 runs. Among players who retired prior to 1910, only Cap Anson, Ed Delahanty, Jesse Burkett, Lave Cross, George Van Haltren, George Davis, and Willie Keeler had more hits.

Ryan's baseball career began in the early 1880s, when he starred for Holy Cross College. He entered professional ranks in 1885 with Bridgeport of the Eastern League and had but 29 games of experience when Cap Anson brought him up to the Cubs at the close of that season. Jimmy played his first big league game at Chicago, Oct. 8, 1885. Although he went only one-for-four as the Phillies beat the Cubs 5-3, the *Chicago Tribune* noted that "Ryan, the young Bridgeport player . . . proved himself a strong batter, a quick fielder, and very clever between the bases." The following day he went four-for-six, but Philadelphia won again, 12-11.

In 1886 Ryan gave Cub fans a hint of things to come when he batted .306 in his first year as a regular. From then through 1900, Jimmy was a Cub mainstay, except for the 1890 season, when he jumped to the Chicago (Players' League) team.

Seeing service in all three outfield positions, Ryan was one of the stellar fielders of his era. Sportswriter Hugh Fullerton, who saw him perform countless times, said, "He was known as the most accurate and clever thrower in the history of the game." The figures bear this out, as Ryan had 33 assists in 1887, a league-leading 34 in '88, 36 in '89, and 28 in '97. His 356 assists in the National League are a league record.

Excluding the 1887 season when bases on balls were counted as hits, Jimmy crossed the .300 level 13 times in his career. Although severely injured in a train wreck in 1893, he bounced back the following year with a .360 average, the highest of his career.

It was as a slugger, however, that Jimmy attained his greatest achievements, smashing 118 home runs at a time when the ball was so dead it practically had rigor mortis. Among players who retired prior to the advent of the lively ball in 1920, only nine others collected 100 or more home runs—Harry Stovey, Dan Brouthers, Sam Thompson, Roger Connor, Ed Delahanty, Hugh Duffy, Mike

28

Tiernan, Honus Wagner, and Gavvy Cravath. Of those, only Connor, Thompson, Stovey, and Cravath hit more homers than Ryan.

Included in Ryan's home run totals were 11 in 1887, a league-leading 16 in '88, 17 in '89, and 10 in '92. His six leadoff homers in 1889 were a major league record until broken in 1973 by Bobby Bonds. Since Jimmy usually batted in the leadoff spot, this prevented him from amassing a more imposing RBI total, his lifetime figure being 1,093. Still, he managed career highs of 89 in 1890, 86 in '96, and 85 in '97.

Jimmy's finest season overall was 1888, when he batted .332 and led the league in assists, home runs, hits (182), doubles (33), and slugging (.515). Furthermore, he is the only Cub player to hit for the cycle twice. He accomplished this in a 21-17 victory over Detroit July 28, 1888, and in a 9-3 win over Cleveland July 1, 1891. He scored 100 or more runs eight times in a Cub uniform, including a whopping 140 in 1889. Finally, Ryan was one of baseball's first successful relief pitchers. Seeing frequent bullpen service during the late 1880s and early '90s, Jimmy won seven games while losing one. In 1888 his pitching record was 4-0, with three of his victories coming in relief.

Ryan was a moody individual. He did not get along well with most of his teammates and manager Cap Anson, but they mellowed after their playing days had ended. Jimmy also had the distinction of being the first Cub player to assault a sportswriter. On July 1, 1892, George Bechel of the *Chicago Evening News* berated Ryan's play, after which Jimmy pummeled him, "using him up pretty badly," according to a newspaper report.

Bill Joyce, then manager of the New York Giants, said of Ryan in 1896, "Baseball patrons in Chicago should appreciate that man, for there are no better players to be found anywhere. I have admired him for years, not only for his ability on the field but as a man." And Chicago fans did appreciate him. On opening day 1899, a group presented him with a gold watch for his years of superlative play.

Following a .277 season in 1900—his lowest to that point—Ryan was released by the Cubs. After serving as player-manager for St. Paul of the Western League the following year, Jimmy made a comeback with the Washington Senators of the new American League in 1902. Although Ryan was now 39 years old, his .320 batting average was the envy of many younger players on the team. The next year, however, he dipped to .249 and left the majors for keeps.

After a one year stint as manager of the Colorado Springs Western League franchise in 1904, Jimmy returned to Chicago, where he operated a semipro team in the Rogers Park neighborhood for the next decade. He played regularly for Rogers Park as late as 1915, when he was 52. Ryan also became active in Chicago civic affairs and was serving as a deputy sheriff at the time of his death. He is buried in Calvary Cemetery (where White Sox founder Charles Comiskey also rests) in Evanston, Ill. Although he has yet to enter baseball's ultimate Valhalla in Cooperstown, where he belongs, Ryan was at last given some of the honor due him in 1982. The fans voted him into the Cubs' Hall of Fame at Wrigley Field.

GEORGE VAN HALTREN

VAN HALTREN, GEORGE EDWARD MARTIN
B. March 30, 1866, St. Louis, Mo.
D. Sept. 29, 1945, Oakland, Calif.
BL TL 5' 11" 170 lb.

To the Cubs, George Van Haltren was "the fish that got away." Joining the Cubs in 1887, he set a major league record by walking 16 batters during a game against Boston on June 27. He also hit two batsmen and heaved a wild pitch as the Braves beat the Cubs 17-11. George redeemed himself on June 21, 1888, by pitching a six-inning 2-0 no-hitter over the Pirates. Actually he pitched seven hitless innings, but the game was called because of rain with the Cubs at bat in the bottom of the seventh, so the top half did not count. As a pitcher, Van Haltren was 11-7 in 1887 and 13-13 in '88. He also roamed the outfields from time to time.

In 1889 Cap Anson made George a full-time outfielder. His true talent began to reveal itself as he batted .309 in 134 games, scoring 126 times. It looked as if the Cubs had another budding superstar, but the Brotherhood rebellion broke out and Van Haltren jumped to Brooklyn of the Players' League. The new league was crushed after one season, but Van Haltren never returned to Chicago. Instead, he drifted from Baltimore to Pittsburgh and finally (in 1894) to the Giants, where he had his greatest years. From 1893 through 1901, he batted over .300 for nine consecutive years, reaching a high of .351 in 1896. Retiring after the 1903 season, George left behind a total of 2,532 hits and a .316 batting average. As a hurler, he was 40-31. Why he has not been elected to baseball's Hall of Fame is a mystery.

HUGH DUFFY

DUFFY, HUGH
B. Nov. 26, 1866, Cranston, R.I.
D. Oct. 19, 1954, Allston, Mass.
BR TR 5' 7" 168 lb.

In 1894 little Hugh Duffy had the biggest batting average in major league history—before or since—an incredible .438. However, by that time he was a member of the Boston Braves rather than the Cubs.

An outfielder by trade, Hugh joined the Cubs in 1888 and showed the shape of things to come when he hit .305 with 12 homers the following year. But like so many others, he jumped to the Players' League in 1890, never to return to the Cubs. One of the league's best hitters in his prime, Duffy was over .300 for 10 straight years from 1889 through '98, mostly with Boston. He finished his major league career in 1906 with a .327 average and 105 home runs, an impressive total for that dead ball era. In 1945 he was elected to the Hall of Fame.

Ad Gumbert joined the Cubs as a rookie in 1888 and won 16 games the following year before jumping to the Boston team of the Players' League in 1890. Back with the Cubs the year after that, he was 17-11 that season and 22-19 in 1892. On June 30 he went the distance in a 20-inning 7-7 tie with the Reds. Gumbert later pitched for the Pirates, Dodgers, and Phillies, finishing in 1896 with a 122-102 record.

AD GUMBERT

GUMBERT, ADDISON COURTNEY
B. Oct. 10, 1868, Pittsburgh, Pa.
D. April 23, 1925, Pittsburgh, Pa.
TR

John Tener was a Cub pitcher in 1888 and '89 posting a 7-5 record his rookie season and 15-15 the next year. He jumped to the Players' League in 1890, but following one disastrous (3-11) season with the Pittsburgh club, John left baseball. He later returned briefly as an umpire.

But Tener's real talent turned out to be politics, and by 1910 he was elected governor in Pennsylvania. He later became president of the National League, serving in that capacity from 1913 to '18. He is the only ex-Cub to be elected governor of a state.

JOHN TENER

TENER, JOHN KINLEY
B. July 25, 1863, Tyrone County, Ireland
D. May 19, 1946, Pittsburgh, Pa.
BR TR 6' 4" 180 lb.

Few baseball fans are familiar with Bill Hutchison today, but in the early 1890s he was the workhorse of the Cub staff, and then some. Possibly the first Cub player with a college degree (Cap Anson had some college but did not finish), Hutchison was a graduate of Yale University, class of 1880.

Hutchison, whose father was a professor at Yale, starred on the school baseball team for three years and belonged to the Yale Glee Club, Delta Kappa, He Boule, Delta Kappa Epsilon, and Scroll and Key. He was one of the most scholarly players of his era.

Upon graduation, Bill went into the cotton manufacturing business in Biddeford, Maine, but gave it up after one year because of ill health. He later worked in an administrative position for the Burlington, Cedar Rapids, and Northern Railroad at Cedar Rapids, Iowa. Playing for the local baseball team as a weekend hobby, he earned a reputation for himself. He was signed to a Cub contract without having played in the minors.

After a 16-17 rookie year in 1889, Hutch reeled off three big seasons with records of 42-25, 43-19, and 37-34. In each of these three years, he led the league in games pitched, games started, complete games, victories, and innings pitched. His 627 innings pitched in 1892 are a club record, and an impressive statistic even considering the 50 foot pitching distance of that time.

Hutchison's best pitch was his fastball. When it was working, it worked miracles, as proven by a league-leading 316 whiffs in 1892. On the other hand, he often had trouble controlling it—a la Nolan

BILL HUTCHISON

HUTCHISON, WILLIAM FORREST
B. Dec. 17, 1859, New Haven, Conn.
D. March 19, 1926, Kansas City, Mo.
BR TR 5' 9' 175 lb.

Ryan—and earned the nickname "Wild Bill." In 1890 alone, he issued 199 free passes.

Ready to work at a moment's notice, Wild Bill made frequent relief appearances in addition to his starting assignments, picking up seven relief wins in 1891. On Memorial Day 1890 he won both ends of a morning-afternoon doubleheader with the Dodgers at Brooklyn 6-4 and 11-7. Hutch went the distance in both games, and only three of the runs made off him were earned.

In 1893 the pitching distance was increased to 60 feet, six inches, and many hurlers could not adjust to the change, Hutchison being one of them. After three great seasons, he suffered three bad ones. A 14-15 mark in 1894 was the best he could deliver. The additional pitching length aggravated Wild Bill's control problems, and his bases on balls were nearly double his strikeouts during his later years.

The Cubs released Hutchison at the end of 1895. He made a try with the Cardinals two years later, but the comeback attempt was a failure. After leaving baseball, Hutchison returned to the railroad industry, where he worked as an agent in freight trafficking until his death. A lifelong bachelor, he left no survivors.

His lifetime major league record was 183-160 with a 3.60 ERA.

JIMMY COONEY, SR.

COONEY, JAMES JOSEPH
B. July 9, 1865, Cranston, R.I.
D. July 1, 1903, Cranston, R.I.
BR TR 5' 9" 155 lb.

Jimmy Cooney, the elder half of the only father-son combo in Cub history, was a slick-fielding but weak-hitting shortstop during the early 1890s. In 1890 and '91 he had the best fielding average of all National League shortstops, and in the former season scored an impressive 114 runs.

Unfortunately for Cooney, Bill Dahlen, who could hit as well as field, was waiting in the wings, so Jimmy's days were numbered. After playing on a part-time basis in 1892, Cooney was sold to Washington, where he finished his abbreviated career the same season. In his three years in the majors, Jimmy was a .242 hitter with 315 hits and 77 stolen bases.

WALT WILMOT

WILMOT, WALTER R.
B. Oct. 18, 1863, Stevens Point, Wis.
D. Feb. 1, 1929, Stevens Point, Wis.
BB TL

In 1890 nearly the entire Cub team defected to the Players' League leaving manager Cap Anson with the task of recruiting a new team. Among the "half-broken colts" he signed to the roster was Walt Wilmot, who had led the National League in triples in 1889 with 19 for Washington, before the franchise folded. Placed in center field, Wilmot responded with a solid season, batting .278 with 14 home runs, 99 RBI and 114 runs scored. His homer total was high in the league, but as a defensive outfielder, Wilmot was only fair.

The Players' League revolt fizzled out after one season, and many former Cubs returned to Chicago in 1891. Some of the replacements of the previous year were discarded or benched, but

Wilmot remained a regular. On Aug. 22 he put himself in the record books by drawing six bases on balls in a single game, as the Cubs beat Cleveland 11-9. This feat has been matched only once, by Jimmy Foxx of the Red Sox in 1938. Three days after his walking marathon, Wilmot collected four hits in a 28-5 romp over the Dodgers.

After slumping badly in 1892, Walt came back with a .301 mark the following year, before enjoying the best season of his career. In 1894 he batted .330 in 133 games, scored 134 runs, and knocked home another 130. He stroked 45 doubles, and his 197 hits set a club record (later broken). When he fell to .283 the following year, Wilmot retired but made a comeback attempt with New York in 1897. After two seasons as a second-stringer with the Giants, he dropped out of the big time, hanging around in the minors for several more years before leaving the game.

During his 10-year stay in the majors, Walt was a .276 hitter.

In the summer of 1894, Bad Bill Dahlen put together one of the finest batting feats ever achieved by a Cub player—back-to-back hitting streaks of 42 and 28 games. His 42-game skein has been exceeded only by Willie Keeler, Joe DiMaggio, and Pete Rose.

BILL DAHLEN

DAHLEN, WILLIAM FREDERICK
B. Jan. 5, 1870, Nelliston, N.Y.
D. Dec. 5, 1950, Brooklyn, N.Y.
BR TR 5′ 9″ 180 lb.

Dahlen's heroics began June 20, when he went one-for-four in a 7-3 loss to Cleveland. At the time, he was batting only .257. By Aug. 4, Bill had hit safely in 40 straight games, bringing his average up to .329. On Aug. 6 it reached 42 with a two-for-four outing in a 12-9 win over the Reds before Cincy collared him the following day.

Not to be silenced, Dahlen embarked on another streak, which reached 28 games, before he was halted by the Dodgers on Sept. 15, thus hitting safely in 70 of 71 contests.

During his 42 game streak, Dahlen collected 74 hits in 186 at bats for a .398 average with 14 doubles, 7 triples, 4 home runs, 66 runs scored, and 44 RBI.

In his 28-game run, his totals were 49 hits in 118 at bats for a .415 mark with 7 doubles, 3 triples, 2 homers, 30 runs scored, and 12 RBI.

However, his 0-for-6 outing Aug. 7 kept his overall average for the period "down" to .397. For that year—his best—Bill hit .362 with 184 hits, 32 doubles, 14 triples, 15 homers, 150 runs scored, and 107 RBI.

His biggest day came July 5 when he went four-for-five, with three doubles, scoring five runs and driving in three in a 13-10 win against Washington.

Dahlen joined the Cubs as a third baseman in 1891 but was soon moved to shortstop, where he became one of the game's best. A rangy glove man, he was "quick as a cat" (Cap Anson's words) and boasted a strong, accurate throwing arm.

Bad Bill also had a weakness for the ponies and often got himself ejected from games deliberately so he could go to the racetrack.

Once the umpires caught onto him, however, they refused to give him the heave-ho no matter how obnoxious he acted . . . so long as he did not get too physical.

In his days as a Cub, Dahlen was a good batter, hitting .301 in 1893 and .361 in '96, along with his super season in '94. A fast man on the bases, Bill swiped many a sack and legged out many a triple. He is the only Cub player to hit three triples in a game *twice* during his career. On May 3, 1896, an overflow crowd of 17,231 at West Side Grounds forced the umpire to declare any ball hit into the crowd a ground-rule triple, with the result that the Cubs smashed nine triples—three by Dahlen—in a 16-7 romp over the Cardinals.

Circumstances made the onslaught rather dubious, but Bill repeated the act on June 6, 1898, leading the Cubs to a 15-2 win over the Dodgers at Brooklyn. Later, as a member of the Brooklynites, he tripled twice in one inning on Aug. 30, 1900.

After missing much of the 1897 season because of injuries (or was it horseraces?), Dahlen came back to bat .290 in 142 games the following year, his last as a Cub. In the winter of 1898-99, he was traded to the Baltimore Orioles (then in the National League) for shortstop Gene Demontreville, a good hitter but a bungler afield. Baltimore, in turn, sent Bill to the Dodgers that same winter. When he left Chicago, Dahlen had an eight-year .304 batting average.

Bill left his hitting shoes behind after leaving the Cubs and wound up a .275 lifetime batter, but he retained his reputation as a top-notch fielder and played regularly for another decade.

After five years of shortstopping with the Dodgers (1899-1903), four with the Giants (1904-07) and two with the Braves (1908-09), Bad Bill returned to the Dodgers as player-manager in 1910. Playing his final game the following year, he remained as nonplaying field boss through the end of 1913.

As a shortstop, Dahlen is first on the all-time list in total chances with 13,325, second in assists with 7,500, third in putouts with 4,850, and fourth in total games with 2,132. He made 2,478 hits in his major league career.

GEORGE DECKER

DECKER, GEORGE A.
B. June 1, 1869,
York, Pa.
D. June 9, 1909,
Compton, Calif.

George Decker was a Cub jack-of-all-trades utility man from 1892 through '97. In 1894, his best season, he batted .313 with 92 RBI. During a 24-6 sinking of the Pirates on July 25, Decker smashed a 500-feet home run at Chicago's West Side Grounds, although it is unclear from the newspaper accounts whether the ball went that far on the fly or on the bounce.

As the Cubs' regular left fielder in 1896 and '97, George batted .280 and .290, enjoying a 26-game hitting streak the former season. After moving on to the Cardinals in 1898, Decker had brief sojourns with Louisville and Washington before leaving the big leagues the following year, a .276 hitter with 753 hits. Ten years later, he died in a mental institution.

The date, Aug. 31, 1896; the place, Washington, D.C. It was the bottom of the 10th inning in a still scoreless duel between the Cubs and the Capitols. Suddenly Washington's Gene DeMontreville smashed a line drive to deep center, but Cub outfielder Bill Lange, never giving up on it, made a diving, somersault catch to the applause even of the partisan Washington crowd.

BILL LANGE

LANGE, WILLIAM ALEXANDER
B. June 6, 1871, San Francisco, Calif.
D. July 23, 1950, San Francisco, Calif.
BR TR 6′ 2″ 200 lb.

Earlier in the same inning, Cub first baseman George Decker had broken his wrist on a bad throw by Cub pitcher Danny Friend. Since there was a hospital adjacent to the ball park, Washington's Kip Selbach battered down several boards of the outfield fence to give Decker a quick exit.

This incident evolved into a popular legend which claimed that Lange had crashed through the fence making a catch off Selbach. Washington finally won the game 1-0 in the 11th, but it was Lange's catch that made history—in a mythological sort of way.

Lange's glovework needed no excuses, nor did his hitting or baserunning. In his brief Cub career (seven years) he made an indelible mark on the team's history. Frank Chance, Bill's teammate during his last two seasons, said, "Bill Lange's equal as a center fielder never lived." Another teammate, pitcher Clark Griffith, regarded Lange as "the greatest outfielder I ever saw."

Coming from the Oakland club of the California League, Lange joined the Cubs as a combination second baseman-outfielder in 1893, batting .281 in 117 games. From the following season until his retirement, the center field job was his, and he never hit under .319 thereafter.

A blond-haired, blue-eyed giant, Lange was a deer on his feet in spite of his 200-pound frame. He became the darling of the fans, especially the females. He stole 84 bases in 1896 and a league-leading 73 the year after.

It should be noted that prior to 1898 a player was credited with a stolen base if he advanced from first to third on a single, but Lange was a first-class thief regardless. At the peak of Ty Cobb's career, Cincinnati sportswriter W.A. Phelon said, "Despite all the praise they lavish on the Georgian today, I cannot see where the gigantic Lange was inferior. . . . I distinctly remember many of Cobb's tricks as exact duplicates of Lange's tricks, forgotten when Bill left the game, and revived long afterward by the Georgian."

In one of the last games he ever played for the Cubs, Oct. 8, 1899, Bill doubled, stole third on the next pitch, then stole home on the one after that, in a 7-3 win over Louisville.

Lange excelled with his bat also, enjoying his greatest year in 1895 when he batted a sizzling .389, scored 120 runs, smacked 10 homers, and drove 98 runs across the plate.

In fact, on Aug. 27 he was robbed of another home run by the scoring rules of that era. Coming to bat against Washington in the bottom of the 10th with a runner on second, Bill smashed one over the fence, but he was only credited with a single since the winning run was already on base. Instead of winning 6-4, the Cubs were victorious by a 5-4 margin.

Following the 1899 season, Lange bade farewell to baseball to marry the daughter of a wealthy San Francisco real estate magnate. It was no wonder that the Cubs had been begging him to stay, as he retired with a .330 batting average, 1,055 hits, and 399 stolen bases.

Once out of baseball, Lange remained just as much a ladies' man as he had ever been. Three times married and twice divorced, he was still flirting with young lasses well into his seventies.

His nephew, George Lange Kelly, had a fine career as a first baseman during the late 1910s and '20s. Although primarily remembered as a Giant, Kelly enjoyed a brief fling with his uncle's alma mater in 1930, near the end of his career.

CLARK GRIFFITH

GRIFFITH, CLARK CALVIN

B. Nov. 20, 1869, Stringtown, Mo.
D. Oct. 27, 1955, Washington, D.C.
BR TR 5' 6½" 156 lb.

Clark Griffith is best remembered as manager and later as owner of the old Washington Senators, where he was known as "The Old Fox." Few are aware that he was pretty foxy as a pitcher, too, having been the ace of the Cub staff during the tailend of the 19th century.

Following a season split between St. Louis and Boston of the American Association in 1891, Griffith drifted back to the minors before being brought up by the Cubs in September 1893. He blossomed beyond expectations, winning 20 or more games for six consecutive years, 1894 through '99.

The only other Cubs to duplicate this feat were Mordecai Brown (1906-11) and Fergie Jenkins (1967-72). Griffith's greatest season came in 1898, when he won 26 games, lost only 10, and posted a league-leading earned-run average of 1.88.

Griff had a tireless arm and generally finished what he started. He hurled 353 innings in 1895 with 39 complete games, a Cub record (since 1893, when the pitching distance became its present length of 60 feet, 6 inches) shared only by Jack Taylor (1899).

He also had an unusual superstition—he considered it bad luck to pitch a shutout! Not until Aug. 13, 1897—his sixth season in the majors—did Griffith record his first whitewash. He blanked the Reds 2-0 in spite of himself. Frank Chance recalled that when he made his Cub debut on April 29, 1898, Griffith ordered him to drop a couple of pop-ups to let a run score. As a result, the Cubs beat Louisville by a "mere" 16-2 margin instead of 16-0.

It is ironic, then, that Griffith holds the record for the longest shutout victory by a Cub pitcher—14 innings on June 19, 1900. In a classic pitchers' duel, Griff locked horns with Rube Waddell of the Pirates at the Cubs' West Side Grounds, with Waddell fanning 12 Cubs along the way. Finally, Griffith himself drove in the winning run with a single in the bottom of the 14th.

Indeed, Clark was not a bad hitter as pitchers go, reaching .319

in 1895 and .303 in 1901. On May 20, 1895, he collected five hits in five trips in a 24-6 romp over the Phillies.

In 1901 Griffith, along with teammates Jimmy Callahan and Sam Mertes, jumped to the Chicago White Sox of the newly formed American League. Not only did Clark pitch but he managed as well, leading the Sox to the league's first pennant with his 24-7 record. In 1903 he moved to the New York Highlanders (later the Yankees), winning 14 games his first year. Thereafter he began to fade, posting his last win in 1906. From there, Griffith drifted on to the Reds and finally the Senators, where he made token appearances as late as 1914.

Lifetime, Griffith was 242-131 with a 3.31 ERA.

BILL TERRY

TERRY, WILLIAM H.
B. Aug. 7, 1864,
Westfield, Mass.
D. Feb. 24, 1915,
Milwaukee, Wis.
BR TR

In the 1880s and early '90s, Bill "Adonis" Terry was a star pitcher for Brooklyn in both the American Association and the National League. After brief stays in Baltimore, and Pittsburgh, Terry came to the Cubs in 1894, slumping to 5-11. He made a strong comeback the following year, though, winning 21 and dropping 14.

As a Cub, Terry was chiefly remembered for an unusual hitting feat rather than as a pitcher. On May 19, 1895, he smashed a double and a homer in an eight-run third inning as the Cubs belted the Dodgers 14-9. His home run was a fluke, coming when the ball rolled into a hole near the outfield fence, enabling him to circle the bases.

Following a 15-13 season in 1896, Terry retired the next year after losing his only start.

Lifetime, he was a 197-195 hurler.

BILLY SCHRIVER

SCHRIVER,
WILLIAM F.
B. June 11, 1866,
Brooklyn, N.Y.
D. Dec. 27, 1932,
Brooklyn, N.Y.
BR TR 5'9½" 172 lb.

On Aug. 26, 1894, Billy Schriver became the first major league player to catch a baseball dropped from the Washington Monument, a distance of over 500 feet. What made it even more remarkable was that he caught it on the first try. The feat was later duplicated by Gabby Street and Billy Sullivan, but neither accomplished it on the first attempt.

That was Schriver's only real claim to fame in his days as a semiregular Cub catcher from 1891 through '94. He played for several other teams also, finishing with the Cardinals in 1901.

He was .264 for his career with 720 hits.

BILL EVERETT

EVERETT, WILLIAM L.
B. Dec. 13, 1868, Fort Wayne, Ind.
D. Jan. 19, 1938, Denver, Colo.
TR 6' 188 lb.

Bill Everett was a 19th century Cub infielder whose name has become obscured by the passage of time. Virtually nothing is known about him other than his statistics.

Yet he still holds the Cub record for highest batting average by a rookie—.358 in 1895. In that season, he collected 197 hits (most by a Cub in the 19th century; shared by Walt Wilmot, 1894). He also scored 129 runs, and drove in 88.

Everett never again reached the lofty totals of his first year, but he hit well over .300 from 1896 through '99. A dependable singles hitter, he led the club in hits four times, and was reputedly a good bunter as well. He was a good pal of Cub teammate Bill Dahlen, and the pair were frequent visitors at Chicago area racetracks.

Unfortunately, Everett appears to have been a liability defensively. As a third baseman, he committed 75 errors in 1895 alone while fielding only .854—a low figure even for that era. Switched to first base in 1898, he topped the league in miscues at that position the following year.

As the century turned, Everett faded from the scene rapidly. On May 17, 1900, the Cubs traded him to Kansas City of the American League (then a minor circuit) for first baseman John Ganzel. Everett played briefly for the Washington Senators in 1901, then retired.

A lifetime .317 batter, Bill collected 902 career hits.

JIMMY CALLAHAN

CALLAHAN, JAMES JOSEPH
B. March 18, 1874, Fitchburg, Mass.
D. Oct. 4, 1934, Boston, Mass.
BR TR 5'10½" 180 lb.

After a look-see with the Phillies three years earlier, Jim "Nixey" Callahan spent two seasons at Kansas City getting seasoned before coming to the Cubs in 1897. As a combination pitcher-outfielder, he created headlines almost immediately.

He was the winning pitcher on June 29, 1897, as the Cubs set an all-time scoring record in trouncing Louisville 36-7. Jimmy helped his own cause (as if he needed any) with five hits in seven trips, including two doubles, and scoring four times. For the season "Nixey" was 12-9 on the mound and batted .292 as a utility infielder-outfielder.

Callahan was used primarily as a pitcher during the next two seasons as he reached his prime, posting a 20-10 mark in 1898 and 21-12 the following year. On April 30, 1899, he blanked the Cardinals 4-0 on 12 hits at West Side Grounds before a throng of 27,489, the largest crowd to attend a baseball game in the 19th century.

After a disappointing 13-16 record in 1900, Jimmy jumped to the Chicago White Sox of the youthful American League. Putting together a 15-8 record, he helped the Sox win the junior circuit's first pennant. On Sept. 20, 1902 he hurled the first no-hitter in White Sox history, halting the Tigers 2-0 at Chicago.

The following year Callahan gave up pitching to become a full-time outfielder and White Sox manager. He batted .292 but the team finished seventh. Jimmy was relieved of his managerial duties early the next season.

In 1906 Callahan left the White Sox to form his own semipro team in Logan Square, a neighborhood on Chicago's Northwest side. It was here that he enjoyed his greatest triumph, shortly after the White Sox defeated the Cubs in the 1906 World Series.

On Oct. 20, Jimmy took the mound to defeat Nick Altrock and the Sox 2-1 going all the way. The following day, with former Cub "Long Tom" Hughes on the mound, Logan Square took the Cubs and Mordecai Brown 1-0 in 10 innings. Callahan played in the outfield, delivering the game-winning single.

In 1911 Callahan sold out his interests in the Logan Squares and returned to the White Sox. Although 37 years old and out of the majors for six years, he batted .281 and stole an incredible 45 bases. Appointed player-manager the following year, he was fired after the 1914 season.

He left behind a career pitching record of 99-73 and a .273 batting average. After managing the Pirates briefly in 1916-17, Jimmy retired from the game. He was a close friend of theatrical magnate George M. Cohan, whom he was visiting at the time of his death.

William "Barry" McCormick was a Cub infielder from 1896 through 1901, playing shortstop, second base, and third. He had no outstanding skills as a batter, fielder, or baserunner and would be totally forgotten were it not for his one day in the sun. It was June 29, 1897, as the Cubs went berserk, setting a major league record for runs scored in a 36-7 carnage over Louisville. In eight trips to the plate, McCormick collected four singles, a triple, and a home run, and he scored four times.

In 1902 McCormick defected to the St. Louis Browns of the American League, and he wound up his career two years later with the Washington Senators. Why he was nicknamed "Barry" is unknown.

BARRY MCCORMICK

MCCORMICK, WILLIAM J.
B Dec. 25, 1874, Cincinnati, Ohio
D. Jan. 28, 1956, Cincinnati, Ohio
TR

WALT THORNTON

THORNTON, WALTER MILLER
B. Feb. 28, 1875, Lewiston, Me.
D. July 14, 1960, Los Angeles, Calif.
TL

Walter Thornton was a Cub pitcher-outfielder of the late 1890s who is remembered for two 1898 contests—one a triumph, the other a disaster.

The disaster came May 18 as Thornton hit three consecutive batters in the fourth inning during an 11-4 loss to the Cardinals. But Walt redeemed himself Aug. 21, hurling a 2-0 no-hitter over the Dodgers at West Side Grounds, in the second game of a doubleheader.

Thornton joined the Cubs in 1895 but spent most of his first two seasons on the bench. He began playing on and off regularly in 1897, batting .321 in 75 games with a 6-7 pitching mark. In his "big" season, 1898, Walt was 13-10 on the mound and .295 at the plate. He was pressured out of baseball at the end of that season because of his frequent altercations with National League umpires.

DANNY GREEN

GREEN, EDWARD
B. Nov. 6, 1876,
Burlington, N.J.
D. Nov. 9, 1914,
Camden, N.J.
BL

Edward Green, nicknamed "Danny" for reasons that have been lost to history, joined the Cubs in August 1898 and displayed rare promise, batting .314 in 47 games.

Primarily a singles hitter, Green was a consistent batsman and a good baserunner, falling just under .300 the next two campaigns. He enjoyed his finest year in 1901, batting .313 with 168 hits and 31 stolen bases. Covering a lot of ground in the outfield, he topped the circuit in putouts that season with 312.

Green then jumped to Charlie Comiskey's White Sox, where he batted .312 in 1902 and .309 the following year before his hitting tapered off. After the 1905 season, he called it quits.

Green was a lifetime .293 batter with 1021 hits.

SAM MERTES

MERTES, SAMUEL
BLAIR
B. Aug. 6, 1872,
San Francisco, Calif.
D. March 11, 1945,
San Francisco, Calif.
BR TR 5'10" 185 lb.

After a brief trial with the Phillies two years earlier, Sam Mertes joined the Cubs in May 1898 and immediately became a regular.

Nicknamed "Sandow" after a popular circus strongman of that era, the muscular Mertes was primarily an outfielder, but he frequently filled in at first base as well. A consistent batter, Sam hit .297 in 1898, .298 the following year, and .295 in 1900.

He was a terror on the basepaths as well, pulling 45 steals in 1899 and 38 in 1900. Mertes was also the only player in Cub history to homer as the game's leadoff man on two consecutive days, accomplishing this on June 8 and 9, 1900.

In 1901 Mertes jumped to the crosstown White Sox, helping them win the first American League flag. Two years later he moved to the Giants, playing on John McGraw's pennant winners of 1904 and '05. He finished his career with the Cardinals the following year.

In his 10 years in the majors, Sam was a .279 hitter with 1,227 hits.

40

Pitcher Herbert "Buttons" Briggs was the only Cub player to serve under both Cap Anson (1896-97) and Frank Chance (1905), making his name a must for trivia freaks.

Briggs broke in with a 12-8 record in 1896 but slipped horribly the following year. He was shipped off to the minors early in 1898. He did not surface again until 1904, when he put together a 19-11 record for the Cubs, posting three shutouts and a splendid 2.05 ERA. His greatest performance came Sept. 18, when he went the distance to edge Cincinnati, 2-1, in 17 innings. Following a so-so year in 1905, Briggs hung up his glove.

In his short career, Briggs was 46-50.

BUTTONS BRIGGS

BRIGGS, HERBERT THEODORE
B. July 8, 1875, Poughkeepsie, N.Y.
D. Feb. 18, 1911, Cleveland, Ohio
BR TR 6'1" 180 lb.

The new century brought new problems for the Chicago Nationals. The youthful American League, declaring itself a major league, began raiding established stars from National League clubs. Among the hardest hit, the West Siders sank to a poor sixth, escaping the cellar by one game.

In 1902 Frank Selee, who had won five pennants for Boston, was named manager. Since he emphasized youth in his rebuilding program, papers began calling the team "Cubs." It took several years for the name to stick, as Colts was still in more common use at the time.

Twenty-two year old Joe Tinker became an immediate regular at short, Jimmy Slagle the center fielder, and Johnny Kling a star catcher. Carl Lundgren was recruited from the University of Illinois to beef up the pitching corps, while Selee converted back-up catcher Frank Chance to first base. Around Labor Day, an underfed Johnny Evers arrived to play second base, and on Sept. 15, 1902, the first Tinker-to-Evers-to-Chance double play was recorded. It was around this time also that Spalding sold out his final interests to James Hart.

By 1904 Selee had brought the Cubs up to second place, their best finish in 13 years. During that season pitcher Mordecai Brown and outfielder Frank Schulte were added to the team; they were joined by pitcher Ed Reulbach the following year.

On Aug. 1, 1905, Selee resigned because of failing health, after which Frank Chance was elected the new manager by the players. Charles A. Murphy, meanwhile, had purchased the club from Hart.

During the off-season the finishing touches were added as Harry Steinfeldt was acquired to play third base, Jimmy Sheckard to patrol left field, and Jack Pfiester to provide a much-needed

SECTION TWO
1901-1915
Don't Evers Tinker with Chance

The Chicago Cubs, 1908 World Champions

left-handed hurler. The pitching was strengthened even further by the acquisition of Orval Overall in 1906.

The result was an unstoppable machine that dominated the league for the next five years, winning pennants in 1906, '07, '08, and '10, plus world championships in 1907 and '08. Ironically, when the Cubs won a record 116 games, in 1906, the nominally inferior White Sox took the World Series in six games. Two years later, however, the Cubs became the first team to win two World Series after taming the Tigers twice.

By 1910 Franklin P. Adams of the *New York World* felt inspired to pen the following lines of verse:

> These are the saddest of possible words—
> Tinker to Evers to Chance.
> A trio of bear Cubs and fleeter than birds—
> Tinker to Evers to Chance.
> Ruthlessly pricking our gonfalon bubble—
> Making a Giant hit into a double—
> Words that are weighty with nothing but trouble—
> Tinker to Evers to Chance.

Wilbur Good hit the first pinch homer by a Cub in 1911.

The poem eventually helped the trio enter baseball's Hall of Fame while Harry Steinfeldt, who played third, lost his chance at immortality.

Following a crushing defeat by the Philadelphia Athletics in the 1910 World Series, age began to creep up on the Cubs as they slipped to second in 1911 and third the year after. When Murphy fired Chance in September 1912, it was the beginning of the end of an era.

Such new stars as Jimmy Archer, Heinie Zimmerman, Larry Cheney, and Hippo Vaughn provided excitement, but the team continued to decline. Managers went in and out on a revolving door basis—Evers in 1913, Hank O'Day in '14, Roger Bresnahan in '15. The club had changed hands again also, as a group headed by Charles Thomas had bought Murphy out after the 1913 season.

By 1915 the Cubs were again playing losing ball. Attendance dwindled to its lowest point in years, and their days as a West Side team were numbered.

JACK TAYLOR

TAYLOR, JOHN W.
B. Sept. 13, 1873,
Straightville, Ohio
D. March 4, 1938,
Columbus, Ohio
BR TR 5'10"
170 lb.

Although virtually forgotten today, turn-of-the-century Cub pitcher Jack Taylor set a major league record by completing 97 percent of the games he started—278 out of 286. During one stretch—from June 20, 1901, through Aug. 9, 1906—he finished all of his 187 starts, not to mention 15 relief appearances.

Taylor, who was nicknamed "Brakeman Jack" (apparently that was his off-season occupation), began his career with Connie Mack's Milwaukee Brewers of the Western League in 1897. He won 28 games the following year. This caught the attention of the Cubs, who brought him to Chicago, Sept. 25, 1898.

Jack made his big league debut a sensational one, pitching five complete games and winning all of them. The *Chicago Tribune* spoke highly of his "fast sidearm ball." In 1899 Brakeman Jack became Iron Man Jack by going 355 innings, finishing all of his 39 starts and two bullpen jobs. That season the Cub staff hurled 147 complete games for an all-time National League record.

Stardom did not come overnight, however. Plagued with control trouble during his early years, Taylor was 18-21 in 1899, followed by seasons of 10-17 and 13-19. In fairness, the mediocre records were not entirely his fault; the Cub infield had more holes than a swiss cheese. In 1900 his ERA was 2.55, third best in the league.

In 1902 Frank Selee was named Cub manager and fortunes improved both for Taylor and the team. Under Selee's tutelage, Jack realized his full potential, winning 22 games while losing only 11. In his 325 innings he threw seven shutouts (including three in succession) and posted a league-leading ERA of 1.33. His victories included a 19-inning, 3-2 win over the Pirates June 22, and a 12-inning, 1-0 whitewash of the Braves July 30. Jack followed up with a 21-14 log in 1903.

Shortly thereafter, the spectre of scandal made its appearance in Taylor's career. Club president James Hart accused him of throwing games to the crosstown White Sox in the "City Series." To be sure, Taylor's record against the seventh-place Sox was a bit suspect.

After mauling the White Sox, 11-0 in the series opener, Taylor lost his other three starts, 10-2, 9-3, and 4-2. Consequently, the series ended in a stand-off with each side winning seven games. Although the charges were never substantiated, Taylor was fined for misconduct. On Dec. 12, 1903, Taylor and catcher John McLean were traded to the Cardinals for Mordecai Brown and Jack O'Neill.

In a St. Louis uniform, Taylor was 20-19 in 1904 and 15-21 the following year with a largely untalented squad behind him. In the autumn of 1905, bribery charges surfaced again when Jack was accused of throwing games to the Browns in the St. Louis City Series. Again, the charges were not proven. Finally, on July 1, 1906, Taylor was sent back to the Cubs for Fred Beebe, Peter Noonan, and an undisclosed sum.

When traded back to Chicago, Taylor was 8-9. He then won 12 of his remaining 15 decisions to finish at 20-12. On Aug. 13 his complete game streak came to an end when lowly Brooklyn knocked him out of the box in the third frame, although the Cubs came back to win 11-3.

After the Cubs clinched the pennant, Taylor was not used in the World Series against the White Sox, probably because of his tarnished image. Dropping to 6-5 in 1907, Jack was released shortly after Labor Day, leaving behind a 150-139 record with a 2.66 ERA, although the latter figure was not compiled until decades later. He lingered on in the minors for six more years, but he was unable to make it back to the big leagues.

FRANK CHANCE

CHANCE, FRANK
LEROY
B. Sept. 9, 1877,
Fresno, Calif.
D. Sept. 14, 1924,
Los Angeles, Calif.
BR TR 6' 190 lb.

Throughout their long history, the Cubs have had many leaders, both real and otherwise, but only one has earned the proud title of "Peerless." He was Frank "Husk" Chance, first baseman and field boss when the Cubs enjoyed the most productive five year span in major league annals.

Chance's career began in 1898 when his fellow Californian, Cub outfielder Bill Lange, saw him playing for the University of Washington, where he was studying medicine. Lange recommended him to Cub president James Hart, who signed Chance to a contract.

Frank made his big league debut at Chicago, April 29, 1898, replacing catcher Tim Donahue in the late innings of a game already won. He dropped two pop-ups as the Cubs crushed Louisville 16-2. Chance did not get to bat until May 11, when he went zero-for-two against the great Cy Young of Cleveland. It was hardly an overpowering start.

For the next several years, Chance went largely unnoticed, spending most of his time on the sidelines as the Cubs second string catcher. While he displayed fair skill as a batsman and baserunner, Frank's glove work left much to be desired, especially his handling of foul tips. After four years in the majors, Chance appeared doomed to be a career back-up man.

In 1902 Frank Selee was named Cub manager, and this was the turning point in Chance's career. In the latter part of the season Selee ordered him to concentrate on playing first base instead of catching. Against his will, Chance accepted the command with the greatest reluctance.

Meanwhile, Joe Tinker had already nailed down the shortstop position, while in September the youthful Johnny Evers was given a trial at the keystone sack. During a contest against the Reds on Sept. 15, 1902, a double play was recorded that went from Tinker to Evers to Chance. Little did anyone know that a new era in Chicago baseball was dawning.

Now that Chance had adapted to his new position, nothing short of murder could tear him away from it. On his mind was one goal—to win at any cost. When Chance faced an opposing pitcher, his normally handsome features transformed into a defiant scowl, as if he were saying, "Try and stop me," to the hurler.

So insatiable was his desire for triumph that he deliberately let himself be hit by pitches to get on base. When hurt, he would merely spit tobacco juice onto the wound and go back into the game. On May 30, 1904, Chance was clipped three times in the first game and twice in the nightcap. He suffered a black eye and a cut forehead, as the Cubs split a twin bill with the Reds, losing 7-1 then winning 5-2.

Despite such abuse, Frank was now having the best performances of his career, batting .327 in 1903, followed by marks of .310, .316, and .319. His 67 stolen bases in 1903—highest by a Cub in the 20th century—were tied for the league leadership, as were his 57 steals in 1906. On June 13, 1904, he hit for the cycle in a 3-2 trimming of the Giants. At long last, Chance was fulfilling his potential.

Appointed team captain in 1904, Chance began learning the tricks of the managerial trade. When Selee's health began to fail the following year, Chance served as interim leader during road trips. With the resignation of the consumption-racked Selee on Aug. 1, 1905, Chance was elected manager by a narrow margin among the players.

At the time the Cubs were in fourth place with a 52-38 log. Spurred on by Chance's leadership, they won 40 of their last 63 games to finish a strong third with 92-61. But the best was yet to come.

With his added responsibilities, Chance's drive to win burned brighter than ever. The tone of the Chance reign was set on April 28, 1906, when he stole home with two out in the bottom of the ninth to beat the Reds 1-0. From that point on, the season belonged to the Cubs as they piled up 116 victories—still the major league record—finishing 20 games ahead of the second place Giants.

Germany Schaefer was the third baseman when Joe Tinker, Johnny Evers, and Frank Chance played their first game together.

On the other side of town, the White Sox were winning the pennant also as Chicago prepared for its only subway World Series. With their anemic team batting average of .230, the Sox—dubbed the "Hitless Wonders"—were expected to be putty in the Cubs' hands. Such was not the case, though. Charles Comiskey's band upset the proud Cubs in six games. Chance, who hated the Sox with a passion, admitted defeat grudgingly:

> The Sox played grand, game baseball and outclassed us in this series. . . . But there is one thing that I will never believe and that is that the White Sox are better than the Cubs.

Undaunted by this defeat, Chance and his warriors marched to further flags in 1907, '08, and '10, with back-to-back World Series victories over the Tigers the two former years. In the 1908 World Series, Frank was one of the batting heroes with a .421 batting average and five stolen bases.

The following year the Cubs barely missed another pennant, winning 104 games as runner-up to the Pirates, who totaled 110 wins. All in all, from 1906 through '10, the Cubs won 530 games and lost only 235 for a .693 percentage, the most lavish five year splurge ever recorded. Small wonder Chance was called "the Peerless Leader."

As a former catcher, Chance was renowned for his finesse at handling pitchers, often holding up a game for minutes at a time to steady a nervous hurler.

He was also a stern disciplinarian, not averse to using his fists to bring a message home to an unruly player. "Play it my way or meet me after the game" was his motto. He once pulverized Heinie Zimmerman, 10 years his junior, for daring to challenge his authority.

Opposing players and fans dared not obstruct his path. Chance started a riot at the Polo Grounds once by slugging Giant ace Joe McGinnity. Another time—on July 8, 1907—Chance became angered at Brooklyn loyalists throwing pop bottles at the Cubs, so he began heaving them back, lacerating one fan in the leg. When the game ended in a 5-0 Cub victory, Husk had to escape the mob in an armored car surrounded by police.

In 1909 Chance suffered a broken shoulder, which was the beginning of the end of his days as a regular. Soon afterward, his mighty Cub machine began to show signs of aging. After being steamrolled by the Athletics in the 1910 World Series, the Cubs slipped to second in '11 and third the year after.

By this time, Frank had surrendered his first base job to Vic Saier. He was also having contract difficulties with owner Charles Murphy. When Murphy charged the team with drinking and carousing too much, Chance countered by calling Murphy a cheapskate, who was only interested in milking the club. On Sept. 28, 1912, Chance was released. Thus he left the scenes of his greatest triumphs in bitterness and recrimination.

In 1913 Chance signed on as player-manager of the Yankees, but without the talent to work with, he lasted for only two unsuccessful seasons. His playing days over, Chance left the majors with a .297 average, 1,276 hits, and 405 stolen bases.

Chance came back in 1923 to manage the Red Sox, but that effort, too, was a failure, lasting but a solitary campaign. That winter he was hired to manage the team he once hated—the White Sox—but his poor physical condition forced him to resign before the season began.

All the beanings of years gone by had caused him severe migraine headaches, which had taken an awful toll on his health. On Sept. 14, 1924, he died at 47, himself the ultimate, ironic victim of his own unquenchable thirst for victory. Twenty-two years later Chance was elected to baseball's Hall of Fame along with his infield partners, Tinker and Evers.

TOM LOFTUS

LOFTUS, THOMAS JOSEPH
B. Nov. 15, 1856, Jefferson City, Mo.
D. April 16, 1910, Concord, Mass.
BR 168 lb.

Of all the Cub managers, Tom Loftus is probably the most forgotten, having piloted the team to a tie for fifth place in 1900 and a poor sixth the following year.

Before his managerial days, Loftus had played for St. Louis in the National League in 1877 and the St. Louis American Association team six years later, batting .182 in nine games.

Prior to coming to the Cubs, Loftus had managed Milwaukee of the Union Association, Cleveland of the American Association, Cleveland of the National League, and finally the Reds in 1890 and '91. Following his term in Chicago, Loftus managed the Washington Senators in 1902 and '03.

His lifetime record as a field boss was 455-583 for a .438 percentage.

48

Whenever great catchers are discussed, more often than not one deserving name is sadly left out. The forgotten man is Johnny Kling, Cub backstop of the 20th century's first decade.

After starring on a local amateur team in his hometown, Kling entered the professional ranks with Houston of the Texas League in 1896, but as a part-time outfielder rather than a catcher. For the next three years he drifted back into semipro status before catching on with St. Joseph of the Western League in 1900. There he hit .301 in 108 games before signing with the Cubs late in the season.

Johnny made his major league debut at New York's Polo Grounds, Sept. 11, 1900, catching the second game of a doubleheader. In a game that was called a 3-3 draw after nine innings because of darkness, Kling went three-for-four, scoring once and driving in a run.

The next day he received his first dose of the rough-and-tumble style that typified big league ball at the turn of the century. In the seventh inning, Giant pitcher Win Mercer was charging in from third, hoping to bowl Kling over. Johnny guarded the plate with his life and seconds later Mercer was carried off the field unconscious. The Cubs coasted to a 9-1 triumph.

Kling began catching on and off regularly in 1901, but he did not become a full-fledged star until Frank Selee became Cub manager the following year. That season, Johnny earned a permanent position with his .286 batting average in 114 games, coupled with superb fielding.

From then through 1908, he was the premier receiver in the National League, topping the league four times in fielding average, six times in putouts, twice in assists, and once in double plays. Enemy baserunners discovered, to their regret, that Kling's arm was a force to be reckoned with.

On June 21, 1907, for example, he nailed all four runners attempting to steal second, as the Cubs took the Cardinals 2-0. The previous year, Johnny had enjoyed his best season at the plate with a .312 average in 107 games. Cub pitcher Ed Reulbach praised him as "one of the greatest catchers who ever wore a mask."

After the Cubs had won three straight pennants and two World Series, Kling won the world pocket billiard title during the winter of 1908-09, and he decided to forsake the green of the diamond for the green of the pool table.

Without Kling, the Cubs dropped to second place in 1909, their 104 victories notwithstanding. Johnny's replacement, Jimmy Archer, later developed into a fine receiver, but was not Kling's equal in his first year.

Defeated in his attempt to retain the pool championship, Kling rejoined the Cubs in 1910, and Chicago returned to the top. Although the Cubs lost the World Series to the Philadelphia A's in five games, the fact that they had won another pennant led many to feel that they would have won five straight had Kling been with them in 1909. Club owner Charles Murphy never forgave Kling for "deserting" the team and traded him to the Braves in June 1911.

Kling hung on with Boston for almost two seasons, batting .317

JOHNNY KLING

KLING, JOHN
GRADWOHL
B. Feb. 25, 1875,
Kansas City, Mo.
D. Jan. 31, 1947,
Kansas City, Mo.
BR TR 5'9½" 160 lb.

in 1912, although he came to the plate only 252 times. He also served as manager that year, piloting an untalented team to a last place finish. The following year he was traded to the Reds, but after 1913 Johnny hung up his mitt. He was a lifetime .271 hitter with 1,151 hits and 123 stolen bases—an impressive total for a catcher.

Kling, who was a convert to Judaism, spent his entire life in Kansas City, operating several pool halls in the area. For a time he also served as president of the local American Association team, before selling his interests to the Yankee organization in 1937.

Unfortunately for Johnny, most of the fanfare after his playing days went to his contemporary, Roger Bresnahan, who had caught for the Giants. Yet when they were active, Kling was universally acknowledged, outside of New York City, as the superior of the two.

In 1945 Bresnahan was named to the Hall of Fame, largely on the claim that he might have invented the shin guard. Kling, who died two years later, has since fallen into relative obscurity except among Cub history buffs. But his accomplishments speak for themselves.

TOPSY HARTSEL

HARTSEL, TULLY FREDERICK
B. June 26, 1874, Polk, Ohio
D. Oct. 14, 1944, Toledo, Ohio
BL TL 5'5" 155 lb.

Outfielder Tully "Topsy" Hartsel played only one season with the Cubs, but it was a spectacular one. As their regular left fielder in 1901, he led the club in batting (.335), hits (187), runs scored (111), and stolen bases (41).

Hartsel, who had previously seen action with Louisville and Cincinnati in the National League jumped to the Philadelphia Athletics of the American League in 1902. He remained there for the rest of his career, which lasted through 1911.

JOHNNY EVERS

EVERS, JOHN JOSEPH
B. July 21, 1881, Troy, N.Y.
D. March 28, 1947, Albany, N.Y.
BL TR 5'9" 125 lb.

When Johnny Evers checked in with the Cubs in September 1902, he weighed 105 pounds with a wet towel around his waist. The Cubs, who had paid $250 for his contract, figured they had been swindled, especially after he batted a measly .222 in what was left of the season.

But whatever the scowl-faced, lantern-jawed Evers lacked in physical prowess, he made up for in aggressiveness and determination. When second baseman Bobby Lowe broke his knee early the following year, Johnny was given the job more out of necessity rather than by choice.

However, after Evers batted .293 and showed a sticky glove, the position was his for keeps. For the next decade, the middle man of "Tinker to Evers to Chance" was the pepperpot of the Cub team.

Appropriately, the three were elected to the Hall of Fame as a unit.

Nicknamed "Trojan" because of his birthplace and "the Crab" because of his hot temper, Evers was a nervous, intense player who seldom got along well with others. His famous on-the-field brawl with Joe Tinker in 1905 left the pair on nonspeaking terms for years.

On another occasion, Johnny was so uptight that manager Frank Chance ordered him to go out and get drunk. He did so, and collected two hits the next day.

The Cubs soon matured into the best team in either league. Johnny's contributions included 49 stolen bases in 1906, 46 the following year, and a .300 average in '08 to pace the club.

It was on Sept. 23 of the 1908 season that Johnny enjoyed his most shining hour. The Cubs and the Giants were tied, 1-1, with two out in the last of the ninth before a packed house at the Polo Grounds. The Giants had Moose McCormick on third base and Fred Merkle on first when Al Bridwell lined a single to right-center. While McCormick raced home with the apparent winning run, Merkle turned halfway up the line and headed toward the clubhouse.

Amid the swarm of humanity engulfing the field, Evers was screaming for the ball. Finally he got ahold of it—or one just as good—and stepped on second base. Umpire Hank O'Day ruled Merkle out on a force play to nullify the run.

Earlier, in a Sept. 4 Cub-Pirate contest with O'Day umpiring, a Pirate runner failed to touch second while the winning run came home from third, over Evers's objections. Although the 1-0 Pirate win was upheld, league officials instructed umpires to keep their eyes open for such situations in the future.

This time, however, the umps had been on the ball. With the diamond in chaos from all the fans emptying out of the stands, it was impossible to resume play, so the contest was ruled a tie, to be replayed if it would have any bearing on the pennant race. The Cubs and the Giants finished in a virtual tie for the lead, requiring a replay. The Cubs won 4-2 and left the Polo Grounds running for their lives.

Although the Cubs continued to shine over the next few years, Evers was not always so fortunate. He missed the 1910 World Series because of a broken leg, and he suffered a nervous breakdown the following year, seeing little action. In spite of it all, he returned triumphant in 1912 with his greatest season ever, .341 in 143 games.

Evers served as Cub manager in 1913, but did not last despite a third place finish in which the team was often called the Trojans in his honor. Johnny was having contract problems with owner Charles Murphy, who used it as a convenient excuse to fire him.

It turned out to be a blessing in disguise. Evers signed with the Boston Braves, becoming the sparkplug of the team. In baseball's most remarkable comeback, the "Miracle Braves" emerged from last place on July 11 to sweep the pennant.

In the World Series, led by Evers's .438 average, the Braves crushed the Athletics in four straight. For his work, Evers was given a Chalmers automobile, the 1914 version of the Most Valuable Player award.

That was Johnny's last season as a regular, and by mid-1917 he was released to the Phillies. For all practical purposes, his playing days were over after that year, save for two token appearances while coaching for the White Sox in 1922 and the Braves in '29. He was a lifetime .270 hitter with 1,658 hits and 324 stolen bases.

Johnny managed the Cubs again for most of 1921 and the White Sox in '24, but both attempts were failures as the Cubs finished seventh and the Sox last. During the next 15 years, he served numerous clubs in various civilian capacities.

After he left baseball, Evers's remaining years were sad and lonely. Suffering a stroke in 1942, he was a cripple for the rest of his life until a second hemorrhage proved fatal. He is buried at Saint Mary's Cemetery in his hometown, Troy, N.Y.

RUBE WADDELL

WADDELL, GEORGE EDWARD
B. Oct. 13, 1876, Bradford, Pa.
D. April 1, 1914, San Antonio, Tex.
BR TL 6' 1½" 196 lb.

Southpaw George "Rube" Waddell was probably the fastest pitcher in baseball during his heyday with the Philadelphia Athletics from 1902 through '07.

Having previously pitched for Louisville and Pittsburgh, Rube's best years were still ahead of him when he appeared with the Cubs in 1901. Even so, he was the top man on the staff with a 14-14 record. Following his brief sojourn in Chicago, he jumped to the American League, where he gained his fame. Traded to the St. Louis Browns in 1908, Waddell finished his career with them two years later. He was elected to the Hall of Fame in 1946.

CARL LUNDGREN

LUNDGREN, CARL LEONARD
B. Feb. 16, 1880, Marengo, Ill.
D. Aug. 21, 1934, Champaign, Ill.
BR TR

Carl Lundgren is the forgotten man of the Cub pitching staff that won four pennants and two World Series between 1906 and '10. Baseball buffs readily recall the "big four" of Three Finger Brown, Ed Reulbach, Jack Pfiester, and Orval Overall, but Lundgren's name, sadly, is seldom heard.

One of the few players of his era with a college education, Carl joined the Cubs shortly after his graduation from the University of Illinois in 1902. On Sept. 15 of that season, he was on the mound when the first Tinker-to-Evers-to-Chance double play was recorded, in a 6-3 win over the Reds at Chicago.

In his brief but impressive stay in the big time, Lundgren was especially effective in cold weather; hence, his nickname, "The Human Icicle." He enjoyed his best seasons in 1906 and '07, with records of 17-6 and 18-7. In 1907 he posted a remarkable 1.17 ERA and hurled seven shutouts. Surprisingly, Carl was not used in either World Series, nor in 1908.

Lundgren left the Cubs early in 1909, after which he hung around in the minors for a few years before retiring. He then became the

Knute Rockne of college baseball, enjoying his greatest personal triumphs. Interestingly, both men were of Scandinavian descent; Rockne a Norwegian from the old country, Lundgren an American-born Swede.

Hired as Princeton's baseball coach in 1912, Carl later moved to the University of Michigan. There his teams won Big Ten baseball championships in 1918, '19, and '20.

During the winter of 1920-21, George Huff, athletic director at the University of Illinois, induced Carl to return to his alma mater. He quickly led the school to championships in 1921 and '22, for a personal string of five straight winners.

In the ensuing years, Lundgren's teams won four more titles, as he became assistant athletic director along with his duties as baseball coach. His untimely death from heart failure deprived college ball of one of its greatest figures.

Lifetime, Carl was a 91-54 pitcher.

FRANK SELEE

SELEE, FRANK GIBSON
B. Oct. 26, 1859, Amherst, N.H.
D. July 5, 1909, Denver, Colo.

In 1901 former haberdasher Frank Selee closed out a highly successful 12-year tenure as manager of the Boston Braves, then known as the Beaneaters. With his walrus mustache and bald noggin, Selee looked more like a silent movie comedian than a major league manager.

He brought pennants to Boston in 1891, '92, '93, '97, and '98. He developed such stars as Kid Nichols, Bobby Lowe, Jimmy Collins, Fred Tenney, Hugh Duffy, and Herman Long. Only once did his team finish below .500. Surprisingly, Selee never played a day of major league ball.

In the meantime, the Cubs had finished an awful sixth in 1901 with a 53-86 record, escaping the cellar by only one game. Badly riddled by American League raids, they were dubbed the "Remnants" by sarcastic sportswriters. Selee's contract with Boston had run out, and the Cubs signed him for the 1902 season. Because Selee emphasized youth in rebuilding the team, certain newspapers began calling them the "Cubs," although the manager himself preferred the established title of Colts.

He began whipping the team into shape immediately. Joe Tinker, then 22, was given the shortstop position, while Carl Lundgren was signed off the University of Illinois campus to aid the pitching corps. Johnny Kling was made the regular catcher and outfielder Jimmy Slagle was brought over from Boston, responding with a .315 batting average. Jack Taylor, for four years an erratic hurler, blossomed into a 22-game winner under Selee's tutelage. Late in the season, Selee arm-twisted Frank Chance into changing from a second-string catcher to a first baseman. Youthful Johnny Evers was purchased to replace the aging Bobby Lowe at second base, and the rest is history.

For the season, the team finished fifth with a 68-69 record, a vast improvement over the previous year. But this was only the beginning. In 1903 the Cubs bolted to third place with an 82-56 record, their best finish in 12 years. Chance and Evers batted .327 and .293 in their first complete season, while Tinker hit .291. The pitching staff was bolstered with the additions of Jake Weimer and Bob Wicker, both winning 20 games. The following year Mordecai Brown, Frank Schulte, and Artie Hofman were added to the roster as the club nudged up to second place, winning 93 games. More importantly, Selee appointed Frank Chance as team captain and began teaching him the tricks of his trade.

Selee's last major discovery, Ed Reulbach, joined the team in 1905, winning 17 games his rookie season. Meanwhile, Selee's lungs had been eaten away by tuberculosis, then an incurable disease.

By midseason he was unable to make road trips due to his failing health, and Frank Chance served in his stead. On Aug. 1, Selee turned the reins over to Chance, then retired to Colorado.

Although the team dropped back to third place, Chance added the finishing touches to Selee's machine during the winter and spring.

Selee lived to see (or at least hear about) the final results of his efforts, but not for long. Consumption overtook him on July 5, 1909, barely three months before his 50th birthday.

JIMMY SLAGLE

SLAGLE, JAMES FRANKLIN

B. July 11, 1873, Worthville, Pa.

D. May 10, 1956, Chicago, Ill.

BL TR

Nicknamed "Shorty" because of his height (unfortunately his exact measurement has been lost to history) and "the Rabbit" because of his speed, Jimmy Slagle was one of the most popular Cub outfielders of the 1900s.

A graduate of Kansas City of the Western League, Slagle made his National League debut with Washington in 1899, batting .272. The club disbanded when the league cut back from 12 to 8 clubs and Jimmy's contract was snatched up by the Phillies. There he batted .287 in 1900. The following year, Slagle split the season between the Phillies and the Braves.

Meanwhile, Jimmy's manager at Boston, Frank Selee, had signed to manage the Cubs in 1902. The first chance he had, Selee took Slagle with him to Chicago, where "the Rabbit" became an integral part of Selee's rebuilding program. In a Cub jersey Slagle enjoyed the best season of his career, batting .315 and stealing 40 bases to lead the club.

In 1903, as the Cubs jumped to third place, Slagle had another fine year, hitting .298, stealing 33 bases, and scoring 104 runs. He was an excellent defensive outfielder since his speed enabled him to cover a great deal of ground.

Jimmy's throwing arm was nothing to be scoffed at either, as attested by his league-leading 27 assists in 1905. It was in that season he was switched from left field to center.

Although his hitting fell off after 1903, Slagle remained in the lineup because of his speed and defensive skills. In 1906 the Cubs

54

won their first pennant in 20 years, but Jimmy was injured shortly before the World Series and could not play.

The following year, however, he became a hero in the autumn classic against the Tigers. The first game was called a 3-3 tie because of darkness after 12 innings. The Cubs then went on to whip Detroit in four straight. Batting .273 in the series, Slagle drove the Tigers mad with his daring baserunning.

His six stolen bases were a series record until broken by Lou Brock of the Cardinals 60 years later. In the second game on Oct. 9, Jimmy drove in what turned out to be the winning run with a fourth-inning single.

The 1907 World Series was, in effect, Jimmy's last hurrah. As his batting average plummeted to .222 the following year, it became apparent that his baseball days were numbered. He was released late in August.

For his decade in the majors, Slagle was a .268 lifetime hitter with 1,339 hits and 273 stolen bases. Never a power hitter, he socked only two home runs in his entire career, one of which came in a Cub uniform in 1904.

Joe Tinker joined the Cubs in 1902, after two years in the minors, and immediately became the regular shortstop. Late in the year, Frank Chance was switched from a second-string catcher to a first baseman, and the youthful Johnny Evers was given the second baseman's job. The result was baseball's most famous double-play combination of all time: Tinker to Evers to Chance.

JOE TINKER

Joe held his position for the next 11 years, playing it like no other Cub before or since. After topping the league in errors his rookie year, Tinker turned into one of the slickest glove men in the game, leading the league five times in fielding average, four times in total chances, three times in assists, twice in putouts, and once in double plays.

As a shortstop, he was rated second only to Honus Wagner among his contemporaries, certainly nothing to be ashamed of. In 1911, Tinker led in every fielding category except double plays.

Tinker was often criticized as a light hitter, but this was only half of the story. While Tinker's lifetime batting average was only .263, Joe was as dangerous as any when it came to hitting in the clutch, as many an overconfident pitcher found out. Furthermore, his batting became more proficient as the years went on.

TINKER, JOSEPH BERT
B. July 27, 1880, Muscotah, Kan.
D. July 27, 1948, Orlando, Fla.
BR TR 5'9" 175 lb.

From 1902 through '07, Joe's average was a mere .248, but from 1908 through '13, he averaged .283. On Oct. 11, 1908, he became the first Cub to hit a home run in a World Series game, connecting with one in the eighth as the Cubs beat the Tigers 6-1.

Swift and aggressive on the basepaths, Joe stole 304 bases in a Cub uniform (fourth highest on the all-time club list), reaching a high of 41 in 1904. On June 28, 1910, he stole home plate twice in one game, during an 11-1 win over the Reds.

Tinker's most unique distinction was his uncanny ability to hit against Giant ace Christy Mathewson, batting .291 lifetime against Matty, which exceeded his overall average by 28 points. For the first few years, Tinker was putty in Matty's hands, but in 1906 he began using a longer bat. From that point on, the roles were reversed, and Tinker became, in Christy's words, "One of the most dangerous batters I have ever faced."

Joe's greatest outing against Mathewson came on Aug. 7, 1911, at Chicago. In four trips, Tinker singled twice, doubled, and tripled, driving in four runs and scoring three in an 8-6 Cub triumph. He added insult to injury by making two double plays and stealing home once.

Usually genial and good-natured, Tinker was a fighter when riled. His renowned, on-the-field brawl with Johnny Evers in 1905 left the pair on nonspeaking terms for several years, but they performed like clockwork on the field. Another time, Joe went at it with a rowdy fan at Cincinnati. During the off-season, Tinker ran a saloon on Chicago's West Side for awhile. Later he made frequent theatrical appearances, proving himself a competent actor. He received good reviews from *Variety,* and at one point considered forsaking the ballfield for the stage.

In the winter of 1912-13, Evers replaced Frank Chance as Cub manager, and Tinker, at his own request, was traded to Cincinnati. As player-manager of the Reds, he hit .317 in 1913 for his best mark at the plate, but the team finished a dismal seventh.

After one season at the River City, Joe was lured to the outlaw Federal League, where he led the Chicago Whales to the pennant in 1915, again as player-manager. The Feds folded, and Joe was back in a Cub uniform the following year, this time as manager, playing only occasionally. The team finished a poor fifth and Joe was given the ax.

Following his exit from the majors, Tinker played briefly for Columbus of the American Association. In 1921, he settled in Orlando, Fla., where he remained for the rest of his life. He was constantly involved in local baseball affairs, and there is a ballpark named after him in that city. With his infield partners, Evers and Chance, Tinker was elected to the Hall of Fame in 1946.

JAKE WEIMER

WEIMER, JACOB
B. Nov. 29, 1873,
Ottumwa, Iowa
D. June 17, 1928,
Chicago, Ill.
BL TL 5'11" 175 lb.

Jake Weimer entered professional ball with Des Moines of the Western League in 1900, spending one season there and two more at Kansas City before joining the Cubs in 1903.

Although he was already pushing 30 when he reached the majors, Weimer broke in with a sensational 21-9 mark his first year, becoming one of only a handful of Cub rookies to win 20 games. Not bothered by the sophomore jinx, he won 20 the following year.

Known as "Tornado Jake" because of his blazing fastball, Weimer fanned 177 batters in 1904, third highest in the National

League that season. His earned-run average was 1.91 in 307 innings and on May 9 he pitched a two-hit 6-0 victory over Boston, the closest he ever came to a no-hitter.

Following an 18-12 record for the Cubs in 1905, Weimer was traded to the Reds for third baseman Harry Steinfeldt. Jake won 19 his first year with Cincinnati but began to fade thereafter. He finished his career with the Giants in 1909.

Weimer made his home in Chicago and was employed by the Chicago Stockyards at the time of his death. He is buried in Mount Olivet Cemetery on the city's South Side.

He was a lifetime 97-72 pitcher.

BOB WICKER

WICKER, ROBERT KITRIDGE
B. May 25, 1878, Lawrence County, Ind.
D. Jan. 22, 1955, Evanston, Ill.
BR TR 5'11½" 180 lb.

On Saturday June 11, 1904, a crowd of 38,000—the largest in baseball history up to that time—shoehorned its way into the wooden stands of New York's Polo Grounds. On the mound for the Giants was Iron Man Joe McGinnity, seeking his 13th consecutive win. Opposing him was Bob Wicker of the Cubs.

Going into the bottom of the 10th, McGinnity had held the Cubs scoreless, but Wicker was even better, having pitched nine hitless innings. With one gone in the 10th, former Cub Sam Mertes singled to spoil the no-hitter, but Wicker bore down and did not allow another hit. Wicker finally won in the 12th 1-0, when Johnny Evers singled home Frank Chance.

In appreciation of Wicker's triumph, the usually partisan New York crowd carried him off the field on its shoulders. It was an appropriate finish to a great pitcher's duel. On Sept. 24, Bob almost did it again, hurling a 4-0 one-hitter over Brooklyn.

Wicker broke in with the Cardinals in 1901 but had little success until he joined the Cubs two years later. He was 20-9 that season, 17-8 in 1904 and 13-7 in '05.

In July 1906 Wicker was traded to the Reds for pitcher Orval Overall. He wound up his career with Cincinnati that season. He had a 64-53 lifetime record.

MORDECAI BROWN

BROWN, MORDECAI PETER CENTENNIAL
B. Oct. 19, 1876, Nyesville, Ind.
D. Feb. 14, 1948, Terre Haute, Ind.
BB TR 5'10" 175 lb.

A farming accident helped turn Mordecai "Three Finger" Brown into one of baseball's greatest pitchers. Brown lost the index finger on his right hand below the second joint in a cornshredder when he was only five.

Originally a third baseman on the coal-mining teams in southern Indiana, Brown switched to pitching when it was discovered that the stub of the finger permitted him to put more spin on the ball. His curve broke down and out and forced batters to beat the ball into the ground.

The miner-turned-pitcher won 23 games for Terre Haute in 1901 and 27 the next season for Omaha. His next stop was the major leagues, breaking in with the St. Louis Cardinals, where he had a 9-13 record.

Frank Selee, then manager of the Cubs, saw the three-fingered flinger as a comer. He traded 20-game winner Jack Taylor to the Cards for Brown and catcher Jack O'Neill in 1904.

The Cubs built a dynasty from 1906 to '10, and Brown was their leading pitcher, forcing the opposition to pound the ball into the gloves of the storied Tinker-to-Evers-to-Chance double-play combo.

Brown went on to win 239 games and lose only 130 for a .648 percentage. Starting in 1906 he was a 20-game winner six straight seasons, posting records of 26-6, 20-6, 29-9, 27-9, 25-13, and 21-11. In 1906, when the Cubs won a record 116 games, Brown won 11 in a row and pitched nine shutouts. For his career Brown had five one-hitters and tossed 58 shutouts, three in World Series competition.

The highlight of Brown's career was his mastery of John McGraw's hated New York Giants and their pitching ace, Christy Mathewson. The two tangled 24 times, with Brown winning 13, including a string of nine in a row.

Perhaps the most important of their head-on clashes was achieved on Oct. 8, 1908, in the replay of the Fred Merkle boner game. Merkle, a Giant rookie, had failed to touch second base in the ninth inning and turned a 2-1 New York victory into a 1-1 tie.

The Cubs and Giants finished the season with 98 wins and 55 losses, so a playoff was in order at New York's Polo Grounds. McGraw, of course, selected Mathewson to pitch, while Cubs' manager Frank Chance surprisingly picked Jack Pfiester instead of Brown.

All of New York was in a frenzy for this game. The stands were bursting with people and the bluffs overhanging the old ballpark were jammed with the overflow. People were atop houses and telegraph poles. The elevated lines couldn't run because people had climbed up to sit on the tracks.

The fire department came and drove them off with hoses. Then the mob set fire to the fences and came bursting through. Mounted police were used to hold them back. Adding to the frayed tempers, the umpires were an hour late.

Mathewson set down the Cubs quickly in the first inning, but Pfiester encountered trouble. There was one run in with two out and two on when Chance summoned Brown from the bullpen. Brown had to shove his way through the crowd before he reached the mound to strike out the next batter.

The Cubs came up with four runs in the third inning when Joe Tinker tripled, Johnny Kling singled, Brown sacrificed, Johnny Evers walked, and Frank Schulte and Chance doubled.

That set off the crowd again. The next inning catcher Kling went back for a foul and had to dodge derby hats and pop bottles to catch the ball. In the ninth inning a big fight broke out and the game was held up until order was restored.

Chance raced to the mound in the final inning and told Brown to get it over quickly and "run for our lives." Brown obeyed orders. He retired the Giants on *Three* pitches. Art Devlin grounded to third baseman Harry Steinfeldt, Moose McCormick flied to outfielder Jimmy Sheckard, and Al Bridwell grounded to shortstop Tinker. The Cubs won 4-2 and clinched the pennant.

Brown and his teammates dashed for the center field clubhouse with the mob at their heels. Chance, Tinker, Sheckard, and Del Howard were roughed up, and Pfiester was slashed on the shoulder by a knife.

Police formed a cordon around the clubhouse and pulled their revolvers to hold back the unruly mob yelling for Cub blood. The team rode back to the hotel in a paddy wagon with cops on the running boards. That night they left for Detroit and the World Series by slipping out the back door and down the alley.

The Cubs won the World Series in five games. Brown won the first and fourth games. In all, Brown won five World Series games to rank among the all-time leaders.

But the Cub dynasty soon crumbled, and Brown faded to a 5-6 record in 1912. The following season he was sold to Cincinnati where he was 11-12. He jumped to the new Federal League in 1914. He became a member of the Chicago Whales where he was a 17-game winner in 1915. When that league folded, Brown rejoined the Cubs in 1916.

In his final major league game, Brown was paired against Mathewson, then pitcher-manager of the Reds. The veterans were exhausted before the contest concluded with Matty winning 10-8, a far cry from their low-scoring duels.

Brown continued pitching and managing in the minor leagues, winding up his career with the Terre Haute Tots of the Three-I League in 1920. He died in Terre Haute on St. Valentine's Day 1948.

Thus Brown never lived to see his name enshrined in baseball's Hall of Fame at Cooperstown, N.Y. He was elected in 1949, joining Tinker, Evers, Chance, McGraw, and his old pitching rival, Mathewson, of that bygone era.

ARTIE HOFMAN

HOFMAN, ARTHUR FREDERICK
B. Oct. 29, 1882, St. Louis, Mo.
D. March 10, 1956, St. Louis, Mo.
BR TR 6' 160 lb.

While such players as Tinker, Evers, Chance, Brown, and Reulbach received most of the accolades, Artie Hofman was one of the team's unsung heroes. As the Cubs super-sub of the 1900s, he played every position except pitcher and catcher.

Hofman made his major league debut with the Pirates in 1903, but went to bat only twice without getting a hit. Brought back by the Cubs late the following season, Artie was used sparingly for the next two years, filling in whenever and wherever he was needed. Somewhere along the line he picked up the nickname "Circus Solly."

Shortly before the 1906 World Series against the White Sox, the

Cubs regular center fielder, Jimmy Slagle, was injured and "Solly" was sent in to replace him. Although the Sox beat the Cubs in six contests, it could hardly be blamed on Hofman, who batted .304 to pace the team.

Hofman was fast becoming the best utility man a club could ask for. In 1907 right fielder Frank Schulte and shortstop Joe Tinker both missed long periods with ailments. Filling in first at short and then in the outfield, Artie made his way into 133 games, batting .267 and stealing 29 bases. By World Series time, however, all the regulars were back, so Hofman was warming the bench.

The Cubs won their third straight pennant the year after but it was a disappointing effort for Hofman, who hit only .243. Nevertheless, he was center fielder for the world title since Jimmy Slagle had been released near the end of the regular season.

The unsinkable Solly again rose to the occasion with heroics. In game one, his two-run single in the ninth inning battered down the door for a comfortable 10-6 triumph over Detroit. Three games later, back-to-back run-scoring singles by Harry Steinfeldt and Hofman gave Mordecai Brown all the bulk he needed to collar the Tigers 3-0. The Cubs went on to take the series in five games, with Artie batting .316 and driving home four runs toward the victory.

The spring of 1909 found Hofman with a starting position for the first time in his career in center field. He responded with a .285 average, tops on the squad, but the Cubs finished second to the Pirates.

Following this one year hiatus, the Cubs were again king of the hill. With it, Solly had his best year, leading the crew with a .325 average, 16 triples, 86 RBI, and 29 stolen bases. In a five-game World Series loss to the A's, he batted .267.

As the team slowly declined thereafter, so did Hofman. Swapped to the Pirates in midseason 1912 for Tommy Leach, Hofman went to Brooklyn and Buffalo of the Federal League. He was briefly with the Yankees before returning to the Cubs in 1916.

Lifetime, he was a .269 hitter with 1,094 hits.

FRANK SCHULTE

Outfielder Frank Schulte joined the Cubs in September 1904, batting .286 in 20 contests. The Cub brass was impressed, and the following year Schulte, who was nicknamed "Wildfire" after his pet horse, became the regular left fielder. Wildfire responded with a .274 average.

In 1906 the Cubs acquired Jimmy Sheckard from Brooklyn to play left field, and Schulte was shifted to right, where he gained his fame. Frank's hitting continued to improve, as he batted .281 and topped the league in triples with 13.

During the World Series against the White Sox that October, Schulte was involved in the most controversial play of the battle. It was the sixth game of the series, with the Sox ahead, three games

SCHULTE, FRANK
B. Sept. 17, 1882,
Cohocton, N.Y.
D. Oct. 2, 1949,
Oakland, Calif.
BL TR 5'11" 170 lb.

to two. In the bottom of the first inning, the Cubs held a 1-0 lead with one gone and Sox runners on first and second. George Davis then smashed one deep to right field. Schulte always claimed that he could have caught the ball but "that a policeman in uniform came up and pushed him while he was waiting," as was reported in the 1907 *Spalding Base Ball Guide.*

Most newspapers also carried this story, while an obscure paragraph in the *Chicago Tribune* blamed the misdeed on "mute, inglorious Milton," an eight-year-old boy. A fuming Frank Chance demanded that Davis be called out because of fan interference, but to no avail. The hit was ruled a double, and the Sox went on to win 8-3 to capture the title.

Following a groin injury in 1907, Frank's hitting suffered the following year, dropping to .236. Nevertheless, he was one of the heroes in the 1908 World Series, batting .389, as the Cubs sheared the Tigers in five games.

In spring training of 1909, Schulte became acquainted with Ring Lardner, then an unknown *Tribune* sportswriter. Like Schulte, the youthful Lardner was a hard-drinking, back-slapping guy with a wry grin and a sense of humor that was sarcastic yet friendly.

The two hit it off well from the start and became close, lifelong friends. They swapped baseball yarns, closed down many a saloon in the wee hours, and, from time to time, even went on the wagon in unison. During the next several years, Schulte dominated many a Lardner column, both in prose and verse.

In fact, many of the poems, though written by Ring, bore Frank's byline. In addition, Schulte and his teammates provided much of the inspiration for the nominally fictitious characters in the short stories which would soon make Lardner famous.

Shortly after becoming Lardner's drinking buddy, Schulte began hitting like his nickname. In 1910 he batted .301 and hit 10 home runs, the most by a Cub in 15 years. At a time when most homers were inside the park, Frank displayed genuine power by belting them over or against the fence at Chicago's spacious West Side Grounds.

The best came the following year. With uncanny consistency in every department, Frank knocked an even .300 average and had 30 doubles, 21 triples, 21 home runs, 105 runs scored, 107 RBI and 23 stolen bases. His homer and RBI count set the pace for the league, as did his .534 slugging average.

Whether he knew it or not, Schulte had become the first player in history to amass 20 or more doubles, triples, homers, and stolen bases in the same season. This feat has since been duplicated only by Willie Mays of the Giants in 1957, making it one of baseball's rarest accomplishments.

The Schulte bat burned like wildfire in other ways, too. On July 20, 1911, he hit for the cycle as the Cubs edged the Phillies 4-3. On Aug. 20 Frank hit his fourth grand slam of the year to lead the Cubs to a 13-6 pillaging of the Braves.

This set a major league record that was not exceeded until another Cub, Ernie Banks, knocked five grand slammers 44 years later. For his efforts, Schulte was presented with a new Chalmers automobile, that era's equivalent of the Most Valuable Player award.

Unfortunately, things went downhill afterward, and the wildfire dwindled to a smoldering ember. After 1911, the best that Frank could muster was a .279 mark with 68 RBI in 1913, although he socked 12 homers the year before and again in 1915.

Late in the 1916 season, Schulte was peddled to the Pirates. After roughly a year with the Bucs and a half season with the Phillies, Frank finished with the Senators in 1918.

Lifetime, he was a .270 hitter with 1,766 hits.

ED REULBACH

REULBACH, EDWARD MARVIN
B. Dec. 1, 1882, Detroit, Mich.
D. July 17, 1961, Glens Falls, N.Y.
BR TR 6'1" 190 lb.

Following four years of training in the minors, during which he studied at Notre Dame during the off-season, Ed Reulbach joined the Cubs in 1905. He won a berth on the starting staff immediately, responding with an 18-13 log his rookie year. One of the taller men on the squad at 6'1", Reulbach was nicknamed "Big Ed."

Whenever there was history to be made, Reulbach was never far away. On June 24, 1905, he went the distance to beat the Cardinals and ex-Cub Jack Taylor 2-1 in 18 innings. Exactly two months later, on Aug. 24, Ed nipped the Phillies in 20 innings by the same score, again going the route.

In 1906 Reulbach upped his record to 19-4 for a league-leading .826 percentage, which included a personal winning streak of 12 games. This was also the first (and so far the only) year in which the Cubs and the White Sox met in the World Series.

Although the Sox trimmed the Cubs in six games, it was no fault of Reulbach's. On Oct. 10 Big Ed hurled a one-hitter to wipe out the Sox 7-1 on their own grounds. The lone hit, a seventh inning single by Jiggs Donahue, had nothing to do with the scoring, as the Sox had tallied their only run the inning previous on an error and a wild pitch.

Reulbach's one-hitter remained unduplicated in World Series play until 1945, when another Cub, Claude Passeau, turned the trick on the Detroit Tigers. These performances were unsurpassed until 1956, when the Yankees' Don Larsen pitched a perfect game against the Dodgers.

Following a 17-4 mark in 1907 and another World Series victory, this time over the Tigers, Reulbach set the stage for his greatest achievements. In 1908 he led the league in won-lost percentage for the third straight year, putting together a 24-7 record for .774. He beat the Dodgers nine times, but that was the least of his accomplishments.

On Sept. 26 Reulbach pulled off what many consider the greatest pitching feat ever displayed. Pitching the morning game of a doubleheader at Brooklyn, Big Ed blanked the Trolley Dodgers 5-0 on five hits.

With one victory in his pocket, the elated Reulbach asked

manager Frank Chance if he could hurl the nightcap as well. Chance had originally planned on using Jack Pfiester or Chick Fraser, but playing a hunch, he yielded to Reulbach's request. He was not disappointed.

Ed was even stronger in the second contest, holding the Dodgers to only three hits in a 3-0 whitewash. It was the only time in baseball history that a pitcher hurled a shutout doubleheader.

Even that was not all. In his previous outing, Sept. 19, Reulbach had collared the Phillies in 10 innings in a game that was called a scoreless tie because of darkness. Thus his Sept. 26 performance gave him three consecutive shutouts. The fourth came Oct. 1, when he shellacked the Reds 6-0. This tied a National League record for most consecutive shutouts set by the Cubs' Mordecai Brown earlier in the same season. These marks—tied by Cub Bill Lee in 1938—remained the league standard until broken by Don Drysdale of the Dodgers 60 years later. Drysdale posted six consecutive shutouts in 1968 to set a major league mark.

The Cubs again won the World Series from the Tigers in 1908, but this time Reulbach was decisionless. The following year he won 19 games—fourteen of them in a row—but the Cubs slipped to second place. During the next three years Ed continued to win games at a healthy pace, but in the 1910 World Series, he again went without a decision.

In 1913 Reulbach's skills began to fade, and in July he was traded to Brooklyn for pitcher Eddie Stack. After a year and a half with the Dodgers, Ed jumped to the Federal League. He made a good comeback, posting a 20-10 season for Newark in 1915. But the Federal League folded, and Ed's contract was given to the Braves. He appeared on a second-string basis for Boston in 1916 and '17 before hanging up his glove with a lifetime 185-104 record.

ORVAL OVERALL

OVERALL, ORVAL
B. Feb. 2, 1881,
Visalia, Calif.
D. July 14, 1947,
Fresno, Calif.
BB TR 6'2" 214 lb.

Orval Overall was the first graduate of the University of California to make it to the majors, having been a member of the school's class of 1903. Known as the "Big Groundhog" during his college days, the burly young Overall majored in agriculture while serving as captain of both the baseball and football teams. A scholar as well, he belonged to Sigma Uu and the Golden Bear, a senior honor society.

With Tacoma of the Pacific Coast League in 1904, Overall was the workhorse of the staff, winning 34 games and losing 25. This caught the eye of the Cincinnati Reds, who brought him up the following year. After a 17-22 record plus a slow start in 1906, Orval was traded to the Cubs that July for pitcher Bob Wicker. Joining a staff that already included Mordecai Brown, Ed Reulbach, Carl Lundgren, and Jack Pfiester, Overall became the final piece in the jigsaw puzzle. He won 12-of-15 decisions as the Cubs took the pennant. In the 1906 World Series, however, he was decisionless as the White Sox beat the Cubs in six games.

Now approaching his prime, Orval had his greatest season in 1907, posting a 23-8 record with a 1.70 ERA. When it came to whitewashing his opponents, Overall was a master, shutting out the enemy eight times. In the World Series against the Tigers that autumn, Orval was the winner of game number four, clipping the Tigers 6-1 on Oct. 11. Holding Detroit to five hits, Overall helped his own cause with a two-run single in the fifth. The following afternoon the Cubs celebrated Columbus Day by whipping the Tigers again to gain the world championship.

After dropping to 15-11 during the 1908 regular season, Overall again became a hero in the World Series, when the Cubs met the Tigers in a rematch. This time he went the distance to beat the Tigers twice, including a 2-0 three-hitter Oct. 14 for the title clincher. Along the way, Orval fanned 10 batters for good measure.

Although the Cubs fell to second place in 1909, Overall was in brilliant form, winning 21 games and shutting out the opposition nine times. With his fastball working better than ever, Orval struck out 205 batters to lead the league. Thus he became the last Cub pitcher to strike out 200 batters in a season until Fergie Jenkins fanned 236 in 1967.

Following a 12-6 season and a loss to the Athletics in the 1910 World Series, Overall retired because he did not get along with owner Charles Murphy. Attempting a comeback in 1913, Overall had by then lost most of his stuff, splitting eight decisions before being released to San Francisco in late August. At the season's close, he quit baseball for keeps. In his seven years in the majors, Overall won 108 games while losing only 70. His 2.24 ERA is eighth best on the all-time list.

After his departure from baseball, Overall went to work for a brewery and later became a citrus farmer. In 1922 he was named to the Board of Directors of the First National Bank of Visalia. When that institution merged with the Pacific Southwest Trust and Savings Bank of Los Angeles seven years later, he moved up the ladder to the vice-presidency. In 1933 Overall became vice-president and manager of the Fresno branch of the Security Bank of Los Angeles. He held that position until his death of a heart attack in 1947.

JACK PFIESTER

PFIESTER, JOHN
THEODORE JOSEPH
B. May 24, 1878,
Cincinnati, Ohio
D. Sept. 3, 1953,
Twightwee, Ohio
BR TL 6′ 170 lb.

Jack Pfiester was the token southpaw of Frank Chance's indomitable pitching corps of 1906-10. Pfiester, whose real name was Pfiestenberger, began his professional career with Spokane of the Pacific Northwest League in 1902. He moved to San Francisco of the Pacific Coast League the year after. The Pirates gave Jack a trial in late 1903 and early 1904. They were unimpressed, so it was back to the minors for Jack.

Pitching for Omaha of the Western League, Jack won 24 games in 1904 and 22 the following year. Among his victories was a no-hit game against St. Joseph on Sept. 18, 1904.

Pfiester's performance at Omaha gave him a second chance in the majors, this time with the Cubs. Coming to Chicago in 1906, he looked good from the start, displaying a fine fast ball and curve. On Memorial Day he set a Cub record by fanning 17 batters in a game, although it took him 15 innings to do it. But it was all in vain. The Cardinals won 4-2.

As the Cubs made history that season, so did Pfiester. On June 7 Jack took to the mound as the Cubs chopped the beanstalk down on the Giants 19-0, scoring 11 runs in the first inning. From that day forward, Jack was known as "Jack the Giant Killer," and he continued to haunt the New Yorkers for the rest of his short but sweet career.

Pfiester won his 20th game Oct. 4 with a 4-0 whitewash over the Pirates. It was also the Cubs' 116th victory of the year, setting a record which stands to this day. For the year Pfiester lost only eight games while his 153 strikeouts were fourth high in the league.

After his spectacular debut, the "Giant Killer" was consistently effective for several more seasons, putting together records of 15-9, 12-10, and 17-6 before he began to wear out around 1910. Released by the Cubs in mid-1911, Jack hung around in the bushes for a couple of years before retiring. His major league totals were 72 wins and 44 losses.

Unfortunately, Pfiester was not as successful in World Series competition. His lone victory was a 3-1 distance job against the Tigers on Oct. 9, 1907. He dropped two to the White Sox in 1906 and one to Detroit in '08. He was decisionless in 1910.

Although best remembered as a Cub, Jimmy Sheckard actually enjoyed his peak seasons with the Dodgers, when they were known as Hanlon's Superbas.

Born of Pennsylvania Dutch heritage, Sheckard was named after the Democratic presidential candidate of 1876 who lost the election to Rutherford B. Hayes even though he received more popular votes. Hayes copped the electoral college, and that was what counted.

Sheckard, who preferred to be called Jimmy, began playing ball in the sandlots of his hometown. He made his professional debut with Portsmouth of the Virginia State League at the end of 1896, batting .296 in 26 games. The following year he graduated to Brockton of the New England League, winning the batting title with a .370 average. Obviously, Jimmy was ready for the big time.

The opportunity came that September when the Brooklyn Dodgers called him up. In 13 games, the youngster hit .327. The following year, in his first complete big league season, Sheckard batted .291.

Then, in a move that was legally questionable, Jimmy was "loaned" to the Baltimore Orioles in 1899. He continued to improve, lifting his batting average to .295 and stealing 77 bases to

JIMMY SHECKARD

SHECKARD, SAMUEL JAMES TILDEN
B. Nov. 23, 1878,
Upper Chanceford, Pa.
D. Jan. 15, 1947,
Lancaster, Pa.
BL TR 5'9" 175 lb.

lead the league. With his cannon-like throwing arm, he set a National League record that still stands: 14 double plays by an outfielder.

Baltimore disbanded after that season, and 1900 found Jimmy back in a Brooklyn jersey. Although he appeared in just 85 games, Sheck batted .300 as the Superbas won their second straight pennant. The next season was his best by far. Hitting .353, he knocked home 104 runs and scored 116. To top it off, he was the league standard bearer in triples with 21, in slugging with .54!, and was sixth in steals with 35. On Sept. 23-24, 1901, he became only the second player in history to smack grand slams in consecutive games—and the last until the coming of the lively ball in 1920.

In 1902 Jimmy, like many other stars, jumped to the newly formed American League, joining the Baltimore franchise. But he had a quick change of heart and after only four games in the young league, he returned to Brooklyn. However, his average dropped to .265.

If comeback player awards were given in 1903, Sheckard would have been a prime candidate. Rebounding with a .332 clip, he set the league's pace in home runs with nine and in stolen bases with 67. Jimmy's 36 outfield assists were also tops.

The Dodgers were now on the decline, tumbling to last place by 1905. In the meantime, the Cubs were searching for a strong-armed outfielder to cement their defense. On Dec. 16, 1905, Chicago gave the Brooklynites Herb Briggs, Jack McCarthy, Doc Casey, and Billy Maloney in return for Sheckard.

Although Jimmy's best years at the plate were now in back of him, he remained the Cubs regular left fielder through 1912, becoming an integral part of the lineup. Sheckard was a favorite of sportswriter Ring Lardner, who regarded him as one of the greatest players he ever saw. Sheck was teamed with Jimmy Slagle in center and Frank Schulte in right, and the trio often hollered instructions to each other in German.

A near tragedy occurred on June 2, 1908, when a bottle of ammonia exploded in Sheckard's face. Prompt remedies saved his eyesight, but the mishap took its toll. Jimmy missed nearly 40 games, and his batting average plummeted to .231, his poorest showing yet. The next two years were sub-par also.

Jimmy fought back, though, enjoying his best Cub season in 1911. Batting .276, his highest mark in six years, Jimmy led the league in runs scored with 121, bases on balls with 147, and topped the Cubs in stolen bases with 32. He also topped the league with 32 assists and 12 double plays. His walk total remained the major league high until it was broken by Ed Stanky in 1945. It is still the Cub record.

In 1912 Sheckard repeated as league leader with 122 walks, but his batting average slipped to .245. The following April he was sold to the Cardinals. After a poor season divided between the Redbirds and the Reds, Jimmy retired, a lifetime .275 hitter with 2,091 hits and 465 steals. He returned as a Cub coach in 1917 for his final fling in the majors.

Harry Steinfeldt was the Cubs' regular third baseman during the apex of the Tinker-to-Evers-to-Chance era.

Originally an actor by profession, the beer-loving Steinfeldt forsook the stage for the diamond when he discovered that his greatest talent lay with the bat and the ball rather than the script and the greasepaint. Joining the Cincinnati Reds in 1898, Harry batted .295 in 88 games his rookie season.

For the next several years he was switched back and forth from second base to third. By 1902 he had settled permanently at third and the following year he had a fine campaign, batting .312, while his 32 doubles led the circuit.

After Steinfeldt suffered a leg injury the following year, however, the Reds figured he was damaged goods. In the winter of 1905-06, Harry was traded to the Cubs for pitcher Jake Weimer. The new uniform did wonders, and in 1906 Steiny had the finest season of his career. His .327 average paced the club as the Cubs won a record 116 games. Harry's 176 hits and 83 RBI led the league, as did his .954 fielding average. In addition, he stole 29 bases. Truly, it was his year.

The Cubs repeated as winners in 1907. Although Harry's batting percentage dropped to .267, his 70 RBI were still high on the team. He once again topped the league in fielding with a .967 average, committing only 16 errors in 150 games. Finally, he was the Cubs' batting hero in the World Series, collecting 8 hits in 17 trips for a .471 mark, as the Cubs turned the Tigers into kitty litter in five games.

For his remaining three years with the Cubs, Steinfeldt never hit over .252, but he continued to perform well at third base. Once, however, he played a 15-inning game without a ball being hit to him.

Now slowing down, Harry was traded to the Boston Braves in 1911. There he suffered a broken finger and left the majors after appearing in a mere 19 contests for the Beantown.

Lifetime, Steinfeldt was a .267 hitter with 1,576 hits.

HARRY STEINFELDT

STEINFELDT, HARRY M.
B. Sept. 27, 1876, St. Louis, Mo.
D. Aug. 17, 1914, Bellevue, Ky.
BR TR 5'9½" 180 lb.

One of the most colorful characters ever to appear in a Chicago uniform, "Heinie" Zimmerman was a Cub infielder from 1907 to '16. Chiefly remembered as a third baseman, he also appeared frequently at second and occasionally at short or first.

Whatever Heinie did, he did in a spectacular way. In 1912 he had one of the greatest seasons ever enjoyed by a Cub. He batted a league-leading .372 with 207 hits (the first Cub to collect 200 hits in a season), 41 doubles, 14 triples, 14 homers, 95 runs scored, and 23 stolen bases. His double and home run totals topped the league.

Runs batted in were recorded haphazardly in those days, so

HEINIE ZIMMERMAN

ZIMMERMAN, HENRY
B. Feb. 9, 1887, New York, N.Y.
D. March 14, 1969, New York, N.Y.
BR TR 5'11½" 176 lb.

discrepancies exist as to his total in that department. Some books list it as 98, others as 99, and still others as 103. As a result, Zimmerman may or may not have been the only Cub to win the Triple Crown, since some credit him with the RBI leadership, while others give the nod to Honus Wagner.

Either way, it was a helluva season, capped by a 23-game hitting streak (April 14 through May 14), during which he collected 39 hits in 90 trips for a .433 mark.

Heinie holds the Cub record for most RBI during one game—nine—on June 11, 1911, with two singles, a triple, and two homers in a 20-2 cakewalk over the Braves. On June 24, 1915, he pulled a daring steal of home with two out in the bottom of the ninth to give the Cubs a come-from-behind 14-13 win over the Cardinals.

Zim set another record of sorts in June 1913 when he was ejected from three games in five days. Finally, a generous but frantic fan, using the *Chicago Tribune* sports staff and umpire Bill Klem as intermediaries, gave Heinie half of a $100 bill, promising him the other half if he would refrain from getting the heave-ho for two weeks.

Heinie kept his cool and received his payoff, but the reform was shortlived. On Sept. 13, 1913, he was suspended by National League president Thomas Lynch for swearing at umpire Bill Byron two days earlier.

Traded to the Giants for infielder Larry Doyle in August 1916, Zimmerman helped the New Yorkers to the 1917 pennant with a .297 average and 102 RBI. However, he became the goat in the sixth and final game of the World Series with the White Sox, when he chased Eddie Collins across home plate with what turned out to be the winning run.

Since nobody was guarding the plate, Heinie's reply was, "Who the hell was I supposed to throw the ball to? Myself?"

Zimmerman played two more years with the Giants, but after the 1919 season, he was implicated in betting scandals to bring his career to a premature end.

Lifetime, Heinie was a .295 batter with 1,566 hits.

JIMMY ARCHER

ARCHER, JAMES PETER
B. May 13, 1883, Dublin, Ireland
D. March 29, 1958, Milwaukee, Wis.
BR TR 5'10" 168 lb.

Roger Bresnahan, the Giants' fine broth of a catcher, was dubbed the "Duke of Tralee." Tralee? Heck, he was born in Toledo. If any catcher was more worthy of carrying a shillelagh to the plate, it was Dublin-born Jimmy Archer of the Cubs.

Bresnahan was credited with the first use of shin guards for catchers. Archer's contribution was the snap throw from a squatting position. Ironically, that kept him from reaching the big leagues for a long while.

All catchers in the early part of the century stood up before throwing. Archer knew he could save time by throwing from the squat, but he was bounced from the Pirates and Tigers for not being a stand-up guy.

Archer was born in Ireland and was only a year old when his parents moved to Montreal. He was educated at De LaSalle Academy and St. Michael College in Montreal.

The restless youngster then headed west to play ball in Manitoba and soon wound up in Boone, Iowa. His contract was purchased by the Pittsburgh Pirates, where he got into seven games in 1904 and batted .150. Then he was banished to the boondocks, batting .298 at Boone.

It wasn't until 1907 that he reappeared in the majors with Detroit. Tiger manager Hughie Jennings's eyes popped when he saw Archer squat behind the plate and not rise to peg the ball. "No catcher can do any good throwing sitting down," declared Jennings.

Archer's .119 batting average wasn't eye-popping though, so he was shuffled off to Buffalo in 1908. Cub manager Frank Chance saw Archer perform in an exhibition game in Buffalo and realized he had a successor for the fading Johnny Kling.

Unlike Jennings, Chance didn't tamper with Archer's throwing technique, although it caused much controversy during that time. "The object is to throw out the runner." said Archer. 'What difference does it make how you throw the ball just so you get it there in time?"

When Kling staged his season-long holdout in 1909, Archer stepped in and gained notoriety as a skillful handler of pitchers. He saved many a game with his accurate arm.

Archer's big drawback was that he was the most banged-up big leaguer of his time. It started when he was a barrel-maker in Toronto. He fell into a vat of boiling tar, scalding his right arm and leg and suffering a compound fracture of his elbow.

His right arm was scarred and seared from the wrist to well past the elbow. The skin was stretched so tightly he could not hold the arm out straight. As a result the tendons shortened and his right shoulder was an inch shorter than the left. And that was his throwing arm.

In addition, when he was with Boone in 1904, Archer crashed into a hitching post chasing a foul and broke his left collarbone. With Atlanta in 1905, he called for a fastball and pitcher Bugs Raymond crossed him up with a curve that cracked his kneecap.

The fingers of his throwing hand were repeatedly broken. The index finger was busted four times and he could not close it on a bat or a ball.

But Archer held on long enough to last nine seasons with the Cubs from 1909 through '17. His batting average was never robust as attested by his lifetime average of .250.

Archer's most memorable performance came on a sweltering August day in 1911. King Cole of the Cubs and Nap Rucker of the Dodgers were locked in a scoreless duel at West Side Park. Archer stepped to the plate with two out in the 11th inning and homered for a 1-0 victory.

Perhaps his finest season was 1912 when he hit five homers, drove in 58 runs, batted .283, and threw out 81 would-be base thieves.

The Cubs released Archer following the 1917 season. He closed out his career with three teams in 1918, bouncing from the Pirates to the Dodgers to the Reds.

Archer quit baseball to become a hog buyer for Armour & Co., at the Chicago plant. He then turned to bowling and started knocking 'em off their pins as promotion director for the Congress Recreation Center of Chicago. He died in Milwaukee on March 29, 1958, at the age of 75.

In later years, sportswriter Ring Lardner was asked to name his all-time baseball team. Ring had the usual names—Ruth, Cobb, Wagner—except when it came to the catching position. He listed Ray Schalk of the White Sox and Jimmy Archer of the Cubs.

KING
COLE
COLE, LEONARD
LESLIE
B. April 15, 1886,
Toledo, Iowa
D. Jan. 6, 1916,
Bay City, Mich.
BR TR

Brought up by the Cubs late in 1909, Len "King" Cole pitched one game—a six-hit shutout—and was signed to a contract. The following year, the rookie wonder helped pitch the Cubs to their fourth pennant in five years with a phenomenal 20-4 record for a league-leading .833 percentage, the best by a Cub (with 15 or more decisions) in the 20th century.

On July 31, 1910, he pitched a seven-inning 4-0 no-hitter against the Cardinals at St. Louis, in a game that had to be called because both teams had to catch a train.

Cole followed this with an 18-7 mark in 1911, then slipped the next year and was traded to the Pirates, where he failed to stick. After that, the best the "King" could come up with was an 11-9 log with the Yankees in 1914, before an early death overtook him.

His lifetime mark was 55-27 with a 3.12 ERA.

LARRY
CHENEY
CHENEY, LAURANCE
RUSSELL
B. May 2, 1886,
Belleville, Kan.
D. Jan. 6, 1969,
Daytona Beach, Fla.
BR TR 6'1½" 185 lb.

In 1912 Cub spitballer Larry Cheney put together one of the greatest seasons ever enjoyed by a rookie hurler, winning 26 games and losing only 10. His 28 complete games were tops in the National League, as was his .722 win-loss percentage. His victory total was exceeded only by Rube Marquard of the Giants, who had 27. Cheney followed this up with a 20-14 record in 1913 and 20-18 the following year. However, his effectiveness was sometimes reduced by wildness, as evidenced by a league-leading 140 walks in 1914.

Cheney's most famous game came on Sept. 14, 1913, as he shut out the Giants 7-0 in spite of allowing 14 hits. This was the most ever allowed in a nine-inning, complete game shutout.

After dropping to 7-9 in 1915, Cheney was dispatched to Brooklyn late in the season. He had one more good season as a Dodger, helping them win the 1916 pennant with an 18-12 record and a 1.92 ERA. Other than that, he could never fully recapture the magic of his early Cub days. After splitting the 1919 season between the Dodgers, Braves and Phillies, Larry hung up his glove, with a lifetime log of 114 wins and 100 losses.

70

Wilbur Good is credited with the first pinch-hit homer in Cub history, connecting in the eighth inning off Grover Alexander on June 19, 1913, at West Side Grounds. But all it did was spoil Old Pete's shutout as the Phillies won 2-1.

Good, who was acquired by the Cubs in 1911 from the Boston Braves in the Johnny Kling trade, was a fleet outfielder who stole 68 bases in a Cub uniform, including 31 in 1914. He played regularly in 1914 and '15, but his highest average was only .272.

WILBUR GOOD

GOOD, WILBUR DAVID
B. Sept. 28, 1885, Punxsutawney, Pa.
D. Dec. 30, 1963, Brooksville, Fla.
BL TL 5'6" 165 lb.

Jimmy Lavender was a Cub spitballer of the 1910s who is recalled for two outstanding performances. On July 8, 1912, he halted Giant pitcher Rube Marquard's record-winning streak at 19 games with a 7-2 victory before 25,000 at Chicago's West Side Grounds. For an encore, Lavender pitched a 2-0 no-hitter against the Giants at the Polo Grounds on Aug. 31, 1915.

Like most throwers of the wet pitch, Lavender often had control problems and was only a fair pitcher overall. His best season was his rookie year, 1912, when he won 15 and lost 13. The best he could muster thereafter was an 11-11 mark in 1914. Following a year with the Phillies in 1917, Lavender departed with a total record of 63-76.

JIMMY LAVENDER

LAVENDER, JAMES SANFORD
B. March 25, 1884, Barnesville, Ga.
D. Jan. 12, 1960, Cartersville, Ga.
BR TR 5'11" 165 lb.

Roger Bresnahan? Was this multitalented athlete fact or fiction?

It is said the famed "Duke of Tralee" learned to pitch by throwing square potatoes in his native Ireland. When he arrived in the U.S., he lost his curve because of oval spuds. Hence he took to catching.

Another tale credits John McGraw's fiery temper with turning Bresnahan into a catcher. According to the story, McGraw was managing the 1901 Baltimore Orioles. Wilbert Robinson was his catcher and Bresnahan his pitcher.

Robby was injured and his substitute, the legendary Tacks Latimer, did such a lousy job of throwing to the bases that Bresnahan complained. "If you think you can do better, get back there yourself," roared McGraw. Hence, a Hall of Fame catcher was born.

Many record books claim Bresnahan was born in Dublin, Ireland on June 14, 1880. Holy Toledo! He was really born in Ohio on June 11, 1879.

Bresnahan was one of the most versatile athletes in baseball, playing every position. He caught in 974 games, played the outfield in 281, third base in 42, first base in 33, second base in 28, pitched in 9 games, and was a shortstop in 8.

ROGER BRESNAHAN

BRESNAHAN, ROGER PHILIP
B. June 11, 1879, Toledo, Ohio
D. Dec. 4, 1944, Toledo, Ohio
BR TR 5'9" 200 lb.

This fine broth of a lad gained prominence as the batterymate of Christy Mathewson, the New York Giants pitching immortal, who won 373 games. Bresnahan always insisted that Matty was the greatest of all pitchers.

Likewise, McGraw always insisted that Bresnahan was the finest catcher. But Bresnahan had a different view. Unlike most old-timers steeped in nostalgia, he had a different view. "I never saw the day I was as good as Bill Dickey," insisted Bresnahan.

Nevertheless, it was Bresnahan who pioneered the art of catching. He witnessed a cricket game and noticed "the bowlers" wearing shin guards. At that time the catcher was protected only by a small mask and a chest pad.

Bresnahan visited a sporting goods store in 1907 and had shin guards made to his specifications. The innovation was not popular, especially among the young toughs who inhabited the wooden bleachers at Chicago's West Side Park. They derided the new protection by calling Roger a "sissy."

Bresnahan began his career as a pitcher in Lima, Ohio, and was signed in 1897 by the Washington club, which was then in the National League. Although he pitched a shutout in his debut, compiled a 4-0 record, and batted .375 in six games, his contract was dropped.

He next caught on with the Cubs in 1900, getting into one game as a catcher and failing to connect in two trips to the plate. From there he joined McGraw at Baltimore for the American League's inaugural season. When McGraw jumped the Orioles in 1902, he took Bresnahan with him to the Giants. In Roger's peak season, 1903, he batted .350 and stole 34 bases for the Giants.

Under the handling of manager McGraw and catcher Bresnahan, Mathewson developed his famed fadeaway pitch. The trio formed the backbone of the great Giant teams of that era. Bresnahan was back of the plate when Matty threw three shutouts against Connie Mack's Philadelphia A's in the 1905 World Series.

Bresnahan stood only 5'9" but weighed 200 pounds. Like most catchers, he had powerful, stocky legs. But unlike most catchers, he could run. Could you imagine a catcher with 212 career stolen bases or a catcher used as a leadoff batter?

Bresnahan was sought by the St. Louis Cardinals as playing-manager in 1909, and McGraw didn't stand in his way. But McGraw demanded pitcher Bugs Raymond, outfielder Red Murray, and catcher George Schlei in return.

At St. Louis, Bresnahan was no longer under the thumb of Muggsy McGraw. His boss was Mrs. Helene Hathaway Robison Britton, the first female club owner in the majors.

The Cardinals didn't flourish under Bresnahan, finishing in the second division the next four years, winning 255 and losing 352 games. Bresnahan was bounced in 1913 in favor of the little-known Miller Huggins, who had less success. Huggins' Cardinals wound up in the cellar with a 51-90 record. Huggins did tack on some victories later by managing the great Yankee clubs with Ruth, Gehrig and Co.

Bresnahan, meanwhile, joined the Cubs in 1913 and shared catching duties with Jimmy Archer, who was really born in Dublin. However, at this stage of his career, Bresnahan no longer wielded a big shillelagh. He got into 58 games and batted .230. He improved his stickwork in 1914, upping his average to .278.

Bresnahan was appointed playing-manager of the Cubs in 1915 and signed a three-year contract. He guided the Cubs into fourth place with a 73-80 mark. It was obvious his active days behind the plate were nearing an end. His average dipped to .204, but he retained his keen sense of humor.

Once finding it difficult adjusting his shin guards, Roger remarked, "Darn them pads. Who invented them fool things, anyway?"

When Charles Weeghman purchased the Cubs in 1916 and moved the club from West Side Park to spanking, new Weeghman Field (now Wrigley Field), Bresnahan was out and Joe Tinker was in as manager.

Roger took the remaining two years of his contract and became an owner himself, purchasing the Toledo Mud Hens of the American Association.

He rejoined McGraw as a Giants coach in 1925 and served three seasons. Bresnahan then hooked on as a coach with the Detroit Tigers in 1930 and '31.

In later years he was a salesman for a brewing company in Toledo, and he dabbled in Ohio politics. Bresnahan died of a heart attack at age 65 on Dec. 4, 1944. Two months later he was inducted into baseball's Hall of Fame, joining McGraw and Matty.

He was a career .279 hitter with 1,252 hits.

HANK O'DAY

O'DAY, HENRY F.
B. July 8, 1863,
Chicago, Ill.
D. July 2, 1935,
Chicago, Ill.
TR

No man could call umpire Hank O'Day's bluff, not even under the shadows of Coogan's Bluff on Sept. 23, 1908. O'Day stood defiant against the hordes of bewildered fans, milling about the Polo Grounds.

He stood his ground against baseball's toughest manager, John "Muggsy" McGraw. O'Day's steel-gray eyes refused to blink. He had just rendered the toughest decision in baseball history.

The Cubs were playing their hated rivals, the New York Giants. The score was 1-1. The Giants were batting in the bottom of the ninth with two out. Moose McCormick was on third base and rookie Fred Merkle was perched on first. Al Bridwell singled to center and McCormick raced home with the winning run.

But Merkle did not go to second base. Instead, he raced to the clubhouse behind center field. Somehow, the Cubs retrieved the ball and Johnny Evers stepped on second. O'Day had his eyes on the play and ruled Merkle out at second, turning a base hit into a forceout and nullifying the run.

Giant fans, thinking their heroes had won 2-1, swarmed the field.

It was impossible to resume play, so O'Day called the game on account of darkness.

The Cubs and Giants eventually finished in a tie for first place in the National League, necessitating a playoff on Oct. 8 at the Polo Grounds. The Cubs won 4-1 to steal the pennant. They went on to sweep past the Detroit Tigers in the World Series.

Poor Merkle was branded a "Bonehead" because O'Day had refused to bend the rules. But he did earlier. The date was Sept. 4, 1908. The Cubs were playing the Pirates in Pittsburgh. The game was scoreless in the 10th inning. Owen Wilson singled with the bases loaded and Pirate player-manager Fred Clarke raced home with the winning run. But Pirate rookie Warren Gill neglected to run from first to second, electing to race off the field.

Evers took the throw from center fielder Jimmy Slagle, stepped on second and yelled, "Forceout." Umpire O'Day refused to listen. But he realized his mistake and vowed never to let it happen again. That led to the Merkle play.

O'Day, one of the greatest judges of balls and strikes, ruled with an iron fist. He was gruff but just, and a visible authority. It is hard to think of him other than an umpire.

At the outset of his career the native Chicagoan was a pitcher, starting in 1884 and concluding in 1890 with a 71-112 record. He had pitched for Toledo and Pittsburgh of the American Association and Washington and New York of the National League. He was a 29-game loser with Washington, but a 23-game winner with New York.

The tall, taciturn O'Day then turned to umpiring. His career as an arbiter spanned from 1891 through 1927 with two seasons off as a manager. He piloted the Cincinnati Reds in 1912, finishing fourth with a 75-78 record, and took over the Cubs in 1914.

As the Cubs' manager, O'Day's top contribution was placing Hippo Vaughn in the starting rotation. The well-traveled lefty rewarded O'Day's patience by posting a 21-13 record.

O'Day had another 20-game winner, Larry Cheney at 20-18, and had other well-known players as Frank Schulte, Roger Bresnahan, Vic Saier, Jimmy Archer, Heinie Zimmerman, and Tommy Leach in the lineup.

O'Day's Cubs could finish no better than fourth with a 78-76 record. That was the season George Stallings's Miracle Boston Braves zoomed from last place on July 4 to win the National League pennant and sweep Connie Mack's Philadelphia A's in the World Series.

O'Day gave up the Cub reins to Bresnahan at the conclusion of the season and resumed his first love, umpiring. Upon his retirement in 1927, O'Day patronized the Cubs and White Sox parks and the local tracks. He always wintered in Florida. He died July 2, 1935, a week short of his 72nd birthday.

O n Jan. 16, 1916, chewing gum magnate William Wrigley, Jr., became a minority shareholder ($50,000) in the Cubs when Charles Weeghman purchased the team. Within two years Wrigley had become the majority holder. By 1921 he was the sole owner.

It was in 1916 also that the Cubs relocated to Clark and Addison Streets in the ballpark that had been built two years earlier for the Chicago Whales of the short-lived Federal League. Then called Weeghman Park, it was later known as Cubs Park before being rechristened Wrigley Field in 1926.

The North Side era did not begin with much fanfare as the Cubs finished fifth. With Fred Mitchell replacing Joe Tinker as manager in 1917, the Cubs ended fifth again, but that season witnessed the greatest pitching duel in history. Jim Vaughn of the Cubs and Fred Toney of the Reds wrestled elbows in a double no-hitter at Weeghman Park for nine innings before Cincinnati eked out two hits in the 10th to win 1-0.

During the winter of 1917-18, some important deals gave the Cubs a much-needed shot in the arm. The Cubs obtained pitchers Grover Alexander (along with his batterymate, Bill Killefer) from the Phillies and Lefty Tyler from the Braves. Charlie Hollocher was brought up from the minors to play shortstop. In another trade, outfielder George Paskert was also picked up from the Phillies.

Thanks to the hitting of Hollocher and the pitching of the "big three"—Vaughn, Tyler, and Claude Hendrix—the Cubs won the 1918 pennant in a war-shortened season. Alexander, who was expected to be the big winner, was drafted into the army after only three pitching appearances.

In the World Series, the Boston Red Sox beat the Cubs in six games in a series that featured strong pitching on both sides. Babe Ruth, then a pitcher, defeated the Cubs twice. Ironically, the Cubs outscored the Red Sox, 10 runs to 9, in the series. For another odd twist, the Chicago contests were played in Comiskey Park because of its larger seating capacity.

Success was fleeting as the Cubs skidded to third in 1919, fifth in '20, and seventh in '21. Grover Alexander, back from the service, supplanted the fading Vaughn as the ace of the staff, but he could not carry the team on his coattails. Meanwhile, the headlines focused on the White Sox. They lost eight star players in September 1920 following their implication in the "Black Sox" game-throwing scandal of the previous year's World Series.

Fred Mitchell left as Cub manager after the 1920 campaign and was replaced by Johnny Evers, who did not even last through the next season, being replaced by Bill Killefer in August 1921.

Under Killefer the Cubs became fairly respectable for awhile, pulling home fifth in 1922, fourth in '23, and fifth in '24. They finished well above .500 all three seasons.

Alexander and Hollocher continued to set the pace. New front liners included first baseman Ray Grimes, muscular outfielder Hack Miller, infielder Sparky Adams, outfielder Jigger Statz, pitcher Vic Aldridge, and third baseman Barney Friberg. Most of them had brief, meteoric careers. Bob O'Farrell, a veteran of the

SECTION THREE
1916-1925
To the North Side, by Gum

Lou Gehrig's first homer in a big league ballpark occurred on June 26, 1920, at Wrigley Field. Gehrig, a junior at New York's High School of Commerce hit a ninth-inning grand-slam homer to beat Chicago's Lane Tech 12-8.

1918 champions, became one of the league's best catchers.

In 1925, however, the Cubs fell to dead last for the first time in their history. In this tumultuous year there were three managers: Killefer, Rabbit Maranville (whose "leadership" generally led the team into speakeasies), and finally, Moon Gibson. Little could fans conceive that a bright new era would begin the following season.

VIC SAIER

SAIER, VICTOR SYLVESTER
B. May 4, 1891, Lansing, Mich.
D. May 14, 1967, East Lansing, Mich.
BL TR 5′11″ 185 lb.

Although not well remembered today, Victor Saier was Frank Chance's replacement at first base during the 1910s. Coming to the Cubs in 1911, the 20-year-old Saier batted .259 in 86 games. The following year he appeared in 122 contests, jacking his batting average up to .288.

Vic enjoyed his greatest season in 1913. Again batting .288, Saier played in 148 games, smashed 14 dead ball homers, scored 93 runs, and drove in 92. In addition, he tied Frank Schulte's 1911 Cub record by hitting 21 triples to lead the league.

He also displayed skill on the basepaths, stealing 26 bases. Ring Lardner, who then wrote the "In the Wake of the News" column for the *Chicago Tribune,* called him "the likeliest youth I have ever seen."

Saier did not do as well thereafter, the best being a .264 season in 1915 with 29 stolen bases. Nevertheless, he continued to hit the long ball, socking 18 homers in 1914 and another 11 the season after.

The Chicago Cubs, 1918 National League Champions

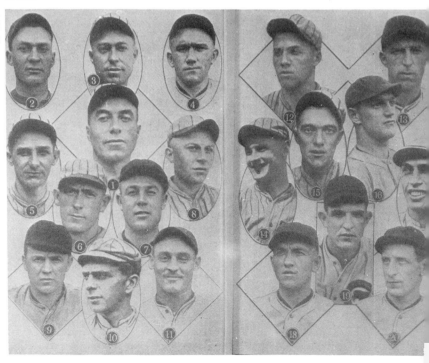

Four of his blasts in 1914 came off Christy Mathewson, the Giant ace who won 373 games lifetime. In fact, Vic's career total of five homers off Matty (he had one more in 1916) were the most hit against him by one player.

April 20, 1916, was the day of the Cubs' first game in the ballpark now known as Wrigley Field. Then it was only a single-decked structure with a seating capacity of 14,000, but 20,000 fans turned out for the season opener.

Vic Saier was the hero as his sacrifice fly in the bottom of the 11th drove home the winning run in a 7-6 squeaker over the Reds. However, the Cubs' first year in their new location turned out to be Saier's last as a regular.

After playing the first six games of the 1917 season, Saier broke his leg. It was the beginning of the end of his career. With Vic in the hospital, the Cubs hastily purchased Fred Merkle from the Dodgers to play first base.

Saier attempted a comeback with the Pirates in 1919, but after batting a weak .223 in 58 games, he retired from the game.

Lifetime, Vic was a .263 hitter with 774 hits.

The Cubs had a live cubby-bear mascot in a cage outside Addison Street in 1917. He was donated by J. Ogden Armour and was named JOA.

T o modern-day fans the worst transaction in Cubs' history occurred on June 15, 1964. That was the day the Cardinals swindled them out of speedy Lou Brock.

The Cubs pulled an earlier boner the day after Christmas in 1917 by gift-wrapping Fred (Cy) Williams to the Phillies for George (Dode) Paskert.

Paskert, an acrobatic center fielder, helped the Cubs win the 1918 National League pennant, batting .286, but he was more a dud. He lasted only three seasons in Cub flannels and hit only nine homers.

Williams, a long-legged bean pole, played 13 seasons with the Phillies and would up with 251 homers. In 1923 Williams matched Babe Ruth in homers, each leading his league with 41. Unfortunately Cy couldn't match the Babe's paycheck.

Williams joined the Cubs in 1912 straight from the Hoosier sandlots. He never played an inning of minor league ball. The Cubs were reluctant to use their free swinger against southpaw pitchers until he hit an eye-popping grand slam off the Dodgers' Nap Rucker, one of the premier lefties, on Aug. 25, 1913, at West Side Park.

Williams didn't become a regular until the 1915 season. Cy celebrated his regular role by leading the club in homers with 13, but finished second to Phillies' Gavvy Cravath, one of the game's unheralded sluggers, who hit 24.

In 1916 Cy hit 12 homers to share the National League homer title with Dave Robertson of the Giants. The following season the Cubs prematurely gave up their young center fielder when he hit only 5 homers and led all batsman with 78 strikeouts. He was

CY WILLIAMS

WILLIAMS, FRED
B. Dec. 21, 1887,
Wadena, Ind.
D. April 23, 1974,
Eagle River, Wis.
BL TL 6'2" 180 lb.

parceled for Paskert on Dec. 26, 1917.

Historians claim Williams, a dead pull hitter, had a soft touch at Philadelphia's ancient Baker Bowl, with its short right field porch. But the height of the fence cut off many homers, frequently holding Williams to a single. Cy's specialties were fierce, low line drives that would rattle off the tin fence.

Indians' manager Lou Boudreau is credited with the famed "Williams Shift" against a latter-day Williams named Ted. Boudreau would bunch his players to the right side against the lanky Red Sox slugger.

But long before Boudreau, the same shift was used against Cy. Cub manager Fred Mitchell instigated the shift during the 1918 season and others followed, including John McGraw of the Giants and Wilbert Robinson of the Dodgers.

Despite the shift, Cy kept swinging away. His 15 homers led the National League in 1920. He ranked second to Rogers Hornsby the following season with 26, but topped them all with 41 in 1923. Cy again led with 30 in 1927, being tied with Cub slugger Hack Wilson.

In addition, Williams cut down on his strikeouts and topped the .300 mark six times, highlighted by a .345 average in 1926.

Williams went on to become the first National Leaguer to reach 200 homers, ranking second only to the Babe overall. He connected for his final homer in 1930. By this time, Cy was relegated to pinch-hitting roles. He had yielded his position to another Hoosier, a young slugger named Chuck Klein.

Williams finished with a .292 batting average, 1,981 hits, and 251 homers (34 as a Cub). He managed the Richmond club of the Eastern League in 1931 and then retired from baseball to become an architect.

He won awards for his designs of hotels, theatres, and a resort in Wisconsin. He died in Eagle River, Wis., on April 23, 1974, at the age of 86.

When the Paskert-Williams trade was consummated, many sang an ode to Dode. But Cub fans later sighed for Cy.

HIPPO
VAUGHN

VAUGHN, JAMES
LESLIE

B. April 9, 1888,
Weatherford, Tex.
D. May 29, 1966,
Chicago, Ill.
BB TL 6'4" 215 lb.

Although he won more games (151) than any other left-hander in Cub history, Jim "Hippo" Vaughn is best remembered for one that he lost. The scene was Wrigley Field, May 2, 1917, where Vaughn and Fred Toney of the Reds battled through the first nine innings without either allowing a hit.

In the top of the 10th, Vaughn retired the first batter, and the tension mounted. Then Larry Kopf singled for the first hit, after which Greasy Neale flied to Cy Williams in center for the second out. Hal Chase followed with another fly to center, but Williams muffed this one, allowing Kopf to take third.

With former Olympic star Jim Thorpe at bat, Chase stole second. Thorpe then dribbled one down the third base line. Vaughn grabbed the ball and fired it to the plate, where catcher Art Wilson was asleep at the switch. The ball bounced off Wilson's chest protector, and Kopf scored. Chase tried to follow him, but Wilson finally recovered the ball and made the tag to retire the side. However, Toney held the Cubs hitless in the 10th to win 1-0.

It was the only double no-hitter (for nine innings) in baseball history, and the chances of it ever recurring with today's lively ball are practically zilch.

Vaughn always took the loss light heartedly. Years afterward he recalled, "There weren't more than 7,000 people in the stands, but I'll bet that 50,000 said they were there and some of them were kids who couldn't have been born at the time."

Vaughn never could catch that elusive no-hitter, but he did pitch a one-hit shutout over the Giants in 1918 and another against the Pirates in 1920.

Before joining the Cubs, Vaughn had been in the majors off and on for five years with the Yankees and Senators, but had accomplished little. He was hurling for Kansas City of the American Association when the Cubs picked him up in August 1913 for pitcher Lew Richie.

In 1914 Vaughn blossomed with a 21-13 log and became an annual 20-game winner through 1919, except for the 1916 season, when he won "only" 17 games. He had good control and a blazing fastball, fanning 195 batters in 1917.

Although Vaughn's victory total peaked in 1917 with 23, the following year was, in many ways, the Hippo's best. In leading the Cubs to the pennant in the war-shortened 1918 season, he topped the league in wins (22), ERA (1.74), innings pitched (290), strikeouts (148), shutouts (8), and games started (33).

He lost two of his three decisions to the Red Sox in the World Series but posted a remarkable 1.00 ERA in 27 innings. His lone win was a 3-0 shutout at Fenway Park, Sept. 10.

For an encore, Jim won 21 games in 1919, and 19 the following year. In a 3-1 victory over the Giants on Aug. 9, 1919, he became the last Cub pitcher to steal home.

In 1921 Johnny Evers replaced Fred Mitchell as Cub manager. He and Vaughn had not gotten along when Evers previously ran the team in 1913, and their mutual dislike had not mitigated over the years. Vaughn slipped to 3-11 and made his last appearance July 9 before quitting the team in disgust.

For many years thereafter, Vaughn pitched for semipro teams in Chicago, becoming a gate attraction in the "pass the hat" circuit. He returned to the Cubs as batting practice pitcher in 1937, after which he called it quits for keeps.

His lifetime record was 178-137 with a 2.49 ERA.

BOB O'FARRELL

O'FARRELL,
ROBERT ARTHUR
B. Oct. 19, 1896,
Waukegan, Ill.
BR TR 5'10" 185 lb.

When Bob O'Farrell was a boy growing up in Waukegan, Ill., he was, like his father, a White Sox fan. White Sox catcher Billy Sullivan was his idol, and the youthful O'Farrell despised the Cubs with a passion.

Then came a June day in 1915 when the local semipro team, which Bob played for, engaged the hated Cubs in an exhibition contest. At the end of the game, the Cubs offered O'Farrell a contract, and a strange transformation came over him: he became a Cub fan.

His father underwent the same metamorphasis. As O'Farrell related decades later in an interview, "I tossed out two Cub runners at second base, and they signed me on the spot. I played my first major league game Sept. 7, 1915, at the Cubs' West Side Park."

For the next couple of years Bob was shuffled back and forth from Chicago to Peoria before settling permanently with the parent club. When the Cubs won the pennant in 1918, Bob served as back-up receiver to Bill Killefer, batting .283 in 52 games.

In the World Series, the Red Sox defeated the Cubs in six games. As O'Farrell recollected, "Babe Ruth was a great pitcher for Boston at that time, and one of the best I ever faced.

"I batted against him twice, and both times I got good wood on the ball and thought I had a hit. But the Red Sox had a great shortstop, Everett Scott. He covered a lot of ground and threw me out both times."

Catching such hurlers as Hippo Vaughn, Lefty Tyler, Grover Alexander, and Claude Hendrix, Bob became a regular in 1920, and by 1922 he was a full-fledged star. That season he batted .324 in 128 games, following it up with a .319 mark in '23, playing 131 contests and driving home 84 runs.

Although a right-handed batter, he was especially adept at punching singles to right-center. With his magnet glove and rifle throwing arm, he topped all National League receivers in putouts and assists both seasons.

But in 1924 Bob suffered a fractured skull from a foul tip, dropping to .240 in 71 games. Gabby Hartnett replaced O'Farrell as the Cubs' first-string catcher and became so good that O'Farrell was no longer needed. Giving up on Bob, the Cubs traded him to the Cardinals for catcher Mike Gonzalez and infielder Howie Freigau on May 23, 1925.

With St. Louis, Bob made a successful comeback, batting .293 in 147 games as the Cardinals won the pennant in 1926. In the World Series, he batted .304 to lead the Redbirds to a thrilling seven-game victory over the Yankees.

It was Bob's throw that nailed Babe Ruth attempting to steal second for the final out of the series. "Throwing out Ruth to end the '26 series is still my greatest thrill," he said nearly half a century later. For his efforts, Bob was named Most Valuable Player in the National League.

As player-manager, Bob brought the Cardinals home second in 1927, but the following May he was traded to the Giants. There he caught Carl Hubbell's no-hitter against the Pirates on May 8, 1929.

"Carl had a great screwball that day," recalled Bob. "Our wives were sitting in a box seat at the Polo Grounds, and as the game progressed they became so nervous that they went up to the grandstand to be further away from the action."

After five years with the Giants, Bob was traded back to the Cardinals in 1933, split the '34 season between the Reds and Cubs, then wound up with the Cardinals again in '35.

During his 21 seasons in the majors—a record for catchers—Bob played in 1,492 contests, batting .273 with 1,120 hits. Following his retirement from baseball, he returned to his home town, where he became a successful businessman.

I f Phil Douglas had been able to defeat John Barleycorn, he might have become one of baseball's greats. Instead, he had a brief, stormy, and ultimately sad career.

PHIL DOUGLAS

DOUGLAS, PHILLIP BROOKS
B. June 17, 1890, Cedartown, Ga.
D. Aug. 1, 1952, Sequatchie Valley, Tenn.
BR TR 6′3″ 190 lb.

Nicknamed "Shufflin' Phil" because of his staggering gait, Douglas specialized in the slippery elm spitball. As no team could hold onto him for very long because of his drinking problem, Douglas bounced from the White Sox (where he started in 1912) to the Reds to the Dodgers—with minor league interludes—before landing with the Cubs late in 1915.

After splitting two decisions, Douglas was sent down to St. Paul for more training, possibly with the hopes of sobering him up.

Brought back up in 1917, Douglas won 14 games for the Cubs but lost 20. Even so, he could throw an effective spitter when he put his mind to it, as evidenced by his five shutouts, 2.55 ERA, and 151 strikeouts. Furthermore, he displayed better control than most spitballers.

The main problem was Phil's own erratic personality. Whenever he was scheduled to pitch, it was never certain that he would show up. He frequently deserted the team for "vacations" which, of course, were extended drinking bouts. There was also the additional cost of drying him out at sanitariums from time to time.

The next season Phil was only a minor factor in the Cubs' pennant drive, contributing a 9-9 record, but he enjoyed what was likely his greatest day in baseball. It was a morning-afternoon doubleheader with the Braves at Chicago. In the opener he came in as fireman and came out the winner in a 10-inning 4-3 victory.

After a couple of hours' rest, Phil went all the way in the nightcap to shuffle the Bostonians 3-2. During the World Series that fall against the Red Sox, however, he lost his only decision.

In 1919 Douglas's spitball was slicker than ever. He went 162 innings without serving a gopher ball. By early August he had won 10-of-16 decisions, but Cubs' brass had grown weary of his all too frequent benders and dispatched him to the Giants for Dave Robertson.

Under John McGraw's iron hand, Douglas won 14 games the following year and 15 in 1921, not to mention two victories over the Yankees in the '21 World Series. By 1922 Phil was on the verge of his best season yet, posting an 11-4 record by mid-August.

Then came an extensive drinking spree even by Douglas's standards. After a fine, suspension, and tongue-lashing by McGraw, Phil fell off the wagon yet again. With St. Louis and New York in a tooth-and-nail battle for the lead, Phil wrote the following letter to outfielder Les Mann of the Cardinals:

> I want to leave here. I don't want to see this guy [McGraw] win the pennant. You know I can pitch, and I am afraid that if I stay I will win the pennant for him.
> Talk this over with the boys and if it is all right send the goods to my house at night and I will go to fishing camp. Let me know if you will do this and I will go home on the next train.

Those words haunted Phil to his dying day. Mann, a YMCA teetotaler, turned the letter over to Card boss Branch Rickey, another abstainer, who gave it to baseball's puritanical czar, Judge Kenesaw Mountain Landis.

Although Douglas was actually more pathetic than hateful, Landis was swift and severe in banning him from organized ball. Shufflin' Phil's pitching days came to an abrupt end. The flawed hurler left behind 93 wins and the same number of losses. He died in the Tennessee hills 30 years later, an impoverished alcoholic.

MAX FLACK

FLACK, MAX JOHN
B. Feb. 5, 1890, Belleville, Ill.
D. July 31, 1955, Belleville, Ill.
BL TL 5'7" 148 lb.

Although hardly remembered today, Max Flack was one of the Cubs more prominent outfielders of the World War I era and immediately thereafter.

Max broke in with the Chicago Whales of the Federal League in 1914, and when the Whales won the pennant the following year, he contributed a fine season, batting .314, scoring 88 runs, and stealing 37 bases.

When the Federal League disbanded after that season, former Whale owner Charles Weeghman purchased a controlling interest in the Cubs and brought many of the Whale players with him, including Flack.

In a Cub uniform Flack dropped to .258 in 1916, but he stole 24 bases and proved himself a competent glove man with his league-leading .991 fielding average, making but two errors in 141 games.

During the years following the war, Flack regained his batting eye, hitting .294 in 1919, .302 in '20, and .301 in '21. In 1921 he was again the top fielding outfielder in the National League with a .989 average.

Then came one of the most bizarre incidents in baseball history. It was Memorial Day 1922. The Cubs were playing the Cardinals in a morning-afternoon twin bill at Wrigley Field.

At that time, Max lived in a house three blocks from the park, and after playing his usual right field position in the morning contest, he went home for lunch. Flack returned to the Cubs' clubhouse ready to suit up for the second game when Cub skipper Bill Killefer told him, "Maxie, boy, you're in the wrong clubhouse."

The Cubs were the first big league team to flash "hit" or "error" on their scoreboard in 1917.

"And I was," Flack recalled years later. "They had traded me to the Cardinals for Cliff Heathcote. So he played for the Cubs that afternoon and I was in right field for the Cardinals.

"There wasn't much radio in those days and, of course, there hadn't been time to have it published in a newspaper. So fans were astonished when they saw us in different uniforms."

Both Flack and Heathcote had gone hitless in the morning game, and the changes of uniforms brought them luck. Flack got one hit for St. Louis, while Heathcote collected a pair for the Cubs. The Cubs won both games 4-1 and 4-2.

Flack had one more good season at the plate with the Cardinals, batting .291 in 1923.

He retired after the 1925 season, a lifetime .278 hitter with 1,461 hits and 200 stolen bases.

A good fielding but light hitting third baseman, Charlie Deal broke in with the Tigers in 1912, then bounced around from there to the Braves, the St. Louis Feds, and the Browns before sticking with the Cubs late in 1916. He remained their regular third baseman until his retirement at the end of the 1921 season.

As a Cub, Deal was a dependable glove man, leading the league three times in fielding average (1919, '20, '21) and once in double plays (1917).

However, he continued to be only a fair batsman, reaching a high of .289 in 1919, which he repeated two years later.

He finished a decade-long career with a .257 average and 752 hits.

CHARLIE DEAL

DEAL, CHARLES ALBERT
B. Oct. 30, 1891, Wilkinsburg, Pa.
D. Sept. 16, 1979, Covina, Calif.
BR TR 5'11" 160 lb.

Claude Hendrix was a Cub hurler of the World War I era. He had a checkered career in more ways than one. Brought up by the Pirates in 1911, he blossomed into a sophomore sensation the following season with a 24-9 record and a .322 batting average to boot, only to slump to 14-15 the year after that.

In 1914 Hendrix jumped to the newly formed Chicago Whales of the Federal League, where he had his greatest season. In a workhorse's 362 innings, Claude notched 29 wins against 11 losses, fanned 189 batters, and threw six shutouts as Chicago finished a

CLAUDE HENDRIX

HENDRIX, CLAUDE RAYMOND
B. April 13, 1889, Olathe, Kan.
D. March 22, 1944, Allentown, Pa.
BR TR 6' 195 lb.

strong second to Indianapolis by one game.

The following year, as Joe Tinker's Whales won the pennant, Hendrix's victory total slipped to 16, but he achieved personal glory with a 10-0 no-hitter over Pittsburgh May 15.

That winter the Federal League disbanded and Whale owner Charles Weeghman bought out the Cubs, taking Hendrix and the cream of the Whale crop with him. Although Weeghman expected a solid contender, he was sadly disappointed as his pitching ace sank to an 8-16 mark while the Cubs finished a poor fifth.

But by 1918 the Cubs were number one, with Claude contributing a 20-7 record for a juicy .741 percentage, tops in the league. The next two years were below average, though, as Hendrix's career took another downslide.

Late in 1920 Hendrix was implicated in a scandal that indirectly triggered the investigation of the 1919 World Series fix. Scheduled to pitch the Aug. 31 contest against the Phillies, Hendrix was benched at the last minute in favor of Grover Alexander, who pitched out of turn and lost 3-0.

It seemed that that morning, club president William Veeck, Sr., had received phone calls and telegrams warning of a set-up, which he revealed to the press Sept. 4.

Later it was alleged that on the day of the game in question, Hendrix had sent a wire to a gambler named Frog Thompson, placing a $5,000 bet against his own team. Although both suspects denied everything, the pitcher was released in February 1921 on grounds that the Cubs were "rebuilding the pitching staff."

Unable to sign on with any other club, Hendrix quietly dropped out of organized ball, a clouded, ambiguous figure.

His lifetime record was 144-116 with a 2.65 ERA.

FRED MERKLE

MERKLE,
FREDERICK
CHARLES
B. Dec. 20, 1888,
Watertown, Wis.
D. March 2, 1956,
Daytona Beach, Fla.
BR TR 6'1" 190 lb.

One fleeting moment shaped the life as well as the baseball career of Frederick Charles Merkle. It happened in the ninth inning against the Chicago Cubs on Sept. 23, 1908, at New York's historic Polo Grounds.

Merkle, a 19-year-old rookie, failed to touch second base and it cost the Giants a pennant. He was labeled a "Bonehead." It was a mistake he was never allowed to forget.

The Giants, Cubs, and Pirates were roaring down the stretch noses apart. The stage was set for the Merkle Boner on Sept. 4, 1908 at Pittsburgh. The Pirates and Cubs were locked in a scoreless tie in the 10th inning. Pittsburgh had the bases loaded when Owen Wilson singled to center.

Manager Fred Clarke raced home with the winning run, but Pirate rookie Warren Gill never ran from first to second, electing to run off the field. Cub second baseman Johnny Evers took the throw from center fielder Jimmy Slagle, stepped on second, and yelled, "Forceout," within earshot of umpire Hank O'Day, who refused to listen.

But O'Day was a good umpire. He realized his mistake and wouldn't allow it to happen again.

The Pirates were out of the race when the Cubs met the Giants 19 days later. The score was 1-1 in the ninth. Moose McCormick singled, and Merkle, playing for the injured Fred Tenney, singled him to third. With two out, Al Bridwell singled to center. Then the fun began.

McCormick crossed the plate and the Giants "won" 2-1. The fans came pouring out of their seats onto the field. Merkle jogged halfway to second, glanced at the fans, and raced off to the clubhouse. He didn't touch second base.

Center fielder Solly Hofman threw the ball in, and it sailed over shortstop Joe Tinker's head. It rolled over to where Giant pitcher Iron Man McGinnity was standing. Tinker and Evers wrestled McGinnity to the ground, but the Iron Man heaved the ball into the crowd.

A middle-aged man wearing a bowler scooped up the ball. Third baseman Harry Steinfeldt and pitcher Rube Kroh raced after him. Steinfeldt begged him, but he wouldn't let go. Kroh solved the problem by pulling the bowler over his eyes, grabbing the ball, and tossing it to Tinker, who relayed it to Evers.

Cubs' manager Frank Chance, meanwhile, was tracking down umpire O'Day. Some say he bit him on the ankle and dragged him to second base. Evers was standing on second and made sure O'Day saw him.

O'Day, remembering the Pittsburgh game, shouted, "The run does not count." Then he walked away. With a jubilant and bewildered crowd on the field, there was no chance to resume the game.

Following bitter arguments, it was ruled that Merkle's failure to touch second base had nullified the run, and the game resorted to a 1-1 tie. The Giants and Cubs finished the season deadlocked for first. The replay was set for Oct. 8 at the Polo Grounds.

The Cubs went on to win the playoff and the pennant, and they swept past Ty Cobb and the Detroit Tigers in the World Series.

Merkle was so broken up he wanted to quit, but Giant manager John McGraw talked him into sticking it out. Merkle became the Giants' cleanup hitter and helped them win pennants in 1911, '12, and '13.

Hard luck again hounded Merkle in the 1912 World Series against the Boston Red Sox. In the 10th inning of the final game, Tris Speaker popped an easy foul. Merkle and catcher Chief Meyers let the ball drop between them. Speaker then singled and later scored the winning run. Again Merkle was blamed as a stupid bonehead.

Merkle actually was above average in intelligence. He was an expert at chess, played bridge, was a shark at algebra, and was one of the first players to shun the pool halls for the golf links.

The tall, stoop-shouldered first baseman was traded to Brooklyn in 1916 and helped the Dodgers win a pennant. During the 1917 season he was acquired by of all teams, the hated Cubs.

He was the Cubs' regular first baseman for four seasons, leading the club in RBI as they won the 1918 pennant. Perhaps his most eventful day in a Cub uniform occurred on Sept. 12, 1919, against the Dodgers when he combined with shortstop Charlie Hollocher for a sixth-inning triple play and then hit a game-winning homer, with the ball going through a hole in the wooden fence at Cubs' Park.

Merkle retired after the 1920 season, but returned as a player-coach with the New York Yankees in 1925 and '26. In 16 seasons, Merkle had 1,579 base hits, hit 59 homers, drove in 733 runs, and batted .273.

In a final appearance as manager of the Class D Daytona, Fla. club in 1929, Merkle walked off the field, vowing never to return. It was reported that a player made a reference to him as a bonehead.

"As a player I became calloused to it after awhile," said Merkle. "But it was tough on my wife, and worse as my three daughters grew up. It finally got on my nerves."

"When I die, I guess they'll put on my tombstone: Here lies Bonehead Merkle." He then went into a self-imposed exile.

It wasn't until July 30, 1950, that Merkle returned to the Polo Grounds. The Giants were staging an old-timers game and he received an invitation. "Yes, I'm going back," he said. "I've got to. My daughter, Marianne, won't let me say no this time. She's going with me to the Polo Grounds."

Merkle was 61, heavy set with gray hair. All the Giants and Cubs were dead—Tinker, Evers, Chance, McGraw, Christy Mathewson. Merkle stepped onto the field to receive a gift, and a crowd of 35,073 rose to its feet for a standing ovation. They had forgiven him.

"All I wanted was a chance to make up for that blunder," said Merkle. "Mr. McGraw gave me that chance. When I would strike out and the fans would shriek, 'Bonehead,' McGraw would say, 'Don't pay any attention to them; you'll hit the next one.'"

"For the youngsters who are playing the game today, don't become discouraged. Don't let a wild throw disturb you and don't let a spectacular play excite you."

Tears ran down his cheeks as the crowd cheered wildly. All the bitterness of more than four decades was washed away. "I didn't want to come back here," said Merkle. "Now, I sort of hate to go back home."

LES MANN

MANN, LESLIE
B. Nov. 18, 1893,
Lincoln, Neb.
D. Jan. 14, 1962,
Pasadena, Calif.
BR TR 5'9" 172 lb.

Les Mann was a Cub outfielder from 1916 through '19, batting .288 for the 1918 Cub pennant winners. In his 16-year career, the well-traveled Mann also played for the Federal League Chicago Whales, the Braves (three times), the Cardinals, the Reds, and the Giants.

Retiring in 1928, he was a career .282 hitter with 1,332 hits.

Turner Barber was a Cub outfielder from 1917 through '22. He had one season as a regular in 1921. He batted .314 in 127 games. Barber had played for the Senators (1915-16) before coming to Chicago, and he finished with the Dodgers in 1923.

Lifetime, he was a .289 hitter in 491 games.

TURNER BARBER

BARBER, TYRUS TURNER
B. July 9, 1893,
Lavinia, Tenn.
D. Oct. 20, 1968,
Milan, Tenn.
BL TR 5'11" 170 lb.

Vic Aldridge was the last Cub pitcher to collect five hits in one game, going five-for-five (all singles) on May 6, 1922. He scored once and drove in one run as the Cubs took the Pirates 11-7.

Aldridge first came to the Cubs in 1917, splitting a dozen decisions. After brief action Aldridge entered the navy the following year, then returned to the minors, not coming back to the big time until 1922. Vic then put in three good seasons for the Cubs, with records of 16-15, 16-9, and 15-12.

In the autumn of 1924, Aldridge was traded to the Pirates in the deal that brought Charlie Grimm to the Cubs. Vic helped the Bucs win pennants in 1925 and '27, posting 15 wins each season plus two victories in the '25 World Series.

He pitched for the Giants in 1928, then hung around in the minors for a few more years. After leaving baseball, Aldridge graduated from law school, passed his bar exam, and later served in the Indiana State Senate.

His career record was 97-80 with a 3.76 ERA.

VIC ALDRIDGE

ALDRIDGE, VICTOR EDDINGTON
B. Oct. 25, 1893,
Indian Springs, Ind.
D. April 17, 1973,
Terre Haute, Ind.
BR TR 5'9½" 175 lb.

FRED MITCHELL

Of all the Cubs' pennant-winning managers, the least known was Fred Mitchell. Perhaps, if he had maintained his real name, Frederick Francis Yapp, he would not have been cloaked in anonymity, especially among trivia buffs.

While some might consider the name appropriate for a ballplayer, Yapp thought it would make him the butt of jokes, so he adopted his mother's maiden name of Mitchell.

Mitchell was an original member of the first American League club in Boston, signing on with the Somersets on Feb. 27, 1901, as a pitcher-infielder. The Somersets, like Yapp, changed names, becoming the Puritans, Pilgrims, Plymouth Rocks, and finally, the Red Sox in 1907.

Mitchell had a 6-6 record as a pitcher, but batted only .159 as a spare infielder that initial season. The following year, Mitchell was traded to the Philadelphia Athletics and wound up with a 5-8 mark. He did improve his stickwork, hiking his average to .184.

Then it was on to the crosstown Phillies in 1903 where he was used exclusively as a pitcher, winning 10 and losing 15. The 1904 season found Mitchell in a Brooklyn uniform. Arm trouble in 1905

MITCHELL, FREDERICK FRANCIS
B. June 5, 1878,
Cambridge, Mass.
D. Oct. 13, 1970,
Newton, Mass.
BR TR 5'9½" 185 lb.

ended his pitching career. He closed with a 30-48 record.

Mitchell was banished to Toronto of the International League, where he became a combination pitcher-catcher and even hurled a no-hitter against Montreal on July 6, 1908.

He bounced back to the majors in 1910, catching 68 games for the New York Highlanders, who later became the Yankees. His batting average? Mitchell was now in the .230 class.

It wasn't enough to keep him in the majors. After two long seasons in the bushes, Mitchell caught on as a coach-pinch hitter with the Boston Braves in 1913. He was now a .333 hitter—but only came to bat three times.

Mitchell, well liked by manager George Stallings, helped coach the pitchers and catchers during the 1914 "miracle season" when the Braves rolled from last place on July 11 to win the National League pennant and sweep Connie Mack's A's in the World Series.

Mitchell replaced Joe Tinker as Cub manager in 1917 and led the team to the 1918 pennant. The Cubs dropped the World Series to the Red Sox in six games, mainly on the strong pitching of a young phenom named Babe Ruth.

As a manager, Mitchell was a devout strategist. In fact, it was he, not Lou Boudreau, who invented the famed "Williams Shift." The Cubs had a dead right field pull hitter named Cy Williams, whom they traded to the Phillies in 1918.

When the left-handed Williams strode to the plate in a Philly uniform, Mitchell ordered his players to shift to the right, leaving only the third baseman and left fielder to the left of the diamond.

Boudreau, managing the Cleveland Indians, employed the same shift against another Williams some 30 years later. The latter-day Williams was a Red Sox slugger named Ted.

When William Wrigley replaced Charles Weeghman as the Cubs' majority stockholder, he elevated Mitchell to the duel role of president and manager and brought in a former sportswriter named William Veeck as vice-president.

It was not long before the National League in looking over its by-laws, found that Mitchell, managing on the field and signed to a players' contract, couldn't double as president. Mitchell then stepped aside and Veeck became president.

After bringing home only one pennant, Mitchell also stepped aside as Cub manager following the 1920 season. In his four years at the Cubs' helm, Mitchell's teams finished fifth, first, third, and fifth. His Cub managerial record was 308 victories and 269 losses.

Mitchell returned to his native Boston, where he guided the Braves for three years. He left the big leagues after the 1923 season and assumed the job for which he is best remembered, Harvard baseball coach.

The ivy halls of Harvard were a perfect setting for the stocky Mitchell, who never ranked among the tobacco chewin' rowdies of the game. The soft-spoken Mitchell led Harvard to 194 victories,

131 losses, and 5 ties during his tenure at Harvard. He retired in 1939. Always the clean-living gentleman, Mitchell lived to the ripe age of 92.

One of baseball's greatest pitchers, Grover "Pete" Alexander won 373 games in his career to tie Christy Mathewson for the all-time National League record. From 1911 through '17, he was the ace of the Philadelphia Phillies' staff, enjoying three consecutive years with 30 or more wins—31-10 in 1915, 33-12 in '16, and 30-13 in '17.

On Nov. 11, 1917, Alex and his batterymate, Bill Killefer, were traded to the Cubs for pitcher Mike Prendergast, catcher Pickles Dilhoefer, and $60,000. Although Alexander's best years had been with the Phillies, he had many fine seasons ahead of him as a Cub. He won 128 games in a Chicago jersey and appeared in many historic contests.

In 1918, Alex won two-of-three decisions before entering the army, where he quickly became a sergeant in France. He was gassed on the battlefield and suffered a partial hearing loss from the cannon fire.

Upon returning to civilian life, Alexander began drinking heavily, and in a short time, he was a full-fledged alcoholic. In addition, he developed epilepsy—often suffering attacks in the dugout, but, strangely, never on the mound. These spectres haunted him to the end of his life, making him one of baseball's most tragic heroes.

Even with his personal difficulties, Alex was a better pitcher when he was drunk than most others were when they were sober. In his bag of tricks, he owned a curve ball, a screwball, a sinker, a change-up, and—in his early days—a wicked fastball. He had pinpoint control, and during one stretch (April 18 through May 13, 1923), he hurled 51 consecutive innings without issuing a free pass, a Cub record.

In his first complete season as a Cub, 1919, Alexander put together a 16-11 record. More importantly, he tied the modern Cub record for shutouts in a year with nine. On Sept. 21, he hurled the shortest game in Cub history, blanking the Braves 3-0 in 58 minutes at Wrigley Field.

Alex's best year as a Cub was 1920. In leading the league in victories with a 27-14 mark, he won 11 straight during April and May.

His 11th victory was a down-to-the-wire thriller on May 31 in which Alex won his own game with a home run in the bottom of the 10th to beat the Reds 3-2.

His 363 innings pitched set a 20th century Cub record, while his 173 strikeouts and 1.91 ERA were tops in the league. On Oct. 1, he went the distance to outlast Jesse Haines of the Cardinals 3-2 in 17 innings.

GROVER ALEXANDER

ALEXANDER, GROVER CLEVELAND
B. Feb. 26, 1887, Elba, Neb.
D. Nov. 4, 1950, St. Paul, Neb.
BR TR 6'1" 185 lb.

Throughout the early and middle twenties, "Ol' Pete" continued to dominate the Cubs' staff, including a 22-12 log in 1923. On Sept. 20, 1924, he reached a personal milestone with his 300th career victory, as he turned back the pennant-bound Giants on their own turf 7-3 in 12 innings.

Number 301 came on April 14, 1925, before an opening day crowd of 38,000 at Wrigley Field. Helping his own cause with a single, a double, and a homer, Alex went the route to sink the Pirates 8-2. The occasion was the first regular season Cub game to be broadcast on radio, with Quin Ryan at the mike from atop the grandstand roof.

After winning 15 games during the regular season, Alex pitched the most grueling duel of his life in a game that didn't even count in his record and ended up a tie. It was Oct. 2, game one of the 1925 City Series between the Cubs and the White Sox. Alexander and Ted Blankenship held each other to a 2-2 draw, called after 19 innings because of darkness.

In a practice that would be unthinkable today, the Cubs made no substitutions during the entire game. The Sox made only one.

In 1926 Joe McCarthy was named Cub manager. To establish discipline on an unbridled team, McCarthy ordered the younger players to follow him back to the hotel after ball games, rather than follow Alex to the speakeasy.

Joe laid down the law, "Ol' Pete" thumbed his nose at it, and the struggle for supremacy was on. On June 15 Alexander was suspended for having been hitting the bottle six times in the last 10 days. A week later, he was sent to the Cardinals on waivers.

With the Redbirds, Alex won 9-of-12 to help them win the 1926 pennant. Then came his greatest moment of glory.

In the seventh game of the World Series against the Yankees, the Cardinals were nursing a 3-2 lead in the bottom of the seventh at Yankee Stadium. There were two gone, but New York had the bases loaded. A thoroughly hungover Alexander came in to relieve the faltering Jesse Haines.

Alex slipped a quick strike past Tony Lazzeri, but on the next pitch the Yankee second baseman sent a powerful drive that curved foul by inches down the left field line. Tony swung again and missed, ending the rally. Alex held the Yankees scoreless for the final two innings, to make the Cardinals champions of the world. "Hell," he said in an interview, "If that second 'strike' had been a few inches the other way, Tony'd be the hero, and I'd be called a bum."

After three more years in St. Louis, Alex returned briefly to the Phillies in 1930 before finishing his career with Dallas of the Texas League the same year. Once out of baseball, he drifted from job to job.

Poor Alex never could cast out the demons that tortured him. His remaining years became a revolving door in and out of sanitariums, in between nightmares of delirium tremens and epileptic seizures.

Elected to the Hall of Fame in 1937, he was present at the

dedication of the Cooperstown shrine two years later. He died in 1950 shortly after posting a final love letter to his lifelong sweetheart.

CHARLIE HOLLOCHER

Were it not for his stomach ailments, real or otherwise, Charles Hollocher might have become one of baseball's immortals. For several years he was one of the best shortstops in the National League.

Hollocher was taught baseball by nationally known sportswriter John B. Sheridan while a member of an amateur boys' team in St. Louis. He made his professional debut in 1915 with Keokuk of the Central Association, later playing with Portland of the Pacific Coast League and Rock Island of the Three-I League.

By the spring of 1918, the Cubs were so impressed with Hollocher's play that they made him their full-time shortstop, filling a gap that had been empty since Joe Tinker left six years earlier.

Charlie took charge immediately and became the sparkplug of the team. He led them to the pennant in a war-shortened season with his .316 batting average, tops on the club and fourth highest in the league.

HOLLOCHER,
CHARLES JACOB
B. June 11, 1896,
St. Louis, Mo.
D. Aug. 14, 1940,
St. Louis, Mo.
BL TR 5'7" 154 lb.

His 161 hits led the league, and he stole 26 bases. Had there been a Rookie of the Year award back then, Hollocher certainly would have deserved it.

Hollocher was a rangy shortstop, covering a lot of territory and winning the accolades of the fans with his spectacular dives. Offensively, he was a hustler every inch of the way, often sliding into first base to beat out infield hits. Pitchers found him nearly impossible to strike out.

Charlie fell victim to the proverbial "sophomore jinx" in 1919, dropping to .270 at the plate. The following year he jacked it back up to .319, but played only 80 games, going AWOL in midseason with alleged stomach pains.

The club tracked him down and located him painting houses in his native St. Louis. The fact that club doctors could find nothing wrong with him led some to believe that Hollocher was either faking it or imagining things. Whatever the case, it was a harbinger of things to come.

In 1921 everything appeared to be back to normal. Hollocher played the full season, batting .289 and setting the pace for National League shortstops with a .963 fielding average. On Aug. 30, he participated in a triple play against the Giants (second baseman Zeb Terry to Hollocher to first baseman Ray Grimes), but New York won 5-3. On the same day the Braves pulled a triple killing on the Reds, but Cincinnati emerged a 6-4 victor. It was the only time in history that two triple plays were performed on the same afternoon.

Reaching his peak, Hollocher had his greatest season in 1922. He batted .340 in 152 games with 201 hits, 37 doubles, and 90 runs scored. For the second straight year, he was the best fielding shortstop in the circuit, and he set a National League record low by striking out only five times the entire season.

On Aug. 13, Charlie became one of only three Cubs in history (with Bill Dahlen and Ernie Banks) to hit three triples in one game, during a 16-5 killing of the Cardinals.

At this juncture Hollocher looked like the best thing to hit shortstop since Honus Wagner, but during the winter he suffered a severe attack of the flu. He had a relapse in spring training. Then the mysterious stomach ailments returned to haunt him.

Once again, physicians who examined Hollocher at the Cubs' request could find nothing wrong with him. Hollocher insisted, however, that a prominent St. Louis physician, Dr. Robert F. Hyland, advised him not to play that season lest it ruin his health.

Consequently, Charlie spent most of the 1923 season on the bench. When he did play, he was still as good as ever, hitting .342 in 66 games.

Illness continued to plague him in 1924, but this time it took its toll on his playing as his average fell to .245. At the season's end, he retired prematurely at age 28. In 760 major league games, Hollocher batted .304 with 894 hits. One can only speculate on the heights he could have attained had his health been better.

Charlie briefly returned to the Cubs as a scout in 1931, but resigned after one season. He later operated a tavern in a St. Louis suburb, but the stomach troubles would not go away and ultimately drove him to self-destruction. His suicide was a tragic end to what might have been an outstanding life and career.

GEORGE PASKERT

PASKERT, GEORGE HENRY

B. Aug. 28, 1881, Cleveland, Ohio.
D. Feb. 12, 1959, Cleveland, Ohio
BR TR 5'11"
165 lb.

George Paskert, nicknamed "Dode" for reasons that have since been forgotten, was one of the best fielding and swiftest outfielders of the pre-World War I era.

Breaking in with the Reds in 1907, Paskert enjoyed his best years with the Phillies. He was more or less over the hill by the time the Cubs obtained him in 1918. Nevertheless, he contributed a .286 average and 20 stolen bases to the Cub championship that year.

In the winter of 1919-20, George became a hero in another way. Risking his life, he single-handedly rescued 15 children from a blazing building in Cleveland.

Although severely burned in the process, he returned to play a full season for the Cubs in 1920, batting .279.

Returning to the Reds the following year, he closed his career after that season.

Paskert was a .268 lifetime hitter with 1,613 hits and 293 stolen bases.

Bill Killefer's lifetime batting average was a mediocre .238. He managed the Cubs from 1921 through '25 and the St. Louis Browns from 1930 through '33, but his success in that capacity was not conspicuous.

BILL KILLEFER

KILLEFER, WILLIAM LAVIER
B. Oct. 10, 1887,
Bloomingdale, Mich.
D. July 2, 1960,
Elsmere, Del.
BR TR 5'10½" 200 lb.

He will be remembered longest as Grover Cleveland Alexander's catcher, forming what many historians insist was the greatest of all batteries.

Born in Bloomingdale, Mich., and raised in the storied town of Paw Paw, Mich., where his father was a probate judge, young Bill followed his older brother Wade into baseball.

Wade was captain of the Kalamazoo club of the Michigan State League when kid brother Bill, just out of high school, got a job with him in the outfield. "But he couldn't hit at all," Wade said. "We had to let him go."

The disappointed youngster then attended Sacred Heart College in Watertown, Wis., and St. Edwards College in Austin, Tex. Killefer switched to catching and surfaced to the big leagues with the Browns in 1909. After hitting only .138 and .124, he was sent to Buffalo.

Nicknamed "Reindeer Bill" because of his lack of speed, Killefer joined the Philadelphia Phillies in 1911, just when Alexander's star was beginning to ascend. With Killefer as his regular catcher, Alexander reeled off three consecutive 30-victory seasons, leading the Phillies to their first pennant in 1915.

After the close of the 1917 campaign, during which Alexander registered a 30-13 record and Killefer batted a surprising .274, the famed battery was sold to the Cubs for a reported $60,000, a fabulous figure for those days.

In 1918 the bugles of World War I sounded and Alexander went off to the army. Killefer remained on the home front as the Cubs won the 1918 pennant. In the World Series, Killefer was no killer, batting a mere .118. The Cubs lost in six games to the Boston Red Sox, led by their pitching phenom Babe Ruth.

Alexander returned in 1919 and the battery was well charged. As a publicity stunt during spring training at Catalina Island, photographers handed Killefer a tomato can and suggested Alexander pitch the ball into the can to test his pinpoint control.

Killefer tossed aside his mitt and went into his catching crouch. Old Pete delivered and hit the open mouth of the can. Alexander was applauded, but no one canonized Killefer.

By this time Killefer had been replaced in the lineup by Bob O'Farrell, a superior hitter. But Reindeer Bill remained to personally handle Old Pete's pitches.

On Aug. 21, 1921, Killefer was appointed Cub manager, succeeding John Evers, who had taken ill. The news was applauded by Cub players, many of whom were in the taciturn Trojan's doghouse. The Cubs were 22-33 under Killefer and finished in seventh place.

The following season, the Cubs rose to 80-74, winding up fifth. Much of the credit went to Killefer, the old tomato-can catcher, who helped develop a tomato-faced young catching prospect named Gabby Hartnett.

In addition, Killefer was the only manager who could handle the alcoholic Alexander. One time, Alex wobbled into the Cubs' clubhouse just before game time and ducked into the washroom.

Killefer followed him and yelled, "You're still pitching." Alexander went out and threw a one-hitter. He got the game over so fast that he was still loaded when it was over.

The Cubs moved up to fourth in 1923 with an 83-71 mark and slid to fifth in 1924, posting a 81-72 record. When they dropped to the cellar in 1925, Killefer was fired in midseason. His overall managerial record was 299-292.

Joe McCarthy, the new Cub manager in 1926, did not take to Alexander's antics. Old Pete missed Killefer's steadying influence and was lost in the new regime. The result? Alexander The Great was placed on waivers.

Killefer, meanwhile, had caught on as a coach with the St. Louis Cardinals. He talked general manager Branch Rickey and player-manager Rogers Hornsby, both teetotalers, into picking up Alexander for the $6,000 waiver price.

The rest is history. The Cardinals won their first pennant, and Alexander was the hero, striking out the Yankees' Tony Lazzeri in the final game of the World Series.

The unsung hero? Reindeer Bill, who made it all possible.

Killefer was named manager of the St. Louis Browns in 1930 and lasted until '33. After leaving the Browns he coached the Cardinals and the Brooklyn Dodgers.

Then in 1941 he was named manager of the Milwaukee Brewers of the American Association. Who was manager of the rival Indianapolis Indians? Older brother Wade. It was the continuation of the family feud that began 40 years ago.

"All brotherly love is lost between us once we hear 'play ball,'" said Wade. "We're both bad losers. We usually get pretty mad at each other during a game. Friendship ceases when we're both out to win."

Reindeer Bill was back in the big leagues in 1942 as coach with his old ballclub, the Phillies. But soon he retired from the game. He died on July 2, 1960, in Elsmere,Del., outlasting Alexander by a decade.

Whenever baseball historians gather to argue and disagree, they usually reach the same conclusion when it comes to famed batteries. Ranked at or near the top is Alexander pitching and Killefer catching.

Along with Bill James and Dick Rudolph, George "Lefty" Tyler was one of the "Big Three" on the 1914 Miracle Braves' pitching staff.

Buried in last place as late as July 11, Boston caught fire and made one of the most dynamic stretch runs in baseball history, not only winning the pennant but also annihilating the defending World Champion Philadelphia A's in four straight. Tyler's contribution was a 16-14 mark.

Tyler broke in with the Braves in 1910 but did not come into his own until 1913, when he posted 16 victories. After four more years with Boston, the best of which was a 17-10 season in 1916, Tyler was traded to the Cubs on Jan. 5, 1918, for catcher Art Wilson, second baseman Larry Doyle, and $15,000.

In leading the Cubs to the 1918 pennant, George enjoyed the best season of his career, putting together a 19-9 mark with a 2.00 ERA and eight shutouts. He tied Cub teammate Jim Vaughn for the league leadership in the last department.

On July 17 he pitched the longest complete game in Cub history, outlasting the Phillies 2-1 in 21 innings.

In the World Series that fall against the Red Sox, Tyler split two decisions, posting a 1.17 ERA. His victory was a 3-1 distance performance Sept. 6 in the second game.

George's most unique talent came not from his pitching arm but from his tongue and lips. Teammate Bob O'Farrell recalled it this way over half a century later:

> He used to fire birdshot from between his teeth by curling up his tongue and shooting a toothpick through it. He peppered a lot of our opponents that way, and a lot of umpires, too. Occasionally, he'd do it to our wives when they were sitting in a hotel lobby, and the girls could never figure out where all that birdshot was coming from.

Tyler's last outstanding season was 1918. Following a 2-2 record for the Cubs in 1919, 11-12 in '20, and 3-2 in '21, the birdshot-spitting lefty retired from the majors.

He served as an umpire for the New England League in 1928, '29, and '30, and for the Eastern League in 1931 and '32. His brother, Fred, was a minor league catcher for many years and appeared briefly with the 1914 Braves.

Lifetime, George was 125-119 with a 2.95 ERA.

GEORGE TYLER

TYLER, GEORGE ALBERT
B. Dec. 14, 1889, Derry, N.H.
D. Sept. 29, 1953, Lowell, Mass.
BL TL 6' 175 lb.

Barney Friberg was a jack-of-all-trades player of the 1920s who saw frequent action at all four infield positions, the outfield, and even solitary appearances at both ends of the battery. Bob O'Farrell, his Cub teammate of the early '20s, described him as "a ballplayer's ballplayer."

Friberg was first brought up by the Cubs in 1919, but after limited service during that season and the next, roaming the outfield and playing second base, he was sent back to the minors for more training. Returning to Chicago in 1922, Friberg shared the right field spot with Cliff Heathcote, batting .311 in 97 games.

BARNEY FRIBERG

FRIBERG, GUSTAVE BERNHARD
B. Aug. 18, 1899, Manchester, N.H.
D. Dec. 8, 1958, Swampscott, Mass.
BR TR 5'11" 178 lb.

The following year was Barney's best. Moved to the third base slot, he batted a solid .318, crossed the plate 91 times, and drove 88 runs across to tie Hack Miller for the club lead.

On July 15, the most memorable hit of his career bailed one out in overtime for Grover Alexander against the Giants. In those days, every game the Cubs and Giants played was a blood match, and this one was no exception. It went into the 10th inning knotted up at five apiece.

With Claude Jonnard on the mound for New York at the Polo Grounds, Charlie Hollocher singled, George Grantham walked, and Bob O'Farrell beat out a bunt to fill the bags.

Up to the plate came Friberg, working Jonnard to a two-and-two count. The next pitch became a souvenir for some one in the bleachers as Barney's grand slammer gave the Cubs a 9-5 victory. It also gave Alexander a 29-28 lifetime edge over the Giants.

Although the hustling Swede dropped to .279 in 1924, he still led the club in RBI with 82. Then came one more great outing, in one of the Cubs' biggest innings. The date was May 28, 1925, and the Cubs tallied 12 times in the seventh inning to trounce the Reds 13-3. Barney contributed a double and a triple to the cause. Shortly thereafter, however, he was sold to the Phillies.

In Philadelphia, Barney became the utility man's utility man, appearing so often that he was almost always in the daily lineup in one position or another. His best years with the Phils were 1929 and '30, when he batted .301 and .341.

During the 1930 season, Friberg played 44 games at second base, 35 in the outfield, 12 at shortstop, and eight at first base, not to mention seven pinch-hit appearances.

After spending the 1933 season as a second-stringer with the Red Sox, Friberg retired.

Lifetime, he was a .281 hitter with 1,170 hits.

TONY KAUFMANN

KAUFMANN, ANTHONY CHARLES

B. Dec. 16, 1900, Chicago, Ill.

D. June 4, 1982, Elgin, Ill.

BR TR 5'11"

165 lb.

A journeyman Cub pitcher of the 1920s, Tony Kaufmann had fairly good seasons in 1923, '24, and '25, when he was 14-10, 16-11 and 13-13. He was the starting and winning pitcher on Aug. 25, 1922, when the Cubs beat the Phillies 26-23, the highest scoring game in history.

Traded to the Phillies in June 1927, Kaufmann was soon sent to the Cardinals. He ended his pitching career there in 1935, having made only token appearances in his later years. He later managed in the minors and served as a Cardinal scout and coach for many years.

His lifetime record was 64-62 with a 4.18 ERA.

Zeb Terry was the Cubs' regular second baseman in 1920, '21, and '22. Basically a run-of-the-mill infielder, Terry bummed around with the White Sox, Braves, and Pirates before coming to the Cubs, where he had his best seasons. After batting .286 in 1922 for a career high, Zeb left the majors, a lifetime .260 hitter in 640 games.

Terry, now approaching 94, is the oldest living member of the White Sox and the Cubs.

ZEB TERRY

TERRY, ZEBULON ALEXANDER
B. June 17, 1891, Denison, Tex.
BR TR 5'8" 129 lb.

Dave Robertson was a Cub outfielder in 1919, '20, and '21. His only season as a regular was 1920, when he batted .300 in 134 games with 75 RBI.

Previously a Giant, Robertson went to the Pirates in mid-1921. He finished up with the Giants the year after.

Dave was a .287 hitter with 812 hits during his nine years in the majors.

DAVE ROBERTSON

ROBERTSON, DAVIS AYDELOTTE
B. Sept. 25, 1889, Portsmouth, Va.
D. Nov. 5, 1970, Virginia Beach, Va.
BL TL 6' 185 lb.

Ray Grimes was a Cub hero of the early 1920s who came from a baseball family. His twin brother, Roy, had a brief trial with the Giants in 1920, and his son, Oscar Ray, Jr., served as a utility infielder with the Indians, Yankees, and Athletics between 1938 and '46.

Grimes signed his first professional contract with Memphis of the Southern League in 1916 but was released to Durham of the Carolina League on April 15—before he played a single game. After Ray stayed the remainder of the season at Durham, batting an unimpressive .247, the league disbanded and he was temporarily out of work.

Signed by the Cleveland organization, Grimes spent the next season at Hartford of the Eastern League before moving onto Bridgeport. In the war-shortened 1918 season, Grimes batted .322 in 55 games but slipped to .275 the next season. It was around this time that he began playing first base on a regular basis.

In 1920 the legendary White Sox pitcher Ed Walsh became the Bridgeport manager, as Ray finally began to find himself as a hitter. Batting .364 in 119 games, he collected 156 hits and scored 90 times. Brother Roy, also with Bridgeport, hit the ball at a .374 clip as the club finished a strong second.

Late in the year the Red Sox brought Ray up for one game but were apparently unimpressed as they did not guard their rights to him. Consequently, the Cubs claimed him for $5,500.

The following spring Grimes found himself holding down the Cubs' first base job with only one game of major league experience

RAY GRIMES

GRIMES, OSCAR RAY, SR.
B. Sept. 11, 1893, Bergholz, Ohio
D. May 25, 1953, Minerva, Ohio
BR TR 5'11" 168 lb.

behind him. Rising to the occasion, the gaunt, raw-boned Grimes batted .321 in 147 games, driving in 79 runs to lead the club.

It was one of the few bright spots in a dismal, seventh place campaign. He was also nicknamed "Bummer" for reasons that are unclear.

The 1922 season belonged to Ray more than any other as the warrior became a one-man army. He carved a unique niche on April 27, when his homer onto Sheffield Avenue in the sixth inning knotted the score 4-4. His two-run single in the seventh paved the way for a 6-4 triumph over the Cardinals.

It was the second consecutive day that Grimes drove in *both* the tying and winning runs. During midseason he had a stretch in which he drove in at least one run for 17 consecutive games, a major league record. For that period he knocked home a total of 27 runs.

By the end of the year, Grimes's statistics spoke for themselves. Leading the Cubs in every major department, he batted .354; slugged 45 doubles, 12 triples, and 14 home runs; scored 99 runs; and drove in another 99. Thanks to the bats of Ray, Hack Miller, and Charlie Hollocher, the Cubs rebounded to a strong fifth, winning 80 games.

The future looked brighter than ever, but such was not the case. Suffering a slipped disc in June 1923, Grimes missed most of the remainder of the season.

Although Ray batted a healthy .329, he appeared in only 64 games and never regained his playing ability. The following year, he played even less, hitting .299 in 51 games. At the close of 1924, the Cubs let him go.

Grimes had one more fling in the majors with the Phillies in 1926, batting .297 in limited service.

He finished an all-too-short career with a .329 average and 505 hits.

SPARKY ADAMS

ADAMS, EARL JOHN

B. Aug. 26, 1894, Newton, Pa.

BR TR 5'5½"

151 lb.

One of the shortest players ever to don a Cub jersey, Earl "Sparky" Adams was an infielder par excellence. He was equally adept at playing second, short, or third, seeing much service at all three positions.

Sparky—so nicknamed by Rabbit Maranville—joined the Cubs in September 1922. He assumed the regular shortstop position the following year when Charlie Hollocher became ill. In 1925 he was moved to second base, and by 1927 he was appearing frequently at third.

Adams was the National League's best fielding second baseman in 1925 with league-leading totals in putouts (354), assists (551), and fielding average (.983).

An excellent leadoff man, Sparky led the league in times at bat in 1925, '26, and '27. His height (or lack of it) made him difficult to pitch to, so he seldom struck out.

As a Cub, his best season at the plate was 1926, when he hit .309 with 193 hits and 95 runs scored. Adams was no slouch on the basepaths, either. He stole 26 bases in 1925, 27 in '26, and 26 in '27.

He was also one of the few Cub players to hit two doubles in one inning, collecting them in the first inning against the Phillies on Aug. 24, 1927. He went on to a five-for-six outing that day in a 13-1 Cub win.

On Nov. 28, 1927, Adams was dealt to the Pirates with outfielder Floyd Scott for outfielder Hazen "Kiki" Cuyler. After two seasons Pittsburgh sent him to the Cardinals, where he batted .314 and .293, leading St. Louis to pennants in 1930 and '31, plus a world championship in '31.

His 46 doubles in 1931 were high in the league, and he was the league's top fielding third baseman both seasons. Sparky slumped off thereafter, winding up with the Reds in 1934.

An avid fisherman and movie buff, Adams also ran an auto repair shop in Tremont, Pa., during his playing days.

He was a lifetime .286 hitter with 1,588 hits and 154 stolen bases.

PERCY JONES

JONES, PERCY LEE
B. Oct. 28, 1899, Harwood, Tex.
BR TL 5'11½"
175 lb.

Percy Jones was a second-string Cub pitcher of the 1920s. He had two fairly good seasons, 1926 and '28, when he was 12-7 and 10-6. Traded to Boston after 1928, he wound up with the Pirates two years later.

Lifetime, he was 53-57.

HACK MILLER

MILLER, LAWRENCE H.
B. Jan. 1, 1894, New York, N.Y.
D. Sept. 17, 1971, Oakland, Calif.
BR TR 5'9" 208 lb.

Possibly the strongest player in baseball history, Lawrence "Hack" Miller was a Cub outfielder of the early 1920s. He thrilled the fans with clutch home runs and weight-lifting exhibitions.

Although born in New York City shortly after his immigrant parents arrived from Germany, Miller was reared from the time he was a year old in a melting pot on Chicago's Near North Side known as "Little Hell."

Growing up in a rough neighborhood, he became streetwise—and tough—at an early age. His father had been a circus strongman in the old country, and the younger Miller inherited more than a bit of the old man's strength.

By the time Lawrence was 18, as an apprentice steamfitter, he would hoist 250 pound radiators on his shoulders and carry them two blocks, then up several flights of stairs for installation.

He began his baseball career with semipro teams in Chicago, earning the nickname "Hack" because of his resemblance to the great wrestler, Hackenschmidt. In 1914 Miller broke into the professionals with Wausau of the Wisconsin-Illinois League, then graduated to St. Boniface and Winnipeg of the Northern League.

The Dodgers brought him up for a cup of coffee in 1916, as did the Red Sox two years hence, but Miller failed to stick either time. It was with Oakland in the Pacific Coast League that his bat really began to boom, reaching .346 in 1919 and .347 the next two years. This caught the eye of the Cubs, who had finished seventh in 1921.

Miller signed with the Cubs and became an immediate sensation. As their regular left fielder in 1922, Hack batted .352 in 122 games, lashing out 164 hits, 12 home runs, and 78 RBI. His batting average was third highest in the National League, as the Cubs moved up to a respectable fifth with an 80-74 record.

In 1923 the stocky slugger upped his homer count to 20 and his RBI total to 88, though his batting average dropped to .301. Miller's bats were monstrous war clubs weighing anywhere from 47 to 67 ounces.

Second to none in the clutch, Miller pulled many a game out of the fire for the Cubs. On Aug. 25, 1922, he smashed a pair of three-run homers to lead the Cubs to a 26-23 battle over the Phillies, the highest scoring brawl in big league history. During another hot streak, he belted four homers in three days.

Hack's greatest day was June 12, 1923, when he knocked home seven runs with two home runs and a single to give the Cubs a 12-11 edge over the Braves at Wrigley Field. His grand slammer in the fifth tied the score at 7-7, and his two run shot an inning later *The Cubs beat* gave the Cubs a temporary two-run lead. On Sept. 12, 1924, Hack's *the Phillies 26-23* pinch-hit homer in the top of the eighth tied the Phillies at six *in baseball's* apiece. The Cubs went on to win 10-8.

highest-scoring As a boy "from the old neighborhood" who made good, Hack *game at Wrigley* was a local folk hero to Cub fans. When he was not winning games *Field in 1922.* with timely hits, Miller would hold fans and teammates breathless with feats of strength. He uprooted trees at Catalina Island, bent iron bars with his hands, and lifted automobiles up by their bumpers.

It is on photographic record that he pounded a forty penny bridge spike through an auto gate at Wrigley Field with his fist, protected only by a rolled up baseball cap. To top it all off, he was a karate expert, a seasoned beer drinker, a good piano player, and a guitar strummer of accomplishment.

Ironically, Miller's muscular build prevented him from realizing his full potential. He could not cover as much ground as most other outfielders, and his heavy frame slowed down his reflex action. When it came to shagging down flies, Hack was adequate, but no Tris Speaker. Consequently, he spent more and more time on the bench.

In 1924 he batted .336 but appeared in only 53 games. The following season, Hack was hitting at a .279 clip, but his days as a Cub were numbered.

In his last appearance, on May 21, 1925, he drove in a run with a pinch-hit triple in the top of the ninth. The Cub rally fell short and they lost to Brooklyn 5-4, but Hack had bowed out in glory. Three days later, he was released. He hung around in the minors for a few more years before retiring in 1927.

In his 349 major league games, Miller collected 387 hits and batted .323. As a pinch hitter he was 15-for-35, a whopping .429 mark. Miller was no Babe Ruth, nor even a Hack Wilson, but what a hero while he lasted.

GEORGE GRANTHAM

George Grantham was the Cubs' equivalent of White Sox outfielder Smead Jolley—all hit, no field. Brought up for a few games in late 1922, George became the Cubs' regular second baseman the following year. He batted an impressive .281 his rookie season, with 43 stolen bases. In 1924 he upped his average to .316 and stole another 21 bases.

GRANTHAM, GEORGE FARLEY
B. May 20, 1900, Galena, Kan.
D. March 16, 1954, Kingman, Ariz.
BL TR 5'10" 170 lb.

Defensively, however, Grantham was not as proficient. His 55 errors in 1923 set a modern National League high for miscues at second base, and his 44 muffs the following season again led the league. His arm was as wild as his glove was slippery; thus George was nicknamed "Boots."

In October 1924 Grantham was sent to the Pirates in a major trade. Pittsburgh often stationed him at first base, hoping he would be less harmful, but he was no ballerina there either. Nevertheless, George continued to hit well and stayed in the lineup.

After two seasons with the Reds and one with the Giants, Grantham retired in 1934 with a lifetime .302 batting average. Once out of a Cub uniform, Grantham quit stealing bases, finishing with only 132 total, half of them in his two-and-a-fraction years as a Cub.

CLIFF HEATHCOTE

Cliff Heathcote was a dependable Cub outfielder of the 1920s whose play, unfortunately, was overshadowed by the more spectacular exploits of such men as Hack Miller, Hack Wilson, Riggs Stephenson, and Kiki Cuyler. Underrated in his day, he has been largely forgotten since.

After attending Penn State University, Heathcote broke in with the Cardinals in 1918 and displayed potential with his bat the next two seasons, batting .279 and .284. On June 13, 1918, he hit for the cycle in a 19-inning 8-8 marathon with the Phillies.

Nevertheless, Cliff's tenure in St. Louis was largely unhappy. The fans had dubbed him "Rubberhead" over a fielding mishap he committed as a rookie, when he lost a fly ball in the sun and it bounced off his head. They never let him live it down, taunting him whenever he took the field.

HEATHCOTE, CLIFTON EARL
B. Jan. 24, 1898, Glen Rock, Pa.
D. Jan. 19, 1939, York, Pa.

On May 30, 1922, the Cardinals were in Chicago for a morning-afternoon doubleheader with the Cubs. In the morning contest Cliff had gone hitless in a 4-1 loss to the Cubs. He then wept openly when he learned that he had been traded to the Cubs between games for outfielder Max Flack.

Heathcote regained his composure quickly, however, collecting a pair of hits in the second game as the Cubs clipped the Cardinals' wings 4-2. It was the only time in major league history that players were exchanged between games of a doubleheader.

Cliff's greatest day at the plate came that Aug. 25, when the Cubs outlasted the Phillies 26-23 in the highest scoring game in big league annals. As the Cubs number one hitting hero, he stole the show with five hits in five trips (including two doubles), five runs, and four RBI.

Heathcote remained the Cubs' regular right fielder for the next several years, enjoying his best season at the plate in 1924, when he hit .309. A good baserunner, he stole 32 bases in 1923 and 26 the year after. His speed also enabled him to beat out many infield rollers and sacrifice bunts.

He was not a power hitter, and many of the home runs he hit were inside the park. As a glove man, Cliff was both a good judge of a fly ball and a strong thrower. In 1926 his .985 fielding average and eight double plays were tops among National League outfielders.

By 1928 the famous outfield of Kiki Cuyler, Hack Wilson, and Riggs Stephenson had become firmly cemented, and Heathcote was relegated to the second-string lineup. He continued to perform well, contributing a .313 average in 82 games, as the Cubs won the pennant in 1929. In his only World Series appearance as a pinch hitter, he struck out.

Dealt to the Reds in 1931, Heathcote finished his career with the Phillies the next season.

In his 1,415 games, Cliff was a .275 hitter with 1,222 hits.

ARNOLD STATZ

STATZ, ARNOLD JOHN
B. Oct. 20, 1897, Waukegan, Ill.
BR TR 5'7½"
150 lb.

Pint-sized outfielder Arnold Statz owns the all-time record for most games played in professional ball with 3,473. However, only 683 were in the majors.

Statz was one of three famous infants to come out of Waukegan, Ill., during the 1890s. The other two were Cub teammate Bob O'Farrell and a would-be violinist named Benjamin Kubelsky, better known to the world as Jack Benny.

Although chiefly remembered as a minor league star, Arnold made his professional debut at the other end. In 1919 Statz broke in with the New York Giants, batting .300 in 21 games.

However, the Giants already had all the outfielders they needed, so Statz was released to the Red Sox. There he played exactly two contests before being sent down to Los Angeles of the Pacific Coast League in mid-1920.

By 1922 Arnold was back in the big time, now in a Cub uniform. Placed in center field, he displayed a strong throwing arm and came through with a .297 average in 110 games. It was at this time that

Cub catcher Bob O'Farrell nicknamed him "Jigger" because he never sat still but was always "jiggling around."

The following year was Statz's dream season. Playing every game, he batted .319 to pace the club, while smacking 33 doubles, driving in 70 runs, and scoring 110. His 209 hits were the most ever by a Cub up to that time, and he displayed skill on the basepaths with his 29 steals.

Although Statz dropped to .277 in 1924, it was during that season that he came through with his most heroic moment. The Cubs were playing the Braves at Boston on Aug. 9 and were behind 6-5 with two out in the ninth. Hack Miller's clutch single knotted the score to send the contest into overtime.

In the 10th inning Statz came to the plate with Bob Barrett, Denver Grigsby, and Gabby Hartnett occupying the bags. The tension mounted. Arnold swung and drove one down the right field line in spacious Braves Field. Barrett, Grigsby, and Hartnett all scored easily while Statz eventually circled the bases himself for an inside-the-park grand slam. The Cubs added one more and went on to win 11-6.

Unfortunately, Statz's days as a Cub were numbered. After falling into a long slump, Arnold was optioned to Los Angeles in June 1925 and never recalled to Chicago. The Dodgers gave him a try two years later, but his stay at Brooklyn was not overly successful. By 1929 Statz again found himself in a Los Angeles uniform—this time for keeps.

In the years that ensued, he became the Ty Cobb of the Pacific Coast League, leading the league four times in runs scored and three times in stolen bases before he retired in 1942 at age 45.

His 18 total seasons with the Angels are a minor league record. Statz's major league totals were 737 hits and a .285 average. In the bushes he was a .315 batter with 3,356 hits.

During his years in Hollywood, Arnold established connections with the motion picture industry and later served as a consultant for several baseball movies, including "Pride of the Yankees" (1942) and "The Stratton Story" (1949). Still later, he returned to his first love, serving as a talent scout for the Cubs for several years.

RABBIT MARANVILLE

Walter "Rabbit" Maranville played only one season with the Cubs, but he left behind a legacy, to say the least.

One of baseball's many short shortstops, Maranville was among the games' best defensive and most colorful performers at that position. Breaking in with New Bedford of the New England League in 1911, Maranville was called up to the Boston Braves late the following season. Soon he had the shortstop job in his back pocket.

By 1914 he was an integral factor in the "Miracle Braves" team that went from last place July 11 to the world championship.

MARANVILLE, WALTER JAMES VINCENT
B. Nov. 11, 1891, Springfield, Mass.
D. Jan. 5, 1954, New York, N.Y.
BR TR 5'5" 155 lb.

Famous for his basket catches, he was nicknamed "Rabbit" for his bunny-hop movements at his station.

After eight seasons with the Braves, Maranville went to the Pirates, where he enjoyed four more productive years. However, the straight-laced Pittsburgh owner, Barney Dreyfuss, grew weary of the Rabbit's nocturnal habits, which were becoming increasingly wild.

On Oct. 27, 1924, Dreyfuss traded Maranville, Charlie Grimm, and Wilbur Cooper to the Cubs for George Grantham, Victor Aldridge, and Al Niehaus.

The year 1925 was the Rabbit's first and only season at Wrigley Field. Artistically, the year was anything but a memorable one. Hampered with injuries, Maranville appeared in only 75 games, batting .233.

However, it was an unforgettable epoch in other ways. The Cubs were in seventh place and going nowhere on July 6 when it was announced that the happy-go-lucky Maranville would be the new Cub manager. Everyone was shocked by the choice, not least of all the Rabbit himself.

The Maranville reign started off with a bang as the Cubs slugged the Dodgers 10-5 at Ebbets Field. Naturally, the Rabbit and several others went out to celebrate.

After doing more than their share of partying, Maranville, Herb Brett, and Clark Pittenger hopped in a taxi to head elsewhere. When they reached their destination at Times Square, the fare was less than one dollar, so the players did not leave a tip. The cab driver became miffed, one thing led to another, and all four ended up in the hoosegow.

From that point on, it was one incident after another. When the Cubs' train pulled out of New York, a slightly inebriated Maranville decided to do some more celebrating. He did so by dumping ice water on every player he found sleeping in his berth.

Another time, he poured a bucket of water out a hotel window onto the head of traveling secretary John O. Seys. On still another occasion, Maranville grabbed Seys himself and dangled him from a window by his legs.

The final straw came when Maranville raced through a Pullman car, annointing the passengers from a spittoon. Shortly afterward, on Sept. 3, the Rabbit was relieved of his command. Under his "leadership" the Cubs had won 23 games, lost 30, and slipped into the cellar, where they finished the season after George Gibson hastily replaced the Rabbit at the helm.

Although it was publicly announced that Maranville resigned, he was actually forced out. The Cub brass had seen enough of the Rabbit's clowning, and in November he was sold to the Dodgers on waivers.

Maranville's career continued to hit the skids. By 1927 he was in the minors with Rochester of the International League. It was at this time that he went on the wagon for keeps. It gave his career a new lease on life.

By the end of the season the reformed Maranville was back in the majors, this time with the Cardinals. Returning to the Braves in 1929, he finished his big league days in Boston in 1935. He later did some managing in the minors.

During his 23 big league seasons, Maranville was a .258 lifetime hitter with 2,605 hits. He was elected to the Hall of Fame shortly after his death in 1954.

F ollowing three seasons with the Cardinals, Howie Freigau was traded to the Cubs in May 1925 with catcher Mike Gonzalez, in exchange for catcher Bob O'Farrell.

He spent about two years as the regular Cub third baseman. He batted .299 in 1925 (.307 as a Cub) and led the league in fielding at his position the following year with a .966 average.

After seeing only part-time service with the Cubs in 1927, Freigau wound up his career the next season with the Dodgers and the Braves.

Lifetime, he was a .272 hitter with 537 hits.

HOWIE FREIGAU
FREIGAU, HOWARD EARL
B. Aug. 1, 1902, Dayton, Ohio
D. July 18, 1932, Chattanooga, Tenn.
BR TR 5'10½" 160 lb.

G eorge Gibson has the distinction of being the only Canadian to manage a big league ballclub. The native of London, Ontario, served as a stop-gap manager for the Cubs late in the 1925 season, winning 12 and losing 14 games.

Gibson, a coach, was rushed in to restore order from the chaos created by Rabbit Maranville during his two-month stint as Cub mentor. The Cubs finished in the cellar for the first time in their 50-year history. Gibson was replaced by the little-known minor league manager, Joe McCarthy, that autumn.

That was Gibby's lone Cub connection. His big league career was spent for the most part with the Pittsburgh Pirates. He joined the Pirates in 1905 and stayed through the 1916 season.

Although known as a fine defensive catcher, Gibson once committed six errors in one game. His batting was a mite defensive, too, a .236 lifetime average.

Perhaps his finest season was 1909 when the Pirates won the pennant and the World Series. The fine Pittsburgh club, led by legendary shortstop Honus Wagner, won 110 games, preventing the Cubs from taking their fourth straight flag. The Cubs finished second, winning 104 and losing only 49.

Gibson played an iron-man role that season, catching 150 games and hitting a respectable .265. He led all catchers with 655 putouts and a .983 fielding average. In addition, Gibson caught Babe Adams's three World Series victories over the Detroit Tigers.

After leaving the Pirates, Gibson was picked up by the New York Giants, but he played sparingly in 1917 and '18. He then became a

GEORGE GIBSON
GIBSON, GEORGE
B. July 22, 1880, London, Ontario
D. Jan. 25, 1967, London, Ontario
BR TR 5'11½" 190 lb.

Giants' coach under John McGraw.

Nicknamed "Moon" because of his facial roundness, Gibson was recalled by the Pirates as manager in 1920. His club wound up fourth, then piled up a substantial lead in 1921 only to lose out to McGraw's Giants in the stretch drive. Pirates' owner Barney Dreyfuss, who was peeved over the loss, fired Gibson early in the 1922 season.

Gibson, a no-nonsense, strict disciplinarian, was the opposite of the fun-loving Maranville, whose escapades included a battle with a Brooklyn cabbie the night he was appointed Cub manager.

Gibson was brought back to Pittsburgh by Dreyfuss in 1932 where he managed the Pirates midway through the 1934 season. His career managerial record was a respectable .546 on 413 victories and 344 defeats.

Upon his retirement, Gibson went back to London, Ontario, where he indulged in hunting, fishing, curling, and gardening. He died at the age of 86 on Jan. 25, 1967.

When "Marse" Joe McCarthy was signed as Cub manager on Oct. 13, 1925, he was given the unenviable task of resurrecting a team that had just finished dead last—and he met the challenge head on. In so doing, McCarthy ushered in a period replete with powerhouse teams and colorful performers.

Marse Joe's first move was to tip off club president Bill Veeck, Sr., on Lewis "Hack" Wilson, whom the Giants had left unprotected in their farm chain. The Cubs drafted him, and for the next five years Wilson set Chicago aflame with his red hot bat and nocturnal escapades.

Other newcomers who paid immediate dividends were pitcher Charlie Root and outfielder Riggs Stephenson. Holdovers from 1925 who came into full bloom under McCarthy's tutelage were first baseman Charlie Grimm, catcher Gabby Hartnett, and pitcher Guy Bush. More important, the Cubs rebounded to fourth place.

To establish his authority over the players, McCarthy quickly came into conflict with alcoholic pitching ace Grover Alexander, who had had things largely his own way under previous managers. McCarthy laid down training rules; Alex defied them—and ended up getting waived to the Cardinals in June 1926. From that point on, everyone knew who was in charge.

In 1927 the Cubs again finished fourth as Woody English supplanted Jimmy Cooney at shortstop and Hal Carlson was added to the pitching corps. Meanwhile, Chicago was going "Cub crazy" as 1,163,347 fans paid their way into the recently double-decked Wrigley Field. It was the first time in history a National League team had drawn more than a million customers.

Pitcher Pat Malone and outfielder Kiki Cuyler joined the Cubs the following year to help boost them to a close third, only four games behind the pennant-winning Cardinals. Championship fever was now in the blood of Cub fans.

William Wrigley, Jr., then loosened his purse strings, shelling out $200,000 plus five run-of-the-mill players to the Boston Braves for batting champion Rogers "Rajah" Hornsby. Hornsby had already left his best years behind him in St. Louis, but he still swung a potent bat.

The addition of the Rajah proved to be the final piece in the jigsaw puzzle, making the 1929 roster possibly the greatest Cub team ever assembled. Fortified by a .303 team batting average and 140 home runs, the Cubs won the pennant by a 10½-game margin over the second place Pirates.

Unfortunately, they met their match in the World Series as Connie Mack's Philadelphia Athletics—led by Al Simmons, Jimmy Foxx, Lefty Grove, and Mickey Cochrane—rolled over them in five games. The Cubs worst humiliation came in game four. They lost an 8-0 lead when the A's rallied for 10 runs in the seventh inning to win 10-8. That destroyed the Cubs' morale, enabling Philly to mop it all up the next day.

It was also a signal that McCarthy's days as Cub manager were numbered. With the Rajah on the bench most of the season with an ankle injury, the Cubs dropped to second in 1930. Wrigley, meanwhile, had mistakenly blamed McCarthy for the Cubs' loss in the series and fired him shortly before the close of the season, a case of bad judgment that would haunt the Cubs for years to come.

Hornsby, who became McCarthy's successor, was not the man for the job. Unlike Marse Joe, who had a firm hand but knew when to turn his head, the taciturn Hornsby continually berated the players, causing undercurrents of resentment. This was especially so with Hack Wilson, whose output plummeted as the Cubs finished a disappointing third in 1931.

That December Wilson, who more than anyone else personified the McCarthy Cubs, was dealt away. In January 1932 William Wrigley, Jr., died, passing the team on to his son, Philip.

JOE McCARTHY

McCARTHY, JOSEPH VINCENT
B. April 21, 1887, Philadelphia, Pa.
D. Jan. 13, 1978, Buffalo, N. Y.

Rival manager Jimmy Dykes once called Joe McCarthy a "push-button manager." Well, McCarthy must have pushed the right buttons because in 24 years of managing, his teams captured nine pennants, won seven World Series, and never finished out of the first division.

McCarthy managed three of baseball's wealthiest ballclubs, the Chicago Cubs, New York Yankees, and Boston Red Sox from 1926 to '50. His .614 percentage on 2,126 victories against only 1,335 losses is the highest in baseball history.

He weathered, with gentlemanly grace and dignity, dramatic showdowns with such temperamental stars as Grover Alexander, Hack Wilson, Rogers Hornsby, Babe Ruth, and Ted Williams.

The stout Irishman with gimlet brown eyes and jut jaw never played an inning of major league ball. He couldn't hit and he couldn't run. His rise came through mental aptitude rather than physical prowess.

As a youth, McCarthy's left kneecap was badly broken as his sled careened against a rock while zooming down a steep hill in the Germantown section of Philadelphia. It left him with loose cartilage that slowed him considerably.

His father, a contractor, was killed in a cave-in when Joe was only three, forcing him to take odd jobs, such as carrying ice. The family situation prevented him from attending high school. Instead, he worked in cotton and woolen mills, earning as much as $5 a week.

Between jobs, McCarthy played sandlot ball as an outfielder. His semipro team traveled the upstate New York coal-mining circuit. Then his baseball ability won a scholarship at Niagara University. "At that time, Niagara was more of a preparatory school, so a high school education was not a prerequisite," said McCarthy.

Marsh Joe got his first trial in organized ball with Wilmington in the Class B Tri-State League in 1906. He played in a dozen games, hit .175, and drew his release within six weeks. McCarthy kicked around the minors, eventually landing his first managerial job with Wilkes-Barre in 1913. Thus, at the age of 26, his managerial career was under way.

He led Wilkes-Barre to a second-place finish and even hit .325 while playing third base and second base. His contract was purchased by the Buffalo club that went on to win the 1915 pennant.

The powerful Bisons began selling their stars such as Joe Judge and Charlie Jamieson to big league clubs. Ironically, McCarthy was offered to the Yankees, but they refused to pay the $3,000 price tag. That was the closest McCarthy came to playing in the majors.

McCarthy's contract was then assigned to Louisville, where he remained for a decade. In 1919 McCarthy was named manager. He developed among others, outfielder Earle Combs, whom he regarded as a perfect player. After hitting .380 in 1923, Combs was purchased by the Yankees for $65,000.

It was then reported that the Yankees were eying McCarthy as a possible replacement for the ailing Miller Huggins. However, Cubs' vice president William Veeck had a secret meeting with McCarthy at French Lick, Ind., in September 1925. They kept the signing secret until the season ended. McCarthy had finally reached the majors.

The Cubs, under three managers, had finished in the cellar for the first time in their history. They had the nucleus with first baseman Charlie Grimm, catcher Gabby Hartnett, and a couple of young pitchers named Charlie Root and Guy Bush. They lacked leadership and it was McCarthy's job to provide it.

He insisted on drafting Toledo outfielder Hack Wilson for $7,500. His next move was to grab Indianapolis outfielder Riggs Stephenson for $20,000 and two players. Wilson went on to lead the league with 30 homers, while Stephenson batted .338. The Cubs were on the move, finishing fourth with an 82-72 record.

McCarthy tried to establish much-needed discipline, and he found a stumbling block in pitcher Grover Alexander, who was constantly on a drinking binge. Alex's days were numbered when McCarthy held a team meeting and he arrived red-eyed and unsteady and then dozed off in the back of the room. The following week Alexander was waived by the Cubs.

McCarthy, meanwhile, was putting the pieces together. That fall, shortstop Woody English was plucked from Toledo. The team showed improvement at 85-68, but again wound up fourth.

The next year he engineered the deal with the Pirates for Kiki Cuyler, who rounded out an all-star outfield with Wilson and Stephenson. Then he bought pitcher Pat Malone from Minneapolis.

Like Wilson, Stephenson, and English, Malone was a player whose future was foreseen by McCarthy when he managed against them in the American Association. Malone, however, almost threw down McCarthy's confidence. "We took him on a look for $2,500," revealed McCarthy. "We could try him until a certain date (June 1) and either return him or pay the balance of the $25,000 purchase price."

The settlement date arrived and Malone had lost seven games without a victory, but McCarthy advised the deal be closed. Malone didn't let McCarthy down. The burly fastballer won 18 games the rest of the way.

The Cubs won 91 games in 1928, but finished four games out in third place behind the Cardinals and Giants. McCarthy figured the team was a player away from the pennant. They got their desired player on Nov. 7, 1928, sending five players and $200,000 to the Boston Braves for second baseman Rogers Hornsby.

The Cubs roared to their first pennant in 11 years. In four seasons McCarthy had lifted the club from the bottom to the top. Hornsby, Wilson, Cuyler, Hartnett, Grimm, Stephenson, and English formed the Cubs' own version of "Murderer's Row," while the pitching trio of Root, Bush, and Malone led them to a 98-54 record.

But one ill-fated inning in the World Series against the Philadelphia Athletics was to undo that all. "That inning in which we ran into those 10 Athletic runs was just one of those things that happen in baseball," said McCarthy.

The Cubs were well on their way to tying the series at two games each, with the advantage of having two of the last three games played in their own park. Root and the Cubs went into the seventh inning leading 8-0.

Wilson lost two fly balls in the sun. McCarthy rushed four pitchers in and none offered any relief. The A's went on to win 10-8 and take the series four games to one. McCarthy could hardly be blamed for the blinding sun or the sudden explosion off Root. Nevertheless, he slid from grace with owner William Wrigley, Jr.

Lefty O'Doul was another factor. Wrigley personally scouted and purchased O'Doul, only to have McCarthy turn thumbs down on the outfielder when he reported to camp. O'Doul, picked up by the

The Chicago Cubs, 1929 National League Champions

110

Phillies, went on to win the National League batting crown in 1929 with a .398 average. One day in Baker Bowl he homered to beat the Cubs. Wrigley didn't need the grim reminder.

Perhaps McCarthy's greatest success was his handling and understanding of the frolicking Wilson. McCarthy knew Wilson couldn't do his best under strict reins, but he saw to it that Hack didn't step too far out of bounds.

During his tempestuous years in which he hit 21, 30, 31, and 39 homers, Wilson was fined only once by McCarthy. In 1930 Wilson hit 56 homers and drove in 190 runs between hangovers. But despite Wilson's record-busting season, the Cubs finished two games behind the pennant-winning Cardinals.

Second place and a 90-64 record wasn't good enough for Wrigley, who axed McCarthy in favor of Hornsby in the final week of the season. Ironically, it was an injury to Hornsby that kept the Cubs behind St. Louis.

The Rajah batted .380 and hit 39 homers to help the Cubs win the 1929 pennant. But after breaking his leg sliding into base early in the 1930 season, Hornsby's playing time was limited to 42 games.

McCarthy had no word from the Cubs of his firing until he read of Hornsby's appointment in the papers. If he didn't feel somewhat bitter he wouldn't have been human. "The club is Mr. Wrigley's," said McCarthy. "I wish him all the luck in the world," added McCarthy, who left behind a 442–321 Cub managerial record. Then he started looking for a new job.

It didn't take long. The following month, Col. Jacob Ruppert handed McCarthy a pen and said, "Joe, if you will sign this contract, it will make you manager of the New York Yankees." McCarthy signed and stepped into another lion's den.

Hack Wilson was a pussy cat compared to Babe Ruth. The Babe, who could hardly manage himself, wanted the Yankee managerial job and felt McCarthy was an interloper. McCarthy wisely decided to do nothing to make a bad situation worse.

He took a firm hold on the rest of the players and let Ruth have his own way. It worked. Ruth was a vital factor, calling his famous home run shot, as the Yankees swept the Cubs four straight in the 1932 World Series. It was sweet revenge for McCarthy, who showed his class by refusing to gloat.

Ruth received his unconditional release following the 1934 season, thus giving McCarthy complete control. He molded the Yankees into baseball's most formidable machine. Known as the Bronx Bombers, McCarthy's Yankees won four straight World Series from 1936 through '39.

The team included such greats as Lou Gehrig, Bill Dickey, Red Ruffing, and Lefty Gomez. It seemed all McCarthy had to do was snap his fingers and the far-flung Yankee scouting system would produce such finished products as Joe DiMaggio, Tommy Henrich, Joe Gordon, or King Kong Keller.

Jimmy Dykes, manager of the impoverished White Sox, called McCarthy a "push-button manager." What everyone overlooked was McCarthy's ability to handle the stars given him. He demanded discipline and was quick-tempered, but he offset that with a native sense of humor and sound strategy.

After dropping to third behind the Tigers and Indians in 1940, McCarthy led his team to three straight pennants, losing his lone World Series to the Cardinals in 1942. When the Yankees passed from the estate of Col. Ruppert to Larry MacPhail, McCarthy's days were numbered. Tired of MacPhail's needling and second-guessing and not in the best of health, McCarthy resigned on May 24, 1946.

In 15 seasons, McCarthy's Yankee juggernauts won eight pennants and seven World Series. They finished second four times, third twice, and fourth once. They won 1,460 games and lost only 703.

Meanwhile, Hack Wilson died a penniless derelict in Baltimore. Wilson's body lay for three days unclaimed. Cub owner P. K. Wrigley secretly paid for the burial and a monument at Martinsburg, W. Va. McCarthy, Cuyler, and Grimm were among those paying last respects.

McCarthy unveiled the monument and soberly said the final words about his favorite slugger, "I know you will say a fervent prayer for the great Hack. And may God rest his soul." He turned to Grimm and Cuyler and added, "He was a wonderful little fellah."

McCarthy was coaxed out of retirement by Red Sox owner Thomas Yawkey in 1948. After runner-up finishes to the Indians in 1948 and the Yankees in 1949, McCarthy resigned in midseason 1950.

He became a gentleman farmer in East Amherst, just ouside of Buffalo, N. Y. His new interests were flowers and birds. He enjoyed putting in tulip bulbs and setting up bird houses.

McCarthy, who was named to the Hall of Fame in 1957, would occasionally appear at Yankee old-timers ceremonies until ill health forced him to remain on the farm. He died on Jan. 13, 1978, at the age of 88.

GUY BUSH

BUSH, GUY
TERRELL
B Aug. 23, 1901,
Aberdeen, Miss.
BR TR 6' 175 lb.

"Y

ou Know Me Al" was Ring Lardner's comic tale of pitcher Jack Keefe, the busher in the big town. Cub pitcher Guy Bush was Jack Keefe in flesh and bone, mostly bone.

Bush was born on his dad's cotton farm, but he didn't cotton to farming. He preferred pitching a baseball. The nearby Tupelo Military Institute had a ballclub, so Bush enrolled there in 1920. He earned his keep by waiting on tables in the mess hall and sweeping the dormitories.

A newspaper item about a game in which Bush struck out 18 batters caught the eye of Harry Ireland, manager of the Greenville (Miss.) team in the Cotton States League and Ireland signed the rawboned "Mississippi Mudcat."

While pitching for Greenville, Bush was spotted by Cubs' scout Jack Doyle, who liked his free motion. "Doyle started talkin' to the club owner about signing me," recalled Bush. "I sat there listening to 'em bargain and finally Doyle got the price up to $1,200. They closed the deal when Doyle offered to throw in a jug of corn whiskey."

But Bush packed his weather-beaten satchel, left town, and pitched under an assumed name in the Kitty League. "I was scared of Chicago," said Bush. "I had heard about all the gangsters and sharp men. I had never ridden an elevator that went up 'n down, and I didn't know about streetcars."

Bush was located three months later and persuaded to go to Chicago. "I missed my first train because the porter said it was a Pullman, and I didn't know what a Pullman was and wasn't going to take a chance on finding out." Bush sat all night in the depot and waited for a day coach.

Spring training in 1924 was quite an adventure for Bush, who was shaking from fright when he reported to manager Bill Killefer. Killefer didn't seem too impressed when he looked over the skinny, hollow-cheeked rookie, who hardly seemed capable of throwing a ball as far as home plate.

While Bush appeared emaciated, he did have broad shoulders and a live fastball. He learned how to throw the curve and screwball from a Cub master, Grover Cleveland Alexander.

Bush was given a uniform and told to pitch batting practice. A friend of Killefer's was working out with the Cubs and was the first to face Bush. The second ball Bush threw was wild and broke the batter's wrist.

Guy was told that he had ruined the star of the team and would be fined. "But I have no money to pay the fine," sighed Bush. "Then you'll be put in jail," replied the teammate.

The Bush-leaguer looked like an easy mark. On the train to Chicago, the players invited Bush to join them in a poker game. When the train pulled into the station Bush had greenbacks sticking from every pocket of his cheap, hometown suit. His winnings totaled $400.

When the Cubs hit New York, Bush pitched and defeated the Giants. Club president William Veeck, Sr., complimented Bush and told him to go over to Broadway and buy the best suit he could find. But Bush strolled to Fifth Avenue instead. They showed him a $75 garment, which was expensive for 1924.

"No, I want a real suit," drawled Bush. They showed him the best suit in the store and Bush took it without hesitating. Imagine Veeck's face when he received the charge for $135.

But Bush's pitching suited Veeck. He was a mainstay on the staff for the next decade, winning 152 games and losing only 101.

Bush was the lone Cub to record a victory in the ill-fated 1929 World Series. After beating the Philadelphia A's 3-1 in the third game, Bush went back to his hotel room and counted 191 wires and telegrams. "Two were from Tupelo, asking me to run for mayor," said Bush.

Off the field he was no longer the country bumpkin. He resembled a showboat gambler with his piercing black eyes, long sideburns, and plastered down black hair.

In addition, the hick from the hominy and hog belt was an enterprising young man in his adopted city. At one time or another, Bush owned a couple of filling stations, a bar, an indoor golf range, was employed in a bank and—are you ready—worked for the transportation department of the Pullman Company.

While Bush ranked among the best right-handers in the league, it always riled him that he never was a 20-game winner. In 1933, he asked Cub fans to send him four-leaf clovers. After he received 25 clovers, Guy went on to win 20 that season.

Following the 1934 season, Bush received a jolt. He was traded with outfielder Babe Herman and pitcher Jim Weaver to the Pittsburgh Pirates for third baseman Fred Lindstrom and pitcher Larry French.

It was Bush who served Babe Ruth's final homers, his 713th and 714th on May 25, 1935. "I threw Ruth my best pitch, the hard one," said Bush. "The Babe caught it in the meat of his bat and sent it over three decks in Forbes Field. I had never seen him hit a long ball and I wanted to challenge him."

After drawing his release from the Pirates in 1936, Bush drifted to the Boston Bees and then the St. Louis Cardinals, where he supposedly closed out his major league career with a 176–136 record.

Then World War II broke out. When young men answered the call to arms, Bush thought it was his patriotic duty to join the call for sore arms. He enlisted his services with the Cincinnati Reds in 1945 at age 44, but he only got into four games and had an 0-0 record.

Bush remained a Chicagoan, working in a sporting goods store and making appearances at old-timers baseball gatherings. He was still thin and wiry, but his patent leather hair was now streaked with gray.

In the 1970s, Bush moved his family back to Mississippi. But they didn't go by Pullman. The Mississippi Mudcat took a jet.

SHERIFF BLAKE

BLAKE, JOHN FREDERICK
B. Sept. 17, 1899, Ansted, W. Va.
D. Oct. 31, 1982, Beckley, W. Va.
BL TR 6' 180 lb.

Journeyman Sheriff Blake, overshadowed by the likes of Charlie Root, Guy Bush, and Pat Malone, is the forgotten man of the 1920s Cub pitching corps.

Blake had his first professional tryout with the Pirates in 1920 but failed to stick, after which it was down to the minors. With Rochester of the International League he was 21-13 with 187 strikeouts in 1921 and 17-9 the following season. Although he slumped to 13-20 with Seattle of the Pacific Coast League in 1923, the Cubs were still interested.

Brought up to Chicago in 1924, Blake won six games his first year but inched his way forward with 10, 11, then 13 victories. Plagued with control problems, however, he always lost more than he won.

Finally, in 1928, the Sheriff put it all together with a 17-11 mark and a sparkling 2.47 ERA, best on the Cub staff and second to Dazzy Vance in the National League. With four shutouts, he was tied with four other pitchers for the league leadership.

When the Cubs ran away with the pennant in 1929, Blake contributed a 14-13 log. Unfortunately, he lost his only World Series decision to the A's on Oct. 12, when the Mackmen rallied for 10 runs in the bottom of the seventh after being behind to the Cubs 8-0.

Blake tailed off quickly after that. He was dealt to the Phillies midway through the 1931 season.

After an absence of six years, he attempted a comeback with the Cardinals and the Browns in 1937. It failed, and Blake retired with a record of 87-102 and a 4.13 ERA. He was operating a farm in West Virginia at the time of his death.

Charlie Root was the losing pitcher when Babe Ruth called his shot in 1932 and the winning pitcher when Gabby Hartnett hit his Homer in the Gloamin' in 1938.

Howard Ehmke strikes out 13 to set a record. . . . Hack Wilson loses a fly ball in the sun and 10 runs clatter across the plate. . . . Babe Ruth calls his shot. . . .

One pitcher was the victim of those three magnified moments in World Series history—Charlie Root. Fortunately, the positive scales for Root outweigh those incidents.

He was the biggest winner in Chicago Cub history, compiling 201 victories from 1926 through '41. In a 1969 newspaper poll, Root was named the greatest right-handed Cub pitcher, beating out such competitors as Mordecai Brown, Grover Alexander, Lon Warneke, and Fergie Jenkins.

Oddly, he was a natural southpaw, doing everything with his left hand, except batting and pitching. Root was born on St. Patrick's Day in Middletown, Ohio, where he learned the pattern makers' trade. His pattern of life was set until he started pitching for the town team.

Root pitched against Carl Weilman of the St. Louis Browns and Hod Eller of the Cincinnati Reds. Both pitchers urged Root to sign with their respective teams. Weilman put up the best argument and Root signed with the Browns, who assigned him to Terre Haute in 1922.

The stocky pitcher earned a trial with the Browns in 1923, but after finishing with an 0-4 record, he found himself with Los Angeles the next season. The Angels were owned by the Cubs and Root's contract was transferred to Chicago.

Cub manager Joe McCarthy made Root feel at ease in his rookie season and told him to cut loose with everything he had on the ball. The result was an 18-17 record in 1926.

Root immediately became the workhorse of the Cub staff, winning 26 games in 1927 and earning the nickname "Strong-

CHARLIE ROOT

ROOT, CHARLES HENRY
B. March 17, 1899, Middletown, Ohio
D. Nov. 5, 1970, Hollister, Calif.
BR TR 5'10½"
190 lb.

heart." He didn't waste time peering at the hitter or squinting for signals. He got the ball back, wound up, and threw it again. When the Cubs had to catch an early train out of any city, Charlie was the getaway pitcher because he could win or lose in an hour and a half.

Root helped pitch the Cubs to the pennant in 1929 with a 19-6 record and was nominated by McCarthy to pitch the World Series opener against the Philadelphia Athletics. Charlie held the A's scoreless for six innings, but Howard Ehmke, a surprise starter, was striking out Cubs with such regularity that he once fanned five in a row. Root allowed only three hits and one run in seven innings, but was tagged with a 3-1 loss as Ehmke went on to strike out 13 for a then-series record.

In the fourth game of that series, Root looked like an easy winner with an 8-0 lead going into the seventh inning. Then center fielder Hack Wilson lost two easy fly balls in the sun to trigger a 10-8 Philadelphia victory. "The glare off the roof in Shibe Park blinded Wilson," said Root.

Root's most historic loss came in the third game of the 1932 World Series against the New York Yankees when Babe Ruth homered off him. Legend says the Babe called his shot by pointing toward the right-center field bleachers at Wrigley Field.

"He didn't point," declared Root. "If he had, I'd have knocked him on his fanny. I'd have loosened him up. I took my pitching too seriously to have anybody facing me do that."

Ruth had hit a three-run homer off Root in the first inning, but the Cubs tied the score 4-4 after four innings. The Cub bench and taunting fans heckled Ruth when he came to bat in the fifth. "I got two strikes on him," Root recounts.

"Babe did lift one finger toward our dugout after the first strike and two after the second. The count was two-and-two when I threw him a curve on the outside and he hit it over my head and into the bleachers. But he didn't point."

According to Root, the whole story was a product of imaginative sportswriters. The newspapers, he contends, didn't say anything about any bat-pointing until three days later. Regardless, it took root and became a part of baseball lore.

Those were his bad games. Fortunately, there were many more good ones. He was McCarthy's meal ticket on a solid pitching staff that included Pat Malone, Guy Bush, and Sheriff Blake. After outlasting that crew, he became part of Charlie Grimm's Big Four that also included Lon Warneke, Bill Lee, and Larry French. Grimm always called Root "Chinski" for unknown reasons.

After sticking around for 16 seasons and helping the Cubs win four pennants, Root finally reached an individual milestone on Aug. 27, 1941. Root was 42 when he took to the mound against the Braves in Boston. The Cubs were trailing 4-3 going into the top of the ninth inning. They then struck for three runs, with Root delivering a clutch single, and went on to win 6-4. It was the 200th victory of Root's career. But at the conclusion of the season, he was handed his release. He was the last survivor of the McCarthy regime.

Root, whose career record was 201–160 (201–156 in a Cub uniform), set out to prove that Strongheart still possessed a strong arm by pitching in the minor leagues until he was 49. He hurled for Hollywood and Columbus, Ohio, winding up at Billings, Mont., in 1948. Root won 111 minor league games; thus he posted 312 victories in 27 years of pitching.

After managing in the minors, Root returned to the Cubs as pitching coach under Frankie Frisch and Phil Cavarretta from 1951 through '53. Then he served as coach with the Milwaukee Braves in 1956–57. He then rejoined Grimm, his old roommate, as Cub coach in 1960.

Root, who had a sprawling cattle ranch and antique business in Hollister, Calif., was invited to Hollywood when the Babe Ruth movie was being filmed. They tried to get Root to put on a Cub uniform and take the mound for that big scene. But Charlie refused, pointing out that Ruth didn't point.

HACK WILSON

Cubs' manager Joe McCarthy took a worm and dropped it into a glass of water. His prize pupil, Hack Wilson, watched it wiggle around. Then McCarthy placed the worm in a glass of whiskey. It sank to the bottom, stone-cold dead.

WILSON, LEWIS ROBERT
B. April 26, 1900, Elwood City, Pa.
D. Nov. 23, 1948, Baltimore, Md.
BR TR 5'6", 190-220 lb. (estimated)

McCarthy beamed and turned to Wilson. "Well, did you see that?" asked Marse Joe.

"Yeah," replied Wilson. "If you drink whiskey you won't get worms."

With apologies to Ernie Banks, Hack Wilson was probably the Cubs' most exciting player on and off the field. He spent only six seasons in a Chicago uniform, but no Cub belted more homers, took more belts, or belted more people in barroom brawls in that span.

The patient McCarthy kept bailing Wilson out of jail, figuring you can't hit homers there.

How could anyone hit homers with a hangover? "I see three balls coming at me and always swing at the one in the middle. It's usually the real one," burped Wilson.

Lewis Robert Wilson acquired the nickname "Hack" from the wrestler Hackenschmidt, whom he resembled physically. The roly-poly slugger was built like a mini-blacksmith, carrying as much as 220 pounds on his squat 5' 6" frame. He swung a long, thin-handled bat that weighed 41 ounces.

Born illegitimately at the turn of the century in the brawling, mining town of Elwood City, Pa., Wilson quit school in the sixth grade and started his tempestuous career in a print shop, earning $4 per week.

Two years later he wielded a sledge hammer in a locomotive factory. Subsequently, Wilson labored in steel mills and shipyards and developed his massive chest, shoulders, and forearms.

Meanwhile, Wilson played baseball, catching for the mine nine. He was signed by Martinsburg (W. Va.) of the Blue Ridge League in 1921, and in his first game, he broke his leg sliding home. Unable to squat behind the plate, Wilson was switched to the outfield.

After hitting .356 and .366 at Martinsburg, Hack went to Portsmouth of the Virginia League and batted .388. There he was spotted by one of John McGraw's many birddogs and was signed to a New York Giants' contract.

Wilson displayed occasional home run power with the Giants, but was sent to Toledo in 1925 for further grooming. McGraw intended to recall Wilson, but because of a clerical error, he was left on the Toledo roster.

McCarthy, who had managed at Louisville, tipped off the Cubs, and Wilson was snared in the draft for $7,500, one of the best bargains in baseball history. As a Cub Wilson hit 190 homers, drove in 768 runs, batted .322, and had a .590 slugging record, highest in Chicago annals.

When not hitting the ball, Wilson hit the bottle and an occasional bottler. A milkman once heckled Wilson and Hack went into the stands and pummeled him. The milkman sued for $50,000. It took a jury, probably all Cub fans, only 20 minutes to tell the dairyman to peddle his bottles. He was awarded $1.

Meanwhile, there were rumblings on the South Side after White Sox first baseman Art "The Great" Shires punched manager Lena Blackburne and broke his jaw.

Wilson was offered $15,000 by promoter Jim Mullen to take on Shires. It was going to be Chicago's biggest fight attraction since Tunney-Dempsey. Wilson was the 7-5 choice until Commissioner Kenesaw Mountain Landis intervened and called it off. He told both ruffians to concentrate on hitting baseballs.

The Cubs concentrated on baseball, winning the 1929 pennant with a potent lineup that included Rogers Hornsby, Gabby Hartnett, Kiki Cuyler, Riggs Stephenson, Charlie Grimm, and Wilson, who slugged 39 homers and drove in 159 runs.

Then followed the darkest inning in Cub history. The Cubs were leading Connie Mack's Philadelphia A's 8-0 in the seventh inning of the fourth game of the World Series.

Mule Haas lofted a long fly to center field. Wilson shielded his eyes, but lost the ball in the sun. Mule wound up with a three-run homer. When the inning ended the A's had sent 10 runs across the plate and eventually won 10-8.

Wilson wore the goat's horns. He was called "Sunny Boy" so often he had to think Al Jolson was his shadow. Nobody mentioned that he hit .471 in the series.

Wilson showed his grit and guts by vindicating himself in 1930, setting an all-time record of 190 RBI. The nearest anyone ever came was Lou Gehrig with 184 in 1931. Next was Hank Greenberg with 183 in 1937. Babe Ruth's top RBI mark was 170 in 1921.

The stumpy Wilson also set a National League record when he clubbed 56 homers that season. Ralph Kiner, Johnny Mize, Willie

Mays, and George Foster took runs at Hack's record and failed. Hank Aaron never came close.

But there was trouble ahead for Wilson. McCarthy left to manage the New York Yankees, and Hornsby, the new Cub manager, wouldn't tolerate Wilson's antics. When Wilson slumped in 1931, he was benched by Hornsby.

After hitting .261, Wilson was traded to St. Louis with pitcher Bud Teachout for pitcher Burleigh Grimes. Wilson soon bounced from the Cardinals to the Dodgers.

Hack Wilson of the Cubs set a National League record of 56 homers in 1930, and none was a grand slammer.

In one game, the Phillies were pounding the Dodgers at ancient Baker Bowl in Philadelphia. Dodger manager Max Carey rushed to the mound to lift pitcher Walter "Boom-Boom" Beck.

The Boomer became enraged, heaved the ball, and sent it rattling against the tin fence. Wilson, obviously nursing another hangover, raced for the ball and threw a strike to second base. He was now playing by instinct.

The Dodgers shunted Wilson to the Phillies late in 1934. There he played seven games, batted .100, and drew his release.

Wilson's baseball career was over and he sank lower and lower on the economic scale. He worked as a bartender, a bouncer in a honky-tonk, a freight-handler, and a stevedore. Wilson wound up as a laborer in the Baltimore park district and died penniless at age 48 on Nov. 23, 1948.

For three decades Wilson knocked on the Hall of Fame door only to have his knuckles rapped. He should have splintered the door long ago with his booming bat.

Finally, in 1979 the Veterans Committee unhinged the door and Wilson marched into the Cooperstown valhalla—a bat in one hand and a bottle in the other.

A career .307 hitter, Hack collected 1,461 hits and 244 homers.

RIGGS STEPHENSON

STEPHENSON, JACKSON RIGGS
B. Jan. 5, 1898, Akron, Ala.
BR TR 5'10" 185 lb.

On June 25, 1977, the Cubs staged a gala Old-Timers Day at Wrigley Field. The old ballpark was overflowing with nostalgia.

The youngsters whistled wildly when such heroes as Ernie Banks, Ron Santo, and Billy Williams were introduced. Older fans cheered when such favorites as Phil Cavarretta, Andy Pafko, and Hank Sauer stepped forward.

But there was only a smattering of applause when a real old-timer advanced to the foul lines in recognition. He was nearing 80, but there was still a spring to his step. Unlike the others, he was attired in civilian clothes.

His face was deeply lined and pugnacious. He bore the cauliflower ears of earlier battles. He waved to the crowd. The "Old Hoss" had returned to the scene where he swooped 'em in the pinch with his game-winning line drives.

Riggs Stephenson was perhaps the most devastating hitter in Cub annals. In fact, he is their leading career batter with a .336 average.

Rescued from the minors by Cub manager Joe McCarthy in 1926, Stevie went on to bat (now hold your breath) .338, .344, .324, .362, .367, .319, .324, and .329 through the 1933 season.

There was a world of admiration and warmth in the nickname Old Hoss. The son of the South had all the qualities of that faithful old family horse of a nearly forgotten age. He was always pulling in the right direction with both shoulders in the harness.

Those cauliflower ears were a reminder of his boisterous days as a fullback at the University of Alabama in the early 1920s. He was heralded as the greatest ball carrier in the South.

At that time the slow-spoken hombre with the pleasant drawl was nicknamed "Rough House." While in school his tuition was paid by the state. He was employed to prevent other frisky students from casting boulders through class windows.

The powerfully built Stephenson also participated in basketball and was a shortstop on the 'Bama varsity nine. Riggs had replaced Joe Sewell, who was called up to Cleveland when Ray Chapman, the Indians' shortstop, had died as a result of a beaning by New York Yankees' pitcher Carl Mays.

The Indians were beset with another accident in 1921. Second baseman Bill Wambsganss had broken his arm and manager Tris Speaker summoned Stephenson. At that time major league teams could sign athletes who were still in school.

Speaker installed Stephenson at second base. He was the unlikeliest looking second baseman with his heavy, muscular, but slightly bowed legs. He had trouble making the pivot because of an old shoulder injury incurred on the gridiron. He was soon switched to left field.

As a utility player from 1921 through '24, Stephenson reeled off batting averages of .330, .339, .319, and .371. But when his average dropped to .296 in 1925, he was dispatched to Kansas City.

He stayed there a month and then was traded to Indianapolis, where he caught the eye of Louisville manager Joe McCarthy. When McCarthy was signed as Cub manager in 1926, he grabbed outfielder Hack Wilson from Toledo and Stephenson from Indy, where he was only hitting .385.

Stephenson, who batted fifth for McCarthy's Cubs, was the least glamorous of that famed North Side Murderer's Row that included Wilson, Gabby Hartnett, Rogers Hornsby, Charlie Grimm, and Kiki Cuyler.

It was quite an outfield. Stephenson in left, Wilson in center and Cuyler in right. In 1929, Wilson drove home 159 runs; Stephenson, 110; and Cuyler, 102, thus becoming the only 100-RBI outfield in National League history.

The following season, Wilson broke the all-time RBI record with a whopping 190 RBI. Cuyler chipped in with 134. And the Old Hoss? He was down to 68. "I batted behind Wilson," drawled Stevie. "He cleaned the sacks and didn't leave any for me."

But Riggs outhit 'em both with his .367 average. Wilson batted only .356 and Cuyler .355.

Stephenson was not a home run hitter. His top mark was 17 in

1929. His specialty was looping doubles to left-center, leading the National League with 46 in 1927 and coming back with 49 in 1932.

The Cubs won pennants in 1929 and '32, but they dropped the World Series to the Philadelphia Athletics in five games and lost four in a row to the New York Yankees. Riggs hit well in both, batting .316 and .444.

It wasn't until 1934 that Stephenson became a benchwarmer. Wilson was gone and the Cubs needed power. They acquired slugger Chuck Klein from the Philadelphia Phillies to fill the void. The Old Hoss got into only 38 games. His average plummeted to .216.

On Halloween he received a trick and a treat. Cub owner P. K. Wrigley summoned Stephenson to Chicago and put on something of a sentimental ceremony, presenting Riggs with a $350 engraved gold watch for his many years of faithful service. It was the most stylish guillotining ever accomplished by a baseball executioner.

But the Old Hoss wasn't ready to be put out to pasture. He went back to Indy in 1935 and hit .340. Then he bounced to Birmingham and batted .355. In the off-season, Stephenson officiated high school games, using his 27-jewel watch with a stop-second attachment to time the matches.

Stephenson permanently discarded his uniform following a semipro game at Demopolis, Ala., on July 4, 1939. Since then he has focused his attention on timber, operating sawmills and a lumberyard in his home town of Akron, Ala.

The Old Hoss was an expert in handling wood on the diamond, so he could easily handle timber in the rough.

Today, Stephenson is retired. He spends his leisure time hunting with Joe Sewell and attending all the Alabama baseball and football games.

And the watch? He presented it to his grandson. Riggs recently received a call from Cooperstown. The Hall of Fame wanted some mementoes, including the watch. Why don't they take a .336 hitter instead?

JIMMY COONEY, JR.

COONEY, JAMES EDWARD
B. Aug. 24, 1894, Cranston, R. I.
BR TR 5'10" 160 lb.

Although he was a Cub less than a year and a half, the younger Jimmy Cooney owns a unique niche in their history—he was the only one to execute an unassisted triple play.

Like his father, Cooney carried a light bat and a sticky glove, topping the league's shortstops in double plays and fielding average in 1926, his only full season with the Cubs.

The big day came at Pittsburgh's Forbes Fields, May 30, 1927, in the morning game of a doubleheader. In the bottom of the fourth inning, the Pirates had Lloyd Waner at second base and Clyde Barnhart at first. Lloyd's brother Paul came to bat.

With the runners on the move, Cooney snagged the elder Waner's line drive, stepped on second to double Lloyd, then tagged

Barnhart coming down the line. It was all over in a matter of seconds. The Cubs went on to win 7-6 in 10 innings, to snap the Bucs' winning streak at 11 straight.

For Cooney it was poetic justice. As a Cardinal on May 7, 1925, he had been doubled off second base by the Pirates' Glenn Wright as the latter pulled an unassisted triple killing. To make the story even more unbelievable, one day after Cooney pulled the trick, Johnny Neun of the Tigers did the same thing against the Indians.

After that, the feat was not duplicated until July 30, 1968, when the Senators' Ron Hansen scalped three Indians again. As of this writing, Cooney's has been the last in the National League.

Only eight days after his heroic moment—on June 8—Cooney was traded to the Phillies for pitcher Hal Carlson. He soon drifted into obscurity, finishing with the Braves in 1928, a lifetime .262 hitter with 413 hits. His brother Johnny was in the majors for 20 years, first as a pitcher and later as an outfielder.

ART NEHF

NEHF, ARTHUR NEUKOM
B. July 31, 1892,
Terre Haute, Ind.
D. Dec. 18, 1960,
Phoenix, Ariz.
BL TL 5'9½" 176 lb.

A star pitcher for the Braves and the Giants during the 1910s and '20s, southpaw Art Nehf won 21 games for John McGraw's New Yorkers in 1920 and 20 the following year.

After a brief interlude with Cincinnati, Nehf was in his pitching twilight when he came to the Cubs late in 1927. Nevertheless, he still had enough juice to post a 13-7 log with a 2.65 ERA in 1928 and an 8-5 mark for the Cub pennant winners of 1929.

He retired thereafter, with a 182–120 record during his 15-year big league career.

HAL CARLSON

CARLSON, HAROLD GUST
B. May 17, 1894,
Rockford, Ill.
D. May 28, 1930,
Chicago, Ill.
BR TR 6' 180 lb.

Hal Carlson is the only Cub to die while an active player during the season. The right-hander broke in with the Pittsburgh Pirates in 1917 and played until his untimely death of a stomach hemorrhage on May 28, 1930.

Various illnesses prevented Carlson from bettering his career record of 114-120. Most of his problems stemmed from being gassed in combat in France during World War I.

Carlson came to the Cubs from the Philadelphia Phillies in 1927. He served as a fifth starter behind Charlie Root, Pat Malone, Guy Bush, and Sheriff Blake.

He would often complain of a sore elbow. One time, Cub trainer Andy Lotshaw took a Coke, poured it into a brown bottle, and told Carlson it was a secret potion. Lotshaw rubbed it on Carlson's elbow, and Hal went out and pitched a complete-game victory. From then on Carlson was hooked on the secret potion.

On the evening of May 27, Carlson was chatting with teammate Kiki Cuyler in the lobby of Chicago's Carlos Hotel. He told Cuyler he wasn't feeling well and went to his room.

A few hours later Carlson summoned assistant trainer Eddie Froehlich, saying he was bleeding from the mouth and was in great pain. Teammates Cuyler, Riggs Stephenson, and Cliff Heathcote also rushed to his room, but Carlson passed away before the ambulance arrived. Carlson had a 30-17 record as a Cub pitcher.

EARL WEBB

Following a look-see with the Giants in 1925, Earl Webb made his genuine rookie season with the Cubs two years later. Playing on and off in right field, Webb batted .301 and smashed 14 home runs. In 1928, however, he played only part-time as his average dropped to .250. By that time Kiki Cuyler had been added to the Cub outfield and Webb was deemed expendable, so back down to the minors he went.

WEBB, WILLIAM EARL
B. Sept. 17, 1898, Bon Air, Tenn.
D. May 23, 1965, Jamestown, Tenn.
BL TR 6'1" 185 lb.

Earl resurfaced with the Boston Red Sox in 1930. The following year he knocked an incredible 67 doubles to set a major league high for a single season. He also batted .333 in 1931 for a career high.

Traded to the Tigers in June 1932, Webb spent almost a year there before going to the White Sox.

He finished his seven-year big league career on Chicago's South Side, a lifetime .306 hitter.

WOODY ENGLISH

The wacky riotous film "Duck Soup," starring the Marx Bros., took place in the mythical kingdom of Fredonia. There actually is a Fredonia, a farming hamlet tucked in a corner of Ohio.

Instead of being inhabited by the likes of Groucho, Chico, Harpo, and Zeppo, there is only Woody. In plain English it's Elwood, but everyone calls him Woody.

Fredonia, a crossroads point of some 50 people, is so small that it hasn't even a post office of its own. For excitement, young English would play checkers in the general merchandise store, or pitch pennies or horseshoes by lamplight.

Of course, in the daytime English would pitch hay or milk the cows on his grandfather's farm. English's father died when he was five, and his granddad helped raise him.

When English wasn't pitching pennies, horseshoes, or hay, he pitched a baseball. Following his school chores, English joined an amateur team representing a Newark, Ohio, tire factory as a shortstop.

ENGLISH, ELWOOD GEORGE
B. March 2, 1907, Fredonia, Ohio
BR TR 5'10" 175 lb.

It was then that English was discovered by Turk Riley, who wanted him for his Zanesville (Ohio) semipro team. But Al Sweitzer (not the guy in Africa, but the Newark manager) wouldn't let him go. Riley bought Sweitzer a new suit and a hat, and Zanesville got a shortstop. That suited all parties, except English, who could've used some new duds.

While starring for Zanesville, English caught the eye of Joe

O'Brien, who owned the Toledo Mud Hens of the American Association. O'Brien anxiously signed English, who immediately disappointed all by hitting only .220 for Toledo in 1925.

The next year, Casey Stengel took over as Toledo manager. He taught Woody to stand back in the batter's box and wait for his pitch. With Stengel's pointers, English boosted his batting average to .301 in 1926.

At that time Toledo had a working agreement with the New York Giants. English was being groomed as the successor to Giants' shortstop Travis Jackson. But the Cubs, on a tip from manager Joe McCarthy, purchased English's contract for $50,000. The Cubs even gave English $1,500 for signing. He thought he was rolling in wealth when he reported to the Cubs in 1927 at the tender age of 20.

English went to Catalina Island with the Cubs in 1927 and won the shortstop job when Jimmy Cooney came up with a sore arm. At first, Woody was erratic and scattered shots over first base with his slingshot arm. But he settled down and even batted .290.

The next season the Cubs acquired second baseman Rogers Hornsby from the Boston Braves for a $200,000 bundle and a bundle of players. The Rajah, a seven-time batting champion, was of such stature that he demanded a "perfect roommate."

Hornsby's preferences were a gent who doesn't talk in his sleep or snore. Or doesn't get up early or come in late. Or doesn't whistle while he's shaving. And most of all—a gent that doesn't keep gin in the room.

Where could a Prohibition-era ballclub come up with such a mild-mannered mouse? Traveling secretary Robert Lewis scanned the Cub roster. He shuddered at the thought of pairing Pat Malone or Hack Wilson with Hornsby. Lewis then beamed and introduced Mr. Elwood English to Mr. Rogers Hornsby.

A new double-play combo was born—the veteran and the youngster. Hornsby took a liking to English and steadied him in the field. He improved Woody's hitting, teaching him wrist action and follow through. By the end of the 1929 season, Hornsby acclaimed "the kid is the best shortstop in the business."

On a team loaded with such sluggers as Hornsby, Wilson, Gabby Hartnett, Kiki Cuyler, and Riggs Stephenson, English became the Cubs' ideal leadoff hitter. His job was to get on base and let the big guns drive him home.

English became so proficient that he set an all-time record for runs scored by a shortstop in a single season, crossing the plate 152 times in 1930. In a three-year period (1929–31) English scored 400 runs.

Woody reached his peak in 1930 with a .335 average that included 214 base hits. In addition, English's 67 extra base hits on 36 doubles, 17 triples, and 14 homers was a Cub record for a shortstop until a fella named Ernie Banks arrived 25 years later and had 83.

Hornsby soon replaced McCarthy as Cub manager, and English was appointed team captain. Then followed some bad breaks. A line drive broke the index finger of Woody's throwing hand in the spring of 1931 and also broke his string of 318 consecutive games. That break brought Billy Jurges into the picture at short. Jurges was so sensational that when English returned he was shifted to third base. Woody also filled in at second base for newcomer Billy Herman.

English remained captain when Hornsby was fired and the managerial job was handed to veteran first baseman Charlie Grimm. Then came a young third baseman named Stan Hack and English was relegated to the bench.

Woody shunted from second to short to third without a whimper as the Cubs' most valued utility player. But lack of steady play dulled his batting eye. Finally, on Dec. 3, 1936, English was traded with pitcher Roy Henshaw to the Brooklyn Dodgers for infielder Linus Frey.

English became a regular again with the 1937 Dodgers, getting into 129 games. He jumped the club in July 1938, and his contract was purchased by the Reds. He decided he would rather go fishing in northern Wisconsin.

The Cubs bought his contract from Cincinnati, but English failed to make the final squad cut during spring training in 1939. He opened a bar on Chicago's North Side and even tried his hand at managing a local ballclub—the Bloomer Girls, who played in Parichy Stadium.

Then it was back to Fredonia. How you gonna keep him down on the farm after he's seen Parichy?

Hecklers at Wrigley Field used to refer to Hack Wilson and Pat Malone as "Whiskey Head and Beer Belly." It was the Prohibition era, and the fun-loving pair gave Cub manager Joe McCarthy many a headache with their escapades.

Wilson and Malone were baseball's odd couple. Wilson was a squat 5′ 6″ roly-poly slugger, while Malone was a strapping 6′ pitcher. Both hailed from the steel and coal regions of Pennsylvania. Neither would qualify as lawyers because they couldn't pass the bar or speakeasy.

Malone was named Perce Leigh after a hard-shelled, two-fisted brakeman by his father, who was a railroad man in Altoona, Pa. But Pat seemed more appropriate than Perce Leigh.

Malone was big for his age and enlisted in the army at 16. While in the U.S. Cavalry at Douglas, Ariz., he acquired the name "Black Knight of the Border." But his parents got him out. Malone then labored as a fireman on the mountain division of the Pennsylvania Railroad.

While playing the outfield for the Altoona team in an industrial league in 1916, Malone cut loose with a throw to nail a runner. George Quinn, the manager, immediately decided a fellow with an arm like that should be a pitcher. Young Perce Leigh then pitched

PAT MALONE

MALONE, PERCE LEIGH
B. Sept. 25, 1902, Altoona, Pa.
D. May 13, 1943, Altoona, Pa.
BL TR 6′ 200 lb.

for Juanita College. Perce Leigh of Juanita? Oh, well.

The black-haired hurler caught the eye of scout Pat Blake, who landed him a job with Knoxville where he was 13-12 in 1921. He then became a chattel of the New York Giants. John McGraw liked the barrel-shaped Malone, but not his off-the-field habits. He kept him on a minor league string for five long seasons.

After a 28-13 season at Des Moines in 1926 and a 20-18 record at Minneapolis, Malone was purchased by the Cubs. Malone lost his first seven decisions in a Cub uniform and would have been back in the sticks if McGraw had been manager. But Cub manager Joe McCarthy stuck by the rookie, who went on to compile an 18-13 record.

The Cubs roomed Perce Leigh Malone with pitcher Percy Lee Jones. Perce Leigh and Percy Lee were a match made in trivia heaven, but in real life it was for the birds. Pat once amused himself by luring pigeons to his window ledge with peanuts and capturing them. He then tucked several under the covers of the sleeping Percy Lee Jones, just to ruffle his feathers.

Malone also used to pigeon-hole sportswriters. He was inclined to fret over newspaper cracks about him and once took a swing at a writer who ducked. But Malone's punch struck another writer, shattering his dentures. Club president William L. Veeck, Sr., gave the writer $1,000 for new store teeth. The writer purchased a new car instead.

McCarthy soon devised his own bed-check method on Malone and Wilson. He'd casually ask Malone for a match, noting its origin on the cover, and know at which speakeasy the two had spent the previous evening. One time they handed McCarthy a pack of matches carrying no identification and challenged their manager to guess which night spot they roamed.

Veeck solved the problem by inviting Mrs. Marion Malone and daughter Pattie on an Eastern road trip. Pat responded by winning seven of eight games on the trip. Apparently, Pattie was a better influence than Hack Wilson.

Malone won 22 and lost 10 and topped the National League in strikeouts with 166 in 1929, leading the Cubs to the pennant. The following season he was 20-9, topping the league in complete games with 22.

Pat should have been one of the greatest pitchers in baseball, but he never was able to achieve that ranking. He never seemed to get himself to realize what ability he had. When McCarthy left the Cubs for the New York Yankees, the pair of Wilson and Malone suffered the most.

Their antics weren't appreciated under the sober and somber regime of Rogers Hornsby. Wilson soon departed and Malone never again won 20. His victory totals dropped to 16, 15, 10, and 14 the next four seasons.

The Cubs underwent a shakeup after the 1934 season and Malone was the first to go. Despite his seven-season ledger of 115–79, he was dispatched to the St. Louis Cardinals for rookie catcher Ken O'Dea.

Malone's career in Cardinal livery was short-lived. He returned his first contract unsigned and yelped, "You made a mistake and sent me the batboy's contract." An irate Branch Rickey found only one taker, McCarthy, who always liked the big fellow with the powerful arm.

After a 3-5 season with the Yankees, Malone bounced back with a 12-4 record in 1936, 9-2 in a relief role. Malone was 4-4 in 1937, his final season, finishing with a 135–92 record.

Malone played briefly in the minors with Minneapolis, Baltimore, and Chattanooga before returning to Altoona to operate a cafe. He died of acute pancreatitis on May 13, 1943, at the age of 40.

KIKI CUYLER

CUYLER, HAZEN SHIRLEY
B Aug. 30, 1899, Harrisville, Mich.
D. Feb. 11, 1950, Ann Arbor, Mich.
BR TR 5'11" 185 lb.

Hazen "Kiki" Cuyler made his debut with the Pirates in 1921 but was shuffled back and forth to the minors for his first three years, seeing only sparse action with the parent club. In 1924 he burst into stardom his first full season with a .354 average in 117 games, going six-for-six on Aug. 9.

Kiki—the nickname was derived from "Cuy" while he was in the minors—followed that season with a .357 mark the following year and .321 in 1926.

He tied a National League record by collecting 10 straight hits on Sept. 18, 19, and 21, 1925. In the seventh game of the 1925 World Series against the Senators, Kiki drove in the tying and winning runs with an eighth-inning double.

A hurricane struck in 1927 when Donie Bush replaced Bill McKechnie as Pirate manager. Bush insisted that Kiki bat second in the lineup instead of his customary third. Highly superstitious, Cuyler refused to bat number two, but said he would accept any other spot.

Bush stuck to his demand and kept Cuyler out of the lineup, benching him during the World Series when the Yankees steamrolled the Bucs in four straight.

On Nov. 28, 1927, Cuyler was traded to the Cubs for Sparky Adams and Floyd Scott, and Pittsburgh's loss was Chicago's gain. The addition of Kiki gave the Cubs their greatest outfield in history—Riggs Stephenson in left, Hack Wilson in center, and Cuyler in right.

Kiki won games with his bat, nailed runners at the plate with his powerful arm, and was a throwback to an earlier era with his daring baserunning.

During his first three seasons as a Cub, he topped the league with 37 steals in 1928, 43 in '29, and 37 in '30. He is the only Cub in history to accomplish this feat even three times, let alone in succession.

In 1929 Cuyler reached a career high average of .360 and drove in 102 runs as the Cubs won the pennant. He hit .300 in the World Series, but the Athletics trimmed the Cubs in five games. His best season overall was 1930. He batted .355 and enjoyed career peaks of 228 hits, 155 runs, 50 doubles, and 134 RBI. For good measure, he smashed 17 triples and 13 homers.

Off the field, Cuyler was an avid hunter and champion dancer, winning several trophies for waltzing. He neither drank nor smoked, but had a weakness for ice cream sodas.

A pious Roman Catholic, he prayed before every game, wore a scapular, and often made the sign of the cross when stepping into the batter's box, one of the few non-Latin players to practice this custom. Judging from his record, it must have worked.

Kiki was the idol of the female fans, and he seldom let them down—especially on June 27, 1930, before the largest crowd in Wrigley Field history.

Of the 51,556 total, there were 30,476 Ladies Day guests, hollering and screaming for their hero, Cuyler. He gave them a thrill they never forgot in the bottom of the 10th, when he homered with a man on to give the Cubs a 7-5 win over Brooklyn.

Cuyler's greatest heroics came in the stretch drive of the 1932 pennant race. Ironically, it had been an off season for him. He missed more than 40 games with a broken foot, and was batting only .262 on the morning of Aug. 27.

The fireworks began in a doubleheader with the Giants at Wrigley Field. In game one, Cuyler smashed a three-run homer as the Cubs crushed New York 6-1 for their eighth win in a row.

Kiki added a single and a run in the second game as the Cubs made it nine. On Aug. 28, he collected three hits, including an eighth-inning homer, then drove in the game-winner with a sacrifice fly in the bottom of the ninth. The 5-4 victory over New York made it 10 straight.

Number eleven came Aug. 30 in a 4-3 win over Bill Terry's men. Cuyler collected two hits, two RBI, including another eighth-inning home run, and a stolen base.

But his greatest day was Aug. 31. With three hits already, Kiki saved the game with a game-tying single in the last of the ninth, knotting the score at five apiece. Then came near-disaster as the Giants exploded for four tallies in the 10th. But with two out in their half, the Cubs fought back and made it 9-7 when Kiki came to bat with Billy Herman and Woody English on base. He smacked one into the center field bleachers to give the Cubs a 10-9 win, their 12th in succession. The joyous crowd nearly mobbed him in adoration!

The streak reached 13 on Sept. 2, as Cuyler's fifth homer in six games propelled the Cubs to an 8-5 win over St. Louis. The following day it hit 14—although Cuyler went hitless—before Dizzy Dean collared them 3-0 in the second game of the doubleheader.

The Cubs continued on their road to glory and so did Cuyler. On Sept. 15, his 11th inning home run gave his mates an 8-7 win against the Giants on the enemy's turf. Back in Chicago five days later, his bases-loaded triple in the seventh provided the margin for a 5-2 victory over the Pirates to clinch the pennant.

From Aug. 27 to the end of the season, he batted .365 to bring his average for the year up to .291.

Cuyler batted .278 in the World Series, but the Yankees swept the Cubs, four games to zip. Cuyler enjoyed two more productive seasons before hitting a prolonged slump in 1935. The Cubs released him July 3 and he signed with the Reds, where he made a comeback in 1936, hitting .326 in 144 games. His skills waned thereafter, and he wound up his playing days with the Dodgers two years later.

Kiki later served as a Cub coach, managed in the minors, and was on the Red Sox coaching staff at the time of his death. He was elected to the Hall of Fame, somewhat belatedly, in 1968.

Lifetime, he was a .321 hitter with 2,299 hits, 127 homers, and 328 stolen bases.

ROGERS HORNSBY

Probably the greatest right-handed hitter of all time, Rogers "Rajah" Hornsby had his best years with the Cardinals, for whom he batted .402 over a five-year period, 1921 through '25.

A winner of seven batting titles, he set a 20th century high with a .424 average in 1924. After leading the Redbirds to the world championship in 1926 as player-manager, Hornsby got into contract difficulties with Cardinal boss Sam Breadon and was traded to the Giants.

But the Giants could not afford the Rajah's contract for more than one year, nor could the Braves, for whom he played in 1928.

Into the scene stepped Cub owner William Wrigley, Jr., who could not only afford Hornsby's salary but was more than willing to pay it. The Cubs had finished a close third in 1928, and the front office was convinced that Hornsby could turn the tide in Chicago's favor.

On Nov. 7, 1928, the Cubs gave the Braves infielder Fred Maguire, catcher Doc Leggett, pitchers Percy Jones, Harry Seibold, and Bruce Cunningham *plus* $200,000 for Hornsby.

In 1929 Hornsby proved himself worth every penny of the investment. Leading a wrecking crew that included Hack Wilson, Kiki Cuyler, Riggs Stephenson, and Charlie Grimm, the Rajah batted .380 (a 20th century Cub high) with 47 doubles, 7 triples, 39 home runs, and 149 RBI. He also set club records with 229 hits and 156 runs scored.

Hornsby's key to success was his remarkable vision. Protective of his eyes to the point of paranoia, he neither read books nor attended movies for fear they might damage his orbs. As a second baseman he made most plays well, but had difficulties with pop flies.

In 1930 the Rajah suffered a fractured ankle, which turned out to be the beginning of the end of his career. Playing only 42 games, Hornsby batted .308 as the Cubs finished a close second to the

HORNSBY, ROGERS
B. April 27, 1896,
Winters, Tex.
D. Jan. 5, 1963,
Chicago, Ill.
BR TR 5'11½"
200 lb.

Cardinals, two games out. A healthy Hornsby would probably have made the difference.

In the meantime, Wrigley had lost faith in manager Joe McCarthy since the 1929 World Series defeat. On Sept. 23, 1930, the reins were turned over to Hornsby. The Cubs won the final four games of the season under his tutelage.

The honeymoon, however, was short-lived. Hornsby had enjoyed success earlier while running the Cardinals, but as Cub field boss he was blunt, crude, sometimes arrogant, and as diplomatic as a sawed-off shotgun. Impatient and sarcastic to the nth degree, he expected perfection and nothing less, regardless of the circumstances.

He berated players for drinking and smoking, while he blew his own money at the racetrack. With his razor tongue, he alienated nearly every player on the club, and a team that could have done a lot better slipped to a distant third in 1931.

Regardless of his shortcomings as a team leader, Hornsby was still an asset as a player. Playing his last season as a regular in '31, the Rajah hit .331 in 100 games, driving in 90 runs. On April 24 he had one of the greatest days of his career, stroking three straight homers and driving in eight runs to beat the Pirates 10-6 at Pittsburgh.

On Sept. 13 he was sitting in the dugout with the Cubs and the Braves knotted at seven apiece at Wrigley Field. It was the last of the 11th and the Cubs had the bases loaded. Coming in cold off the bench, the Rajah smashed a grand slammer for an 11-7 Cub win.

When asked why he put himself on the line in such a tight spot, he replied in typical Hornsbian fashion, "I needed the best hitter on the team, so I put myself in."

As the 1932 season got under way, Hornsby did most of his managing from the bench, rarely appearing in the lineup. But William Wrigley had died during the winter, and relations with both the players and the club president William Veeck, Sr., had deteriorated.

Rumors—and finally an investigation—concerning the Rajah's gambling habits did not help either. Finally, with the team five games behind and floundering, Hornsby was replaced by Charlie Grimm on Aug. 2.

Grimm brought the Cubs home first, while Hornsby rejoined the Cardinals in 1933. Four years later, he ended his career as player-manager of the Browns, posting a lifetime batting average of .358, second only to Ty Cobb. In 1942 he entered baseball's Hall of Fame.

After serving as a Cub television announcer in 1949, Hornsby briefly managed the Browns and the Reds in the early fifties, without much success.

In 1958 he returned to the Cubs as a coach and batting instructor. Before his death he was influential in the development of two other Cub greats—Ron Santo and Billy Williams.

By mid-1932 the Cubs were a distant second and going nowhere. Resentment against Hornsby's rule was boiling over, and the players were approaching open revolt. Finally, the front office saw the smoke signals and replaced him with Charlie Grimm on Aug. 2.

In contrast to the Cromwellian Hornsby, Grimm let the team run itself whenever possible, cracking the whip only when necessary. His immense popularity with his teammates did not hurt matters either.

That season also witnessed the emergence of three young and rising stars—pitcher Lon Warneke, second baseman Billy Herman, and shortstop Billy Jurges. Plus the acquisition of former Yankee Mark Koenig gave them a shot in the arm in the stretch drive. Consequently, the team won 37 of its last 57 games to take the pennant.

The World Series, however, was sweet revenge time for Joe McCarthy, who now managed the power-laden Yankees of Ruth and Gerhig. They flattened the Cubs in four straight, capped by Babe Ruth's alleged "called shot" off Charlie Root.

The next two years were a rebuilding period. The Cubs slipped to third in 1933 and again the year after. Ex-Brooklyn slugger Babe Herman was picked up in '33 for pennant insurance, but he was not the answer, nor was Chuck Klein, whom they obtained from the Phillies the following year.

Meanwhile, a massive changing of the guard was taking place. After seeing only limited action the previous two seasons, Stan Hack secured the third baseman's job on a regular basis in 1934 and held onto it for the next 12 years. Outfielder Frank Demaree, who also came up in 1932, was back for keeps by '35. Pitcher Bill Lee and outfielder Augie Galan (originally a second baseman) joined the team in 1934, and both were stars by the following year. Late in the season, the youthful Phil Cavarretta was brought up as the eventual replacement for Charlie Grimm at first base.

During the winter of 1934–35, veteran hurlers Guy Bush and Pat

SECTION
FIVE
1932–1940
Grimm 'n
Gabby
Glory

The Chicago Cubs, 1938 National League Champions

Malone were dealt away. Riggs Stephenson retired. Larry French and Tex Carleton replaced Bush and Malone, while Freddie Lindstrom was picked up to help in the outfield. By mid-1935 Kiki Cuyler was gone also.

Thus when the face-lifted Cubs won the '35 pennant, thanks largely to a 21-game winning streak in September, there were only four players left from the 1929 Murderer's Row—Grimm, Hartnett, Root, and English. Of those, only Hartnett and Root were still seen on a regular basis.

Although the Cubs won 100 games, they again met defeat in the World Series, this time at the paws of the Tigers, who roared away with the title in six games. Only Lon Warneke could tame them.

Despite a 15-game winning streak early in the season, the Cubs had to settle for a tie for the runner-up slot in 1936, and a close second the next year. Between seasons Lon Warneke was traded to the Cardinals for first baseman Rip Collins in a questionable deal.

If 1951 was the year of the "Miracle Giants," then 1938 was the season of the "Miracle Cubs." Off to their slowest start in several years, the Cubs were on a third place treadmill when Charlie Grimm voluntarily stepped down as manager July 26, turning the reins over to Gabby Hartnett.

Changing horses in midstream worked again. The Cubs charged to the top with a 10-game winning streak in the last week and a half of the race. Gabby's famed "Homer in the Gloamin' " on Sept. 28 wiped out the first place Pirates psychologically, enabling the Cubs to propel themselves to the pennant.

Thereafter, Hartnett's Irish luck began to wane. In the World Series Joe McCarthy got more revenge as his Yanks again drubbed the Cubs in four straight. The following year the Cubs dropped to fourth, in a season highlighted by the arrival of pitcher Claude Passeau and future home run king Bill Nicholson.

In 1940 the Cubs sank to fifth place, their first losing season and second division finish in 15 years. When Hartnett was fired that November, the door was closed forever on the fabulous days that had begun under McCarthy.

GABBY HARTNETT

HARTNETT, CHARLES LEO
B. Dec. 20, 1900, Woonsocket, R. I.
D. Dec. 20, 1972, Park Ridge, Ill.
BR TR 6'1" 215 lb.

THE DATE: WEDNESDAY SEPT. 28, 1938.
THE TIME: 5:37 P.M.
THE PLACE: WRIGLEY FIELD.
THE EVENT: A BASEBALL GAME; THE MOST MEMORABLE IN CHICAGO CUBS HISTORY.

The Pittsburgh Pirates entered the September stretch with a seven-game lead over the Cubs. But now, four days before the season's end, Pittsburgh clung to first place by only half a game.

The shadows of evening fell on Wrigley Field as the Cubs and Pirates were tied 5-5 in the ninth inning. It had been a dark afternoon. Now, it was getting difficult to see. The umpires

132

conferred and decided to let the game continue one more inning.

Veteran Cub pitcher Charlie Root set the Pirates down in order in the top of the ninth inning. It was now the Cubs last turn at bat. Mace Brown, the Pirates burly relief ace, retired Phil Cavarretta on a long fly to center. Carl Reynolds grounded out.

Gabby Hartnett, who had replaced Charlie Grimm as Cub manager midway in the season, then strode to the plate in the dusk. "I swung once and missed," recalled Hartnett. "I swung again and got a piece of it, but that was all. A foul and strike two. I had one more chance. Brown wound up and let fly.

"I swung with everything I had and then I got that feeling, the kind of feeling you get when the blood rushes out of your head and you get dizzy.

"A lot of people have told me they didn't know the ball was in the bleachers. Well, I did. Maybe I was the only one in the park who did. I knew it the moment I hit it."

Plate umpire George Barr peered through the darkness and signaled a home run. Pandemonium broke loose. The Cubs had beaten the Pirates 6-5. They took over first place and went on to win the National League pennant.

Hartnett's homer was a lifetime in an instant. It became known as "The Homer in the Gloamin'."

On his way to second base he was mobbed by his teammates, the fans, the vendors, the ushers, even the cops. Gabby would've been lost in the throng except for that "Tomato Face" that glistened with sweat and a wide grin.

"I don't think I saw third base," said Hartnett. "And I don't think I walked a step to the plate—I was carried in. But when I got there I saw Ump Barr taking a good look. He was going to make sure I touched home plate."

Charles Leo Hartnett was born in Woonsocket, R. I., the eldest of 14 children. Gabby's dad was a street car conductor in Woonsocket and then in Millville, Mass., just outside of Boston, where the family moved when he was only three weeks old.

"My dad was a pretty good semipro player, and a catcher at that," said Hartnett. "He's the fellow who really made a ballplayer out of me. Not many kids are that fortunate."

When Hartnett was a small boy, a bully picked him up by the arm, threw him over his shoulder, and broke his right arm. Gabby carried a pail of sand for three months to regain the strength in his arm.

The ruddy-faced Irishman went on to catch for Dean Academy. He played semipro ball and was the "best berry picker in that part of New England." In 1921, he gave up berries to pick knuckleballs and spitballs out of the dirt for Worcester of the Eastern League, where he batted .264, and caught the eye of Cub scout Jack Doyle, who purchased his contract for $2,500.

At 21, Hartnett was signed and sealed for Cub delivery to Catalina Island. Before boarding the train for California his mother bade him to keep his mouth shut. Hartnett sat silently next to Dean Sullivan, sports editor of the *Chicago Herald Examiner,* who finally remarked, "You're certainly a gabby guy." A nickname was born.

Cub manager Bill Killefer assigned Hartnett to catch Grover Cleveland Alexander in an exhibition at Los Angeles. Hartnett got a single, a double, and a homer and high praise from Old Alex, who said, "He'll do. In fact, that kid is going to be all right."

Alexander insisted Hartnett catch him in the opener at Cincinnati. The Cubs won 5-3, but Hartnett went zero-for-four. The next day Killefer benched Hartnett in favor of regular catcher Bob O'Farrell.

Hartnett got another chance in the next series in St. Louis. He pinch-hit for pitcher Vic Aldridge in the sixth inning, worked the count to three-and-two against pitcher Billy Bailey, and then banged a long drive to right-center.

The youngster was so busy watching the flight of the ball that he tripped over first base and went sprawling. He scrambled to his feet and slid into third with a triple, his first big league hit.

In a game against Pittsburgh, first baseman Ray Grimes pulled up lame, and Killefer selected Hartnett as his man. It wasn't long before a Pirates batter hit a slow bouncer to the infield. The runner, Hartnett, and the harried throw all came together at first base. Hartnett went one way, his glove another, the runner another, and the ball, for all purposes, is still rolling.

Killefer galloped out of the dugout, collected all the scattered equipment, and decided Hartnett was a catcher. Gabby served most of the season as a backup to O'Farrell, catching only 31 games and hitting a meager .194. The next season he got into 85 games, batted .268, and then supplanted O'Farrell, who was traded to the Cardinals in 1925.

Once he became a regular catcher, Hartnett's batting improved steadily. And he caught on with Chicago fans, who loved his constant chatter behind the plate, finally living up to the name Gabby. His rifle-like shots to the bases to nab runners won him the respect of opponents, and his deft handling of pitchers won him their support.

Hartnett was easily the best catcher in the National League and was rated along with American Leaguers Mickey Cochrane and Bill Dickey as the Big Three behind the plate. In 1925, Hartnett hit 24 homers, a record for a catcher.

As Gabby improved with age, so did the Cubs. Under manager Joe McCarthy, the Cubs became a pennant contender. After hitting .302 in 1928, Hartnett was in his prime. He reported to Catalina Island for the start of the 1929 season with the advance guard and the early birds.

Tired of catching, Hartnett went to third and relayed the ball with an underhand twist. The next day his arm was painfully sore and stayed that way every time he attempted to throw. He only caught one game that year, the season the Cubs won the pennant.

The dead arm that kept him inactive returned to life, and the 1930 season found him cutting loose of old. He piled up a batting average of .339, walloped 37 homers, and drove in 122 runs.

Hartnett always seemed to be in the middle of historical episodes. In one City Series game against the White Sox at Comiskey Park, Hartnett was called over to a front-row box by a man he recognized. It was Scarface Al Capone, who was accompanied by a nephew and hordes of bodyguards. Capone wanted an autograph for the youngster.

Old Tomato Face obliged and a photographer snapped a picture. Commissioner Kenesaw Mountain Landis didn't like the published photo and reprimanded Gabby. Hartnett reportedly told Landis, "If you don't want anybody to talk to the Big Guy, Judge, you tell him."

Hartnett was also closest to Babe Ruth when he supposedly called his home run shot in the 1932 Cubs-Yankees World Series. It was in the fourth inning of the third game when Ruth homered after pointing toward a spot in the right-center field bleachers at Wrigley Field.

"I don't want to take anything away from the Babe," said Hartnett, "But he didn't call the shot. He held up the index finger of his left hand, looked at our dugout, not the outfield and said, 'it only takes one to hit.' "

Then there was the All-Star Game of 1934 at the Polo Grounds, with Giants' pitcher Carl Hubbell in the spotlight. Hartnett, who was to catch the first five All-Star Games for the National League, was behind the plate with Hubbell pitching.

"After the first two batters got on base in the first inning, I called time and went out to Hub and said, 'Why don't you throw the screwball? It always gets me out.' " Hubbell went on to strike out Babe Ruth, Lou Gehrig, Jimmie Foxx, Al Simmons, and Joe Cronin in succession.

In 1935 Hartnett had another enjoyable season and the Cubs won the pennant. He batted .344 and gained the Most Valuable Player award. After slipping to .307 in 1936, Gabby came up with a .354 average, the highest of his career in 1937. It was late in that season that Gabby got his first taste of managing.

Cub manager Charlie Grimm was ailing and turned over the reins to team captain Hartnett, who took the club out of a mild tailspin. Hartnett replaced Grimm as manager on July 26, 1938, and rallied them to the pennant, capped by his famed homer. But after dropping into the second division, the Cubs' first time since 1925, Hartnett was fired after the 1940 season.

Gabby finished his playing career the following year as a reserve catcher and pinch hitter with the Giants. He then managed in the minor leagues at Indianapolis, Jersey City, and Buffalo before devoting full-time attention to his bowling alley in Lincolnwood, a Chicago suburb. Hartnett, at one time, boasted a 190 average.

In 1955 Gabby was voted into the Hall of Fame. On that occasion, he told reporters, "This is one day of my life I'll never forget. It's a wonderful feeling to be an immortal." To Cub fans, Hartnett became an immortal on that dusky day in 1938.

Hartnett came out of retirement in 1965 as a coach for Charlie

Finley's Kansas City A's. It was only a one-season shot. He had been in ill health most of the decade and died of a kidney and liver ailment on Dec. 20, 1972—his 72nd birthday.

Hartnett had a lifetime average of .297 and five times batted over .300. He set a National League record for endurance, catching 100-or-more games in a dozen seasons. He slugged 236 homers. Of that total, 231 were with the Cubs and included one that was hit at 5:37 p.m. on Sept. 28, 1938.

CHARLIE GRIMM

GRIMM, CHARLES JOHN
B. Aug. 28, 1898,
St. Louis, Mo.
D. Nov. 15, 1983
Scottsdale, Ariz.
BL TL 5'11½"
173 lb.

Wilhelm Grimm, Charlie's father, left Bavaria because his father wanted him to become a priest. Instead, Wilhelm came to America, where he became a house painter in heavily Teutonic St. Louis. Young Charlie, in turn, did not want to become a house painter, so he became a ballplayer instead. It was a wise decision, for the humdrum existence of a house painter never would have fit the free-spirited Grimm.

Grimm's first connection with baseball was as a peanut vendor at old Robison Field in St. Louis. He learned the game by shagging flies for Roger Bresnahan, Ed Konetchy, and other Cardinal players during batting practice. By 1916 Charlie was given a trial with the last place Philadelphia Athletics. Although he was on the roster all season, Grimm appeared in only 12 games, batting .091.

Optioned to the A's farm club in Durham, N. C., Grimm was equally unimpressive. Then the club folded, and it was back to the paint brush and turpentine in St. Louis.

Charlie Barrett, a Cardinal scout, recruited Grimm for the locals, and by the spring of 1918, Charlie was playing for home town crowds. However, his jaunt with the Cardinals was not a success, and after 50 games, Grimm found himself in Little Rock of the Southern League.

In late 1919 Grimm caught on with the Pirates, where he finally began reaching his potential. As the Bucs' regular first baseman in 1920, Charlie batted only .227 but proved himself a full-fledged major leaguer as a glove man, making only eight errors in 148 games. His .995 fielding average topped the league.

Having proven that he could field, Charlie now concentrated on his hitting, lifting his average to .274 in 1921 and .292 the year after. By 1923 he enjoyed his greatest season at the plate, batting .345 with 194 hits and 99 RBI, all of which were career highs.

The not-so-grim Charlie also earned a reputation as a happy-go-lucky back-slapping guy who loved singing, banjo-playing, beer, and German food. But Grimm's easy-going style did not set well with the Pirates' conservative owner, Barney Dreyfuss.

Said the staid Dreyfuss, "I've decided it is about time we got rid of our banjo players." With that, Grimm, his drinking buddy Rabbit Maranville, and Wilbur Cooper were traded to the Cubs for

George Grantham, Vic Aldridge, and Al Niehaus on Oct. 27, 1924.

At the Cubs' spring training camp at Catalina Island the following year, Charlie met a musically inclined trio. Hack Miller played a taped-up guitar, Barney Friberg the mandolin, and Cliff Heathcote the ukelele. With banjo-playing Charlie on the team, the trio became a quartet, starting a Cub string band tradition that lasted into the early 1940s.

Club owner William Wrigley came over one morning, saw Miller's patched-up guitar, and said "You boys need new instruments." From that moment, Charlie knew he had found the right club.

It was a good season for Grimm, who batted .306 and knocked home 76 runs to pace the club in both departments, but not for the Cubs, who finished last for the first time in their history.

In 1926 Joe McCarthy was named Cub manager and fortunes improved for the club as Grimm continued to prosper. Moreover, he came through on countless occasions when he was needed the most.

Such was the case on May 17, 1927, when the Cubs and the Braves locked horns in one of the most grueling battles ever witnessed. In the top of the 22nd inning the game stood as a 3-3 stalemate. Finally, the ever-dependable Charlie stroked Hack Wilson across the plate with the lead run. The Cubs held on to win 4-3 for a hard-earned victory.

By 1929 the Cubs were number one, winning the pennant by 10½ games over the second place Pirates. In a lineup that starred the famed "Murderer's Row" of Rogers Hornsby, Hack Wilson, Kiki Cuyler, and Riggs Stephenson, Grimm was just one of the supporting cast.

Even so, he batted .298 and drove in 91 runs, his top mark as a Cub. Although the Cubs bowed to the Athletics, four games to one, in the World Series, Charlie was a hero in defeat, batting .389 and knocking in four runs.

After missing 40 games of the 1930 season due to minor ailments, Charlie bounced back in '31 with his highest batting average as a Cub (.331) sharing the club leadership with Hornsby.

Hornsby, by the way, had replaced McCarthy as Cub manager, much to the chagrin of the players, who found him acid-tongued and impossible to work for. After Wrigley's death in January of 1932, Hornsby and club president William Veeck, Sr., began to fall out.

The inevitable parting of ways came Aug. 3, when Veeck announced that Grimm was the new Cub field boss. The Cubs were a distant second with a 53–44 record and no apparent pennant hopes.

Unlike Hornsby, who ran the team like a Puritan schoolmaster, the jovial Grimm took the outlook of the Bavarian peasant stock he descended from, letting the team run itself as much as he could, applying the whip only when necessary. Perhaps as a good omen of things to come, the Cubs slapped the Phillies 12-2 on Jolly Cholly's first day in the driver's seat.

By Aug. 16 the team had loosened up and was ready for Charlie Grimm Day at Wrigley Field. With the Cubs behind, 3-0 in the last of the ninth, shortstop Billy Jurges shouted, "C'mon, guys, we can't lose this one for Charlie!" They rallied and won 4-3 with Jurges driving home the game winner.

Spurred on by a 14-game winning streak and the hot bats of Kiki Cuyler and the recently acquired Mark Koenig, the Cubs crashed into the lead and clinched the pennant Sept. 20. Grimm was no slouch himself, contributing a .307 average with 80 RBI.

In the World Series, the much-favored Yankees overpowered the Cubs in four straight. One of Grimm's few consolations was his own .333 batting average.

In 1933 Charlie's playing skills began to wane as he devoted more time to the task managing. In this capacity, he developed a penchant for giving odd nicknames to his players. Charlie Root was "Chinski," Stan Hack was "Stanislaus," while Grimm himself was "Der Kapitan." Phil Cavarretta, whom Grimm began grooming as his replacement at first base in late 1934, was "Phillibuck." In later years, Lou Novikoff would be "The Mad Russian;" Dom Dallessandro, "Dim Dom;" Andy Pafko, "Prushka;" and Hal Jeffcoat, "Hotfoot Hal."

Following two third-place finishes, Grimm assembled another winner in 1935. It was this bunch that Charlie called "the best group I ever managed." Gabby Hartnett was Most Valuable Player, while Billy Herman, Stan Hack, Frank Demaree and Augie Galan also hit well over .300.

The young Cavarretta filled Grimm's shoes with ease, and newcoming pitchers Bill Lee, Larry French, and Tex Carleton picked up the slack left by the departure of Guy Bush and Pat Malone. Thanks to a 21-game winning streak in the stretch drive—during which Grimm nailed a tack in his shoe every day—the Cubs won 100 games. But that elusive World Series victory would still not come as the Tigers beat the Cubs in six games.

The Cubs slipped to runner-up in 1936, despite a 15-game winning streak early in the year. Grimm hung up his spikes for good after that season, finishing with a .290 lifetime average and 2,299 hits. He had led the league nine times in fielding average, to set an all-time record for first basemen. His 1,708 double plays are still the National League standard.

Following a close second-place finish in 1937, Grimm turned the managerial reins over to Gabby Hartnett in the middle of the 1938 season. The Cubs came back to life under Gabby, winning the pennant in storybook finish.

Jolly Cholly then embarked on another career, teaming up with former White Sox player-manager Lew Fonseca to do radio broadcasts of Cubs and Sox home games over station WJJD during the 1939 and '40 seasons. Although the duet was an instant hit, Charlie's heart was still in the dugout, and when the Cubs offered him a coaching position, he jumped at it.

The job, however, turned out to be short-lived. Bill Veeck, Jr., in his first major enterprise, purchased the ailing Milwaukee Brewers of the American Association in June 1941, taking Grimm with him as manager. Charlie spent three fun-filled years with Veeck, and the German-Polish-Bohemian crowd that made up most of Milwaukee's fandom gave him a hero's welcome.

Nevertheless, Charlie's road always led back to Chicago. In the early 1940s, the Cubs had fallen into mediocrity. By May 7, 1944, they had lost 12 in a row when Grimm was recycled as Cub manager. The streak reached 13 the next day before Charlie began turning things around. Helped by a strong second half, they wound up a respectable fourth.

That winter witnessed one of Charlie's most colorful capers. Grimm and Cub traveling secretary Bob Lewis were having a few drinks at Chicago's Morrison Hotel, where the 1945 Diamond Dinner was to be held that evening. In an inspired moment, Charlie ordered two doormen's uniforms and a helmet.

That night after the banquet, Lewis appeared on stage as Herman Goering, wearing a helmet that was about two sizes too big. Grimm, complete with a fake toothbrush mustache, was *Der Fuhrer* himself.

Speaking in a half-German, half-English guttural tone, Grimm out-Hitlered Hitler in demagoguery. He berated Lewis for the losses on the Russian front, poking him on the jaw after each tirade. Lewis then retreated into the wings, only to return with another part of his clothing removed. And another blasting and wallop from *Der Fuhrer.*

Finally, Lewis was down to his undershorts. Again came the ringing denunciation. This time, however, Lewis poked Charlie, and Grimm did a pratfall to conclude the act, much to the delight of the audience.

When springtime came, most writers picked the Cardinals to win their fourth straight pennant in 1945. Grimm, however, knew he had a good lineup by wartime standards and was certain the Cubs had a chance. Although the team started off sluggishly, they gathered momentum in July. On the impetus of an 11-game winning streak, they pulled into the forefront.

The pennant clincher came Sept. 29 as the Cubs edged the Pirates 4-3 to beat out the Redbirds by three games. This time the World Series went the full seven games before the Tigers outlasted the Cubs. Charlie was always convinced that the Cubs would have had a world championship if ace pitcher Claude Passeau had not lost a fingernail from his pitching hand in a freak accident during game six.

The aging Cubs declined rapidly after the war, falling to the cellar by 1948. In spite of it all, Grimm never lost his sense of humor. During one game that was hopelessly out of reach, he buried his scorecard by third base, to give the Wrigley Field fans a much-needed laugh. It was in 1948 also that Grimm was immortalized in Norman Rockwell's famous painting, *The*

Dugout, along with Bob Rush, Phil Cavarretta, Johnny Schmitz, and the Cub batboy.

Frankie Frisch replaced Charlie as field boss in June 1949, and Grimm was kicked upstairs to the front office for the remainder of the season. The following year he managed Dallas of the Texas League, and by 1951 he was back in Milwaukee with the Brewers.

By now the Brewers had become part of the Boston Braves' farm chain, so by June 1952, Charlie was called up to run the parent club. When the Braves moved to America's beer capital the following year, Charlie was given a bigger welcome than ever. Although Grimm was relieved of his command in June 1956, his efforts soon bore fruit. The Braves won back-to-back pennants under Fred Haney.

Having left the Braves, Charlie—you guessed it—returned to the Cubs, this time as an executive vice-president. In 1960 he even served briefly as field manager before switching places with radio color man Lou Boudreau. He coached for awhile the following season, when Phil Wrigley came up with the bizarre scheme of replacing the manager with a "college" of rotating coaches.

Not long thereafter, Charlie and his wife relocated to Arizona, where Grimm lived in semiretirement while retaining his title with the Cubs. He was honored with another Charlie Grimm Day at Wrigley Field in 1966.

Finally, in 1968, Jolly Cholly's long awaited autobiography was published. In it, Charlie summed up the meaning of his career by saying, "Pittsburgh was great. So was Milwaukee. But my heart belongs to Chicago and the Cubs."

Grimm died in Arizona at the age of 85. His final wish was to have his ashes strewn about Wrigley Field.

JOHNNY MOORE

MOORE, JOHN FRANCIS
B. March 23, 1902, Waterville, Conn.
BL TR 5'10½"
175 lb.

Johnny Moore spent his first four years (1928–31) trying to break into a Cub outfield that included Riggs Stephenson, Hack Wilson, and Kiki Cuyler. Moore finally succeeded in 1932, hitting .305 and leading the Cubs in homers with a meager 13.

He went to Cincinnati in the Babe Herman deal immediately after the Yankees swept the Cubs in the 1932 World Series. Moore had some outstanding seasons with the Reds and Philadelphia Phillies, closing out his career in 1937 with a .308 lifetime average.

After an eight-year absence, Moore came back to the Cubs in 1945, but he wasn't much of a factor in their drive to the pennant, collecting a single and 2 RBI in six at bats for a .167 average.

Lon Warneke was another of those lanky squirrel shootin' tobacco chewin' pitchers from the foothills of the Ozarks that appeared on the major league scene during the Depression.

His hair was reddish brown and unmanageable, and he learned

how to pitch "jest naturally" by throwing stones at jackrabbits near his native Mt. Ida, Ark.

But Warneke was more than a gangling country boy with a good chew of plug tobacco bulging from one side of his mouth. Nicknamed the "Arkansas Hummingbird," Warneke had speed, control, a brain, and a heart. He won 193 games and lost only 121 in 15 seasons by usually keeping the ball right down at the knees where nobody wanted it.

In 1928, the 19-year-old Warneke decided to see some of the world, so he pedaled his bicycle to Houston where one of his sisters was living. There he got a job as a messenger boy for Western Union.

One day he pedaled past the Houston ballpark where they were holding tryouts. There was a shortage of batting practice pitchers. When asked if he could pitch, Warneke spit out a plug, and said, "Sure, when do I start?"

WARNEKE, LONNIE
B. March 28, 1909,
Mt. Ida, Ark.
D. June 23, 1976,
Hot Springs, Ark.
BR TR 6'2" 185 lb.

Warneke was shipped to Laurel of the Cotton States League, where he won 6 and lost 14. The Cubs bought him for $10,000 and he caught the eye of manager Rogers Hornsby during spring training.

The Rajah saw possibilities in the raw-boned rookie and turned him over to catcher Zack Taylor. Hornsby and Taylor noticed that Warneke always dropped his head with each pitch and looked at the ground instead of the batter. He was taught to "follow through." Control followed and so did success.

In 1932 the Cubs won the pennant, and Warneke led the National League in victories with 22; winning percentage, .786; and earned-run average, 2.37.

The lean right-hander soon became a Chicago favorite. But every winter he headed back to Mt. Ida. "Heck, I can live a whole winter down home for $50," drawled Warneke. "I can't live a week up here for that."

Warneke was an 18-game winner in 1933 and then bounced back with 22 victories in '34. He started the 1934 season with back-to-back one-hitters against the Reds and Cardinals. Adam Comorosky's single with one out in the ninth spoiled his 6-0 win in the Cincy opener, and Ripper Collins's sixth-inning double was the lone hit in the 15-2 triumph in his next start.

The Cubs won the pennant in 1935 on the strength of a 21-game winning streak in September. And Warneke contributed four of his 20 victories during that stretch.

Warneke was the Cubs' lone bright spot in the World Series, beating the Tigers 3-0 and 3-1, but Detroit took the other four games. When asked about his success, Warneke simply replied, "Another row of cotton to be chopped and another bunch of cows to be milked."

The following season Warneke's victory total dwindled to 16, but he had the distinction of being the only major leaguer to strike out Walter Alston of the Cardinals. Incidentally, it was Alston's only at bat in the biggies.

Then in a surprise move the Cubs traded Warneke to St. Louis in 1937 for first baseman Ripper Collins and pitcher Tarzan Parmelee. Lon was sorry to leave the Cubs, but he fit in well with the Gashouse Gang.

Lon joined Pepper Martin's Mudcat Band on the "git-tar" and enjoyed spraying tobacco juice on Dizzy Dean's newly polished shoes. He also gained some revenge by tossing a one-hitter against the Cubs on April 28, 1939. Stan Hack hit a slow roller in the seventh inning and beat Warneke to the bag for the lone safety.

About that time a nervous, lanky shortstop joined the Cardinals. Warneke was pitching when the rookie botched an easy grounder. Lon was livid. He called time and summoned the rookie to the mound to chew his tail.

Then Warneke looked into the youngster's eyes and saw his hangdog expression. Warneke instead put his arms around the kid and said, "Forget it. I saw Travis Jackson, Billy Jurges, and Leo Durocher blow easier ones." On the next play, the kid shortstop went into the hole and came up with a spectacular double play. That was the making of Marty Marion.

On June 11, 1941, Warneke again missed a no-hitter. This time it was a single by Emmett Mueller, the first batter for the Phillies. And then it happened. After four close calls, Warneke hummed a no-hitter against the Reds on Aug. 29, 1941.

In midseason 1942 the Cubs reacquired Warneke on waivers. He was handed his old No. 19 jersey and stayed with the Cubs until their pennant season of 1945.

Warneke came back to the major leagues in 1949 as an umpire. "I tried every place to get a blue serge suit," sighed Warneke. "But I'm doggoned, they just aren't to be had." Lon settled for a dark, grim, forbidding black suit, which made him look more like an undertaker for his umpiring appearance.

He remained an ump until 1955, when he decided to enter politics as a judge in the Garland County Courthouse in Hot Springs, Ark. He ran as an independent against Henry Murphy, a Democrat.

"I ran on the platform 'Everything for the good of the people!' and shook hands with everyone. Heck, Adlai Stevenson wore a hole in one shoe," said Warneke. "I walked so far I had holes in both shoes." Warneke beat Murphy 5,693 to 5,496.

The elongated Warneke looked dignified in judicial attire. He had come a long way from taking pot shots at squirrels back in Mt. Ida.

ROLLIE HEMSLEY

HEMSLEY, RALSTON
BURDETT
B. June 24, 1907,
Syracuse, Ohio
D. July 31, 1972,
Washington D.C.
BR TR 5'10" 170 lb.

Best remembered as a heavy drinker and one of the American League's better receivers of the 1930s, Rollie Hemsley broke in with the Pirates in 1928 and had his best years still ahead of him when the Bucs peddled him to the Cubs early in 1931.

In his two seasons as second fiddle to Gabby Hartnett, Hemsley batted .289 and .238, but left behind some memorable moments

142

during off hours. Bill Veeck, Jr., whose father was Cub president at that time, recalled one such incident nearly 40 years later.

"On my first trip to New York with the Cubs we had trouble getting Rollie Hemsley to bed. An hour later Lewis [Cub traveling secretary Bob Lewis] was called to spring him from jail. We went and did it.

"Another hour passed, and Hemsley was in trouble in another borough of New York. Again we sprung him and put him in the feathers. In the wee, wee hours Lewis got another call. It was a third borough—Brooklyn, I think—and the desk sergeant reported that he had a Mr. Hemsley, and Lewis said, 'To hell with it. Lock him up.'"

After leaving the Cubs in 1933, Rollie caught for the Reds, Browns, Indians, Reds again, Yankees, and Phillies, enjoying his best seasons in St. Louis and Cleveland.

Retiring in 1947, he had a lifetime .262 average with 1,321 hits.

FRANK DEMAREE

DEMAREE, JOSEPH FRANKLIN
B. June 10, 1910, Winter, Calif.
D. Aug. 30, 1958, Los Angeles, Calif.
BR TR 5'11½"
185 lb.

Frank Demaree got his first break when outfielder Kiki Cuyler broke his leg in spring training in 1933. Demaree had a good rookie season, hitting .272, but was sent back to the minors in 1934. At that time, Cub outfielders were expected to hit over .300.

The soft-spoken Californian went to Los Angeles and compiled one of the most sensational seasons in Pacific Coast annals, leading in every batting category but triples. In 186 games, Demaree scored 190 runs, had 269 base hits, 51 doubles, 45 homers, and 173 RBI, while batting a lusty .383. He was now ready for the Cubs.

Born Joseph Franklin Dimaria in the fruitful Sacramento Valley, young Demaree preferred sports to ranch life. In school he was a member of the track and basketball teams and excelled in tennis. But baseball ranked first.

The blue-eyed, brown-haired Demaree was a shortstop on a semipro club in Sacramento. He was then switched to the outfield, where he could use his speed to better advantage.

Demaree was sought out by the Sacramento Solons of the Pacific Coast League at the end of the 1930 season. The 21-year-old Demaree hit .312 and .364 with the Solons and his contract was purchased by the Cubs.

He reported to the Cubs on Aug. 1, 1932, and immediately paid a dividend. The Cubs, scrappin' for the '32 pennant, engaged the Boston Braves in a marathon on Aug. 17 at Wrigley Field. The Cubs won 3-2 on Demaree's long fly with the bases loaded in the 19th inning.

The Cubs went on to win the pennant, and Demaree hit his first major league homer off the Yankees' Johnny Allen in the fourth game of the World Series. It was quite a thrill, despite the four-game New York sweep.

After filling in for Cuyler in 1933 and his demon season with the

Angels, Demaree was in the big leagues to stick, helping the Cubs win the 1935 pennant with his .325 average.

Demaree hit two homers in a losing cause against the Tigers in the '35 series, giving him three, a Cub record in World Series play.

Cub manager Charlie Grimm installed Demaree in the cleanup spot in 1936 and he responded with his best season, banging out 212 hits and batting .350. A .350 average would lead the league nowadays, but in 1936 Demaree could rank only fourth behind Paul Waner's .373.

Demaree seemed to save his big punch for doubleheaders. Twice he collected eight hits in twin bills. He had three hits as the Cubs dropped a 13-12 slugfest to the Phillies on Aug. 31, 1935, but bounced back with five hits in the second game as the Cubs romped 19-5.

Perhaps his biggest day was July 5, 1937, when the Cubs swept the Cardinals 13-12 and 9-7 before 39,240 at Wrigley Field. Demaree had six hits in seven trips in the opener, but managed only two hits in the nightcap.

The 1937 season was another lusty campaign for Demaree. His base hit total fell to 199 and his average dropped to .324, but he drove in 115 runs with 36 doubles, 6 triples, and a career-high 17 homers.

When the Cubs restructured their bleachers in 1938, most observers were worried about the outfielders playing the caroms off the curved ivy walls. Demaree, who was switched to right field, played it to perfection, but his batting average dipped to .273.

The Cubs won the 1938 pennant, but this time Demaree was held to a lone single in a four-game Yankee sweep. Following the series Demaree was traded along with shortstop Billy Jurges and catcher Ken O'Dea to the New York Giants for outfielder Hank Leiber, shortstop Dick Bartell, and catcher Gus Mancuso.

Demaree continued to hit .300, batting .304 and .302 with the Giants the next two seasons. He then served as a sub outfielder with the Braves and Cardinals the next four seasons, finishing in 1944 with a .299 career average. However, his lifetime Cub record is .309.

Demaree then scouted for the White Sox, managed at Fresno and Wisconsin Rapids before closing out his baseball career with San Bernardino in 1950. He was employed by United Artists studios, when he died of an intestinal hemorrhage at the age of 48 in Los Angeles.

Billy Jurges was just another kid trying to break into the Cub infield during spring training at Catalina Island in 1931. Manager Rogers Hornsby was not impressed. The Rajah always leaned toward youngsters that could hit.

The nimble shortstop snared a ball behind second base and

threw out a runner. He then went behind third base and tossed out another. Jurges was all over the diamond.

Scribes covering the Cubs during the exhibition games continued to write pieces about the lad's ability to cover ground at that most demanding position. Even Hornsby dropped his skepticism and eventually paired him with second baseman Billy Herman.

Herman and Jurges became the Cubs storied double-play duo throughout the 1930s. It was a perfect match; Herman, the farm boy from Indiana; and Jurges, the street-wise kid from Brooklyn.

Actually, Jurges was born in the Bronx. But at two his family moved to the Highland Park section of Brooklyn. Young Billy attended Richmond Hill High School, which later sent another shortstop to the big leagues, a fellow named Phil Rizzuto.

Jurges had a horse and cart and worked as a delivery boy for a grocery while playing sandlot ball. He then became a bank messenger and joined a Long Island semipro team called the Hawtree Indians. It was while playing a doubleheader ankle deep in sand for $10 that he attracted the attention of a Newark scout.

The Newark Bears sent Jurges to Manchester (N. H.) of the New England League, where he batted .255 in 1927. That winter, Jurges wanted to increase his strength and went into the woods and spent weeks chopping down trees. The next season Jurges chopped down the pitchers with a .332 average.

The Cubs immediately signed Jurges and planted him at Reading for the next two seasons. There was no doubt about his fielding, but could he hit? Hornsby was of the old school that contends hitters are born, but fielders can be made.

Hornsby soon relented and switched shortstop Woody English to third to make room for Jurges, who got into 88 games in 1931. Swift on his feet and clever with his hands, Jurges became a regular the following season, hiking his average from .201 to .253.

However, in midseason Jurges was sidelined after being shot in the ribs and hand by Violet Popovich Valli, a spurned showgirl. The shooting took place July 6, 1932, in Jurges's room at the Carlos Hotel, two blocks north of Wrigley Field.

It all began at 9:45 that morning when Miss Valli phoned Jurges's room and said, "Come down to my room, I've got something for you."

Jurges replied, "If you have anything to tell me, come up to my room."

Miss Valli entered Room 509 and attempted suicide with a .25 calibre gun. Jurges tried to stop her, and in the scuffle three shots were fired. One bullet entered Billy's right breast, was deflected by a rib, and passed out at the side of his back. Another hit the palm of his left hand. The third pierced the heel of Miss Valli's right hand and lodged in her wrist. Miss Valli fled to her room, while Jurges stumbled into the hall, calling for help.

Residents of the hotel quoted her as saying she would "get Jurges" and that she also would shoot Cub teammate Kiki Cuyler because he was "always interferring."

Jurges and Valli were taken to Illinois Masonic Hospital. Dr.

BILLY JURGES

JURGES, WILLIAM FREDERICK
B. May 9, 1908, Bronx, N. Y.
BR TR 5'11" 175 lb.

John F. Davis, the Cubs' physician who was in the lobby during the gunplay, said Jurges was not seriously hurt and that he would be back in the lineup in about three weeks.

Miss Valli was transferred to Bridewell Hospital, where she was in custody on a charge of assault with intent to kill. She explained that the shooting was the result of "too much gin."

Jurges failed to prosecute and Miss Valli went on to sign a 22-week contract to sing and dance at various clubs and theatres. She was billed as "Violet (I Did It For Love) Valli—The Most Talked Of Girl in Chicago."

When Jurges returned, he found many changes. The Cubs purchased Mark Koenig, a former New York Yankee shortstop, to fill in for Jurges, and Charlie Grimm had replaced Hornsby as manager. Koenig's bat sizzled as the Cubs won 18 of 20 games in August.

But Jurges also contributed. Aug. 16, 1932, was set aside as Charlie Grimm Day. The Cubs were losing 3-0 to the Boston Braves going into the bottom of the ninth inning at Wrigley Field. Jurges said, "C'mon, we can't lose this one for Cholly." The Cubs rallied and won on Billy's two-run single.

The Cubs went on to win the pennant with Koenig hitting .353 down the stretch. Jurges batted .364 in the World Series, but the Yankees swept the Cubs in four games.

With Grimm at first, Herman at second, Jurges at short, and newcomer Stan Hack at third, the Cubs had one of the finest infield quartets in baseball. Of the four, Jurges was the most artistic fielder, but the poorest batsman. The Cubs finished 1-2-3 the next half dozen seasons with Jurges as the infield mainspring.

Then followed his big mistake. Cub owner P. K. Wrigley wanted to replace Grimm as manager in midseason 1938. His chauffer-driven limosine drove up to Jurges's house. Wrigley alighted and asked Jurges to manage the Cubs.

Jurges told Wrigley he had a potential manager catching—Gabby Hartnett. Hartnett replaced Grimm, hit his famed "Homer in the Gloamin' " and led the Cubs to the pennant. Two months after dropping the World Series four straight to the Yankees, the Cubs traded Jurges to the New York Giants in a package deal.

Departing for New York along with Jurges were outfielder Frank Demaree and catcher Ken O'Dea. In return the Cubs received outfielder Hank Leiber, catcher Gus Mancuso, and shortstop Dick Bartell. It was a trade the Cubs later regretted.

The New York born Jurges was a Chicago favorite and anchored the Giants infield the next seven seasons. The Chicago-born Bartell was the target of Wrigley Field boobirds with his many bobbles. He lasted only one season in a Cub uniform.

Jurges returned to the Cubs in 1946. He was no longer the kid that darted about at Catalina Island, gobbling up every ball and throwing with deadly accuracy. But the Cubs had missed Jurges those seven agonizing seasons.

During that span the Cubs employed such household names as Bartell, Bobby Mattick, Billy Myers, Bobby Sturgeon, Lennie

Merullo, and Roy Hughes. None could match the acrobatic Jurges.

Jurges, however, was now a utility player and drew his release following the 1947 season. He took the usual route as a scout and minor league manager and didn't surface to the majors until 1956 as a coach with the Washington Senators.

Jurges finally landed a big league managerial job with the Boston Red Sox, replacing Pinky Higgins midway in the 1959 season. But he, too, was replaced halfway through the 1960 season. Jurges's lifetime managerial record was 78-83.

Jurges was employed by the Cubs as a scout until the Dallas Green takeover in 1982.

BABE HERMAN

HERMAN, FLOYD CAVES
B. June 26, 1903, Buffalo, N. Y.
BL TL 6'4" 190 lb.

In his days as one of the "Daffy Dodgers" of the late 1920s and early '30s, Floyd "Babe" Herman was the idol of Ebbets Field. A powerful hitter, he challenged the hated Bill Terry of the Giants for the batting title with a blazing .393 average in 1930 to Terry's .401.

One could never predict what the colorful Herman was going to pull off next, especially in his attempts at playing the outfield. Scores of stories have been told about fly balls going over his head, off his shoulder, in and out of his glove, and off his head.

During one game, he was one of three Dodger runners on third base concurrently. Another time, while being interviewed by a reporter, Babe pulled a lit cigar out of his pocket.

Herman was tailor-made for Brooklyn and never seemed to fit in anyplace else. After six seasons with the Dodgers and one with the Reds, Babe came to the Cubs in 1933. Although he batted .289 with 16 homers and 93 RBI, Herman became the target of the Wrigley Field boobirds.

Even smashing three homers in one game and hitting for the cycle in another did not save him from becoming the scapegoat. In 1934 he lifted his batting average to .304, but he was still booed, so the Cubs traded him to the Pirates.

After brief action in Pittsburgh and a repeat performance in Cincinnati, Babe finished with the Tigers in 1937. Eight years later, with rosters depleted by the war, Herman made a short comeback with his beloved Bums as a pinch hitter before calling it quits for good.

Herman's lifetime totals included a .324 batting average, 1,818 hits, and 181 homers. His fielding ability, or rather the lack of it, has been the major factor keeping him out of the Hall of Fame.

147

Billy Herman was carried off the field in his major league debut. It wasn't in triumph—it was on a stretcher. After singling for the Cubs off Si Johnson of the Cincinnati Reds his first time up, he was plunked behind the left ear by a foul ball off his own bat in his second trip. Herman was bleeding and unconscious when he was carted away by his teammates. So much for debuts.

Herman was born on a farm in New Albany, Ind., just across the Ohio River from Louisville. His father, obviously a Democrat, named him William Jennings Bryan Herman.

But baseball not politics was his forte. As a youngster he pitched his Sunday School team to a championship and won a trip to Pittsburgh to see the Pirates play the New York Yankees in the 1927 World Series.

Herman, then 18, entered a sandlot tournament in Louisville and was the only one plucked out of a group of 200 amateurs and signed by Cap'n Bill Neal, general manager of the Louisville Colonels. Neal had an eye for raw talent. He discovered pitcher Grover Cleveland Alexander 15 years earlier.

Neal converted Herman from a third baseman to a second baseman and shipped him to Vicksburg (Miss.) of the Cotton States League where he batted .332 in 1928. He then advanced to Dayton of the Central League and socked .329 before being promoted to Louisville.

Herman, who had brown bulging eyes and was often called "Owl Eyes," maintained his keen batting eye at Louisville where he batted .323, .305, and .350. He was now ready for the big leagues.

A scout for the Yankees took a look at Herman and bypassed him in favor of infielder Jack Saltzgaver, who went for a reported $50,000 and three players. The Cubs then grabbed Herman for $50,000.

Incidentally, in that deal the Cubs agreed to loan Louisville a player for the remaining two months of the 1931 season. That player was Billy Jurges, who later teamed with Herman as the Cubs' double-play combo of the 1930s.

Herman had big shoes to fill in Chicago. His predecessor was player-manager Rogers Hornsby. That didn't seem to awe Herman, who hit .327 and reduced the Rajah to pinch-hitting roles.

The Cubs won the pennant in 1932 with Herman hitting .314, collecting 206 hits, and combining with Jurges as the fastest pair in the majors around the keystone sack.

Smarter than most infielders, Herman played a "roving" second base. For left field pull hitters like Wally Berger and Chick Hafey, he played directly behind the bag. For big, fat, slow runners like Shanty Hogan and Ernie Lombardi, he would play back on the grass. And for right field pull hitters like Arky Vaughan and Mel Ott he would swing over toward first base.

That made Herman the busiest second baseman in the business. His 466 putouts in 1933 remains a National League record and that included a record 16 in a doubleheader against the Phillies on June 28. He is the only second baseman to exceed 900 total chances in five different seasons.

Going into the September stretch drive of 1935, the Cubs were third behind the Cardinals and Giants. "Old Popeyes" rallied his team by saying, "Hey, we could win this thing." The Cubs went on to win 21 in a row and steal the pennant with Herman batting .341 and leading the league with 227 hits.

Although not a power hitter, Herman collected his share of extra base hits. He had 57 doubles in 1935 and duplicated that total the next year for a record 114 in two consecutive seasons.

When veteran infielder Woody English was traded to the Dodgers in 1936, Herman was named team captain. A hard bargainer at the salary table, Herman became the highest paid Cub, surpassing even Gabby Hartnett and manager Charlie Grimm.

But when Grimm was fired in midseason 1938, it was Hartnett, not Herman, who was named manager. Herman continued collecting his 200 hits and batting .300, and the Cubs won the 1938 pennant with Hartnett hitting his famed "Homer in the Gloamin'." "It was so dark, that to this day, I never saw the ball," said Herman. "And I don't think anyone else did either."

Hartnett received his walking papers after the Cubs tumbled out of the first division for the first time in nearly two decades. Herman seemed the logical choice to be named manager for the 1941 season.

But the Cub brass selected Jimmy Wilson, a coach with the Cincinnati Reds. Wilson's first move was to strip Herman of his captain's stripes. The next move was obvious. Herman moved to Brooklyn.

In exchange for Herman, the Cubs received infielder Johnny Hudson, outfielder Larry Gilbert, and a reported $25,000, walking around money for Cub owner P. K. Wrigley.

The trade meant a pennant for the Dodgers and oblivion for the Cubs. Herman reported to manager Leo Durocher on May 7, donned his Dodger jersey and banged out four straight hits in a 7-3 romp over the Pirates.

But while Herman and the Dodgers were winning, it wasn't always rosy between Owl Eyes and Leo the Lip. As a Cub, Herman was always free to choke the bat, crowd the plate, drive outside pitches to right and inside pitches to left.

"In one game we were trailing by one run and had the bases loaded," recalled Herman. "The count was two balls and no strikes. Third base coach Charlie Dressen, under Durocher's orders, gives me the take sign. I took it and it was a strike.

"Again, I get the take sign and it's ball three. Now, I'm ready to swing away at a fat pitch. But I get another take sign. I follow orders and let a perfect strike go by.

"Now the count is full. I finally get to swing. I hit into a double play and the inning is over. I'm seething. First baseman Dolph Camilli tosses me the ball to start the warmup drill. I threw it right at Durocher in the dugout.

"The ball skipped off the grass like a rocket and hit Leo square in the forehead. Down he goes. Albie Glossup looks at me in horror and says 'Billy, you just hit Durocher right between the eyes.'

"Now, I'm grinning. That's exactly where I was aiming."

Leo couldn't take a .330 hitter out of the lineup, but the U.S. Navy could. Herman, 34, reported to the Great Lakes Naval Training Station after the 1943 season.

Following two years in the Pacific, Herman returned to the Dodgers and found brash Eddie Stanky planted firmly on second base. Stanky was cut from the same mold as Durocher, and Herman was soon cut adrift to the Boston Braves. Then came his big moment.

He was appointed manager of the Pirates in 1947. His dream had come true. But it soon turned to a nightmare. Despite 76 homers by Ralph Kiner and Hank Greenberg, the Pirates finished dead last and Herman was fired the last day of the season.

Herman became a baseball nomad, managing in the minors and coaching in the majors until he was named manager of the Boston Red Sox in 1964. After two ninth place finishes Herman was out.

Finally in 1975 Herman gained entrance to the Hall of Fame. Baseball did give a hoot for old Owl Eyes.

Billy was a lifetime .304 hitter with 2,345 hits.

CHUCK KLEIN

KLEIN, CHARLES HERBERT
B. Oct. 7, 1904, Indianapolis, Ind.
D. March 28, 1958, Indianapolis, Ind.
BL TR 6' 185 lb.

Wall Street and Mae West were the biggest busts of the Depression era. As far as the Cubs were concerned, you can add slugger Chuck Klein to that list.

Charles Herbert Klein, the third of four sons, was an all-around athlete at Indianapolis' Southport High where he starred in track, basketball, football, and baseball.

After Chuck got out of school he found employment in an Indiana steel mill foundry, handling hot objects with tongs. His job required a strong grip and he soon developed his forearms and wrists. On weekends he played baseball with the Silver Nook Independents.

When the mill shut down he was talked into professional baseball by a prohibition agent, who touted the manager of the Evansville club about the hard-hitting youngster.

Klein was no gazelle in the outfield, but he hit .327 in 1927. The following season Klein moved up to Ft. Wayne, where he was hitting .331 with 26 homers when he was purchased for $7,500 by the Philadelphia Phillies.

Klein had played barely 100 minor league games when he joined the Phillies 10 minutes before game time at Baker Bowl. Manager Burt Shotton penciled him in the cleanup spot against—of all pitchers—Grover Cleveland Alexander. Klein got a double in three trips off Old Alex, but the Cardinals pounded the Phillies 18-5.

In what was left of his first season, Klein ripped into National League pitching for a .360 average. For the next five seasons his averages were .356, .386, .337, .348, and .368, winning the batting title with the latter mark in 1933.

The left-handed muscleman with the blacksmith arms shook the rust off the tin-walled Baker Bowl, an ancient relic of a ballpark that measured only 280-feet down the right field line. During those five and a half seasons, Klein smashed 191 home runs, collected 1,209 hits, scored 699 runs, and drove home 727 runs.

Klein was coveted by the Chicago Cubs, who needed an awesome slugger to replace Hack Wilson. The Cubs, at one time, dangled as much as $250,000, but their offer was spurned.

Finally, on Nov. 21, 1933, Klein became a Cub. The Phillies' treasury was bare and owner Gerald Nugent accepted $65,000 from the benevolent Cubs, who also threw in three players, Mark Koenig, Gink Hendrick, and the little-known Ted Kleinhans.

Cub partisans were ecstatic. If Klein set slugging records with a perennial doormat, what would he do with a contender? They saw him as the much-needed pennant ingredient. The Cubs had the pitching, defense, and hitting. Klein would fill the power void.

But both Klein and the Cubs flopped in 1934 as the Cardinals' Gashouse Gang won the pennant with the Giants two games in arrears. The Cubs were eight games behind in third place.

Klein's Baker Bowl homers were long outs in Wrigley Field. The cheers at the outset of the season turned to murmurs. At the end, the murmurs had turned to catcalls. Chuck proved to be a mere mortal, hitting .301 with 20 homers and 80 RBI. As a Phillie, Klein missed only eight games in five and a half seasons. As a Cub, assorted injuries kept him out of 39 games in one season.

Klein's decline continued in 1935, his batting average dropping below the .300 level for the first time. A .293 average with 21 homers and 73 RBI are respectable, but not what one would expect from the former Philly ogre-in-chief.

The Cubs did win the pennant, thanks to a 21-game winning streak in September. In the World Series Klein's two-run homer helped Lon Warneke win the fifth game 3-1 against the Tigers, who took the series in six games.

Klein was hitting .294 when the Cubs shipped him back to Baker Bowl on May 21, 1936. The deal was Klein and pitcher Fabian Kowalik to the Phils for outfielder Ethan Allen and pitcher Curt Davis. The Cubs even kicked in $50,000 to unload Klein. Thus, it cost the Cubs $115,000 and four players to find that Klein was only human.

And wouldn't you know it. Two months later, Klein hit four homers in one game against the Pirates. In addition, he hiked his RBI total to 104 while hitting 27 homers.

The Phillies abandoned Baker Bowl to share Shibe Park with Connie Mack's Athletics in 1938, and Klein's average dipped to .247. He and his 42-ounce bat went to the Pirates on waivers in 1939.

After being released by Pittsburgh, Klein rejoined the Phillies in 1940 and was honored by the fans on Sept. 5. Most players are presented cars or motorboats on their special days. The Phillies were impoverished and Chuck was presented a box of coins and a ham from a local admirer.

The Clouting Kraut stayed on as player-coach during the war years, finishing in 1944 with a lifetime .320 average and 300 homers, which ranked him seventh behind such greats as Ruth, Foxx, Ott, Gehrig, Simmons, and Hornsby. Klein's other achievements were three home run titles, an MVP award in 1932, and the Triple Crown in 1933.

Out of baseball since 1945, Klein returned to Indianapolis and obscurity. He had been in ill health and unable to work. He was a semi-invalid when he died of a cerebral hemorrhage on March 28, 1958, at the age of 53.

Although Klein left a bundle of National League records, including 107 extra base hits and 158 runs scored in 1930, he was ignored in the Hall of Fame balloting. His detractors claimed the tight confines of Baker Bowl ballooned Klein's statistics.

It wasn't until 1980 that baseball's Old-Timers Committee relented and Klein gained entrance to the Hall of Fame—but not for his underachievements as a Cub.

BILL LEE

LEE, WILLIAM
CRUTCHER
B. Oct. 21, 1909,
Plaquemine, La.
D. June 15, 1977,
Plaquemine, La.
BR TR 6'3" 195 lb.

General Lee was a tall, stately Southerner and a familiar sight in Cub woolens for a decade. He would stroll to the mound and look the world square in the eye. And he had an abundance of talent, kicking up his left leg to extreme heights before delivering his pitch, thus gaining speed and deception.

When Lee was 14 he weighed 180 pounds and worked in a sawmill near his home in Plaquemine, La. He played shortstop on his high school team and filled in as a pitcher. At Louisiana State University he gained a reputation as a varsity tackle, but he didn't care for football.

He had no regrets. "Most of the fellows who played football with me are running filling stations or driving trucks," said the black-haired, blue-eyed pitcher. "I'm glad I chose baseball."

Lee attracted the attention of the Cardinals' famed Branch Rickey, who invited him to the St. Louis training camp in 1930. After a brief trial at St. Joseph of the Western League, Lee finished the season with Greensboro of the Piedmont League.

While with Greensboro, Big Bill pitched a 2-0 shutout in the first game and turned in five more scoreless innings before winning the nightcap. In addition, he made five consecutive hits. The next afternoon he pinch-hit and drove home the tying run. It was obvious that Lee was ready for faster company.

The Cardinals shipped the General to Scottsdale of the Middle Atlantic League in 1931. There he won 22 and struck out 246, a league record. Rickey moved Lee to Columbus near the end of the season and he won two games, fanning 17 in one and 18 in the other.

In 1932 he achieved 20 victories for Columbus. In one game

against Wheeling, he stepped to the mound in relief and struck out the side on nine pitches. But somehow, Lee remained buried in the Cardinals' far-flung chain gang. The next season Lee won 21 and lost 9, while teammate Paul Dean won 22 and lost 7.

Rickey elected to call up Dean to the Cardinals and sell Lee to the Cubs for $40,000. That was Lee's big break. He was an immediate success, pitching successive shutouts in his first two major league starts, tossing a four-hitter at the Phillies in a 2-0 victory and a two-hitter in a 5-0 taming of the Dodgers, both at Wrigley Field.

Lee was 13-14 in his rookie season, but high-kicked his way to a 20-6 record as the Cubs won the 1935 pennant. Five of his victories came during the team's 21-game winning streak in the September stretch, including the pennant clincher.

After winning 18 and 14 the following two seasons, Lee had one of those rare seasons in 1938. Lee pitched the Cubs to the National League pennant on the strength and skill of his good right arm.

He won 22 and lost 9 and led the league with a 2.66 ERA and nine shutouts. From May 19 through June 3 the General marched through five consecutive victories, pitching three straight shutouts, 32 consecutive scoreless innings, allowing one run in 47, and one extra base hit, a double.

The lone run, driven in by pitcher Lou Fette of the Boston Bees in the fourth inning on May 23, prevented Lee from reeling off five straight shutouts. But the best was yet to come.

Within the space of 17 days in September, Lee racked up four successive shutouts, beating the Pirates 3-0, the Reds 2-0, the Giants 4-0, and the Phillies 4-0. Between the first and second shutouts, Lee pitched an inning and one-third of runless relief against the Cardinals. He thus zipped through 37⅓ runless innings against five teams.

In the showdown series with the Pirates, Lee pitched in all three games. On Sept. 27 the Pirates came to Wrigley Field with a one and one-half game lead. Manager Hartnett called on Dizzy Dean to pitch the opener. The Cubs led 2-0 and 'Ol Diz stopped the Pirates through eight innings with his "nothing ball." After retiring the first two batters in the ninth, Dean walked Woody Jensen, and Lee Hendley doubled.

With men on second and third, Hartnett summoned his ace, Bill Lee, who cut loose with a wild pitch to cut the lead to 2-1. But Lee righted himself and struck out Al Todd to preserve the victory.

The following day, Lee pitched the eighth inning as Hartnett won it in the ninth with his famed homer. Lee started the next day and whipped the Pirates 10-1. The pennant race was over.

Lee was 19-15 in 1939, closing out the decade with a 106-70 record, clearly establishing himself as the ace of the Cubs' staff. In addition, he had even surpassed Dean as the highest salaried Cub pitcher.

The 1940s were something else. Big Bill became Bespectacled Bill. It was soon disclosed that Lee was nearsighted and couldn't see the catcher's signals. The man behind the windshield experienced lean years in 1940 and '41, going 9-17 and 8-14.

He was 13-13 with a mediocre team in 1942 and was 3-7 when he was traded to the Phillies for catcher Mickey Livingston on Aug. 3, 1943. From the Phils, Lee bounced to the Braves, never regaining his Cub prowess. Lee returned to the Cubs on waivers in 1947, but was 0-2.

He finished with a 169–157 mark, 139–123 as a Cub. The General then retreated to his Plaquemine homestead, where he raised prize beagles and enjoyed hunting.

In his later years, Lee underwent delicate surgery for detached retinas in both eyes, eventually losing his sight. He died on June 15, 1977, at the age of 67.

ROY HENSHAW

HENSHAW, ROY K.
B. July 29, 1911,
Chicago, Ill.
BR TL 5'8" 155 lb.

University of Chicago graduate Roy Henshaw pitched three seasons with the Cubs (1933, '35, and '36). One of them was memorable, and it could not have come at a better time. It was 1935 as Roy posted a 13-5 mark to do his share toward the Cub pennant. He won two games and helped put out the fire in another during the Cubs' 21-game September winning streak that catapulted them to the top.

He was the victor in win number 21, a 5-3 distance job over the Cardinals on Sept. 27. In his only appearance in the World Series against the Tigers, Roy was decisionless.

Henshaw later pitched for the Dodgers, Cardinals, and Tigers, finishing with a 33-40 mark. But Cub fans remember with gratitude his one season in the sun.

AUGIE GALAN

GALAN, AUGUST
JOHN
B. May 25, 1912,
Berkeley, Calif.
BR TR 6' 175 LB.

Augie Galan holds two records that can never be broken. He was the *first* player to go an entire season without grounding into a double play and the *first* to hit homers batting left-handed and right-handed in one game.

Galan was also the original hard-luck kid. He attained stardom while taped like a mummy and wearing special braces. Briefly, his mishaps after reaching the majors included two sprained ankles, a broken finger, three knee injuries, a tonsilectomy, a dislocated elbow, an operation to remove film from his eye, a broken knee cap, and even typhoid fever.

It all began when Galan was 11. While playing ball on the Oakland sandlots, he fell heavily on concrete, shattering his right elbow. Little Augie concealed the injury from his parents, fearing their reaction. The elbow was never set in a cast and never healed properly.

Known to his teammates as "Goo-Goo," Galan played shortstop on his high school team in San Francisco and later played semipro ball while working for his father's cleaning and dying establishment. Galan was always proud of his ability to iron fancy dress shirts.

The black-haired switch-hitter turned pro in 1931 with Globe (Ariz.) of the Texas League. He batted .291. Galan again batted .291 with San Francisco in 1932. The following season he was voted the Most Valuable Player on the Seals with such eye-catching statistics as 164 runs scored, 265 base hits, 51 doubles, 22 triples, and a .356 batting average.

Galan was purchased by the Cubs in 1934 and filled in for infield stars Billy Herman, Billy Jurges, and Stan Hack. He hit .260 in 66 games and then was converted to an outfielder by manager Charlie Grimm in 1935.

The Cubs went on to win the pennant with Galan in center field. He never revealed that he played much of the time with no feeling in his right arm. But his presence was felt at bat and on the basepaths.

He led the league in stolen bases with 22 and runs scored with 133. His 203 hits included 41 doubles, 11 triples, 12 homers, and a .314 average. When the season concluded, it was discovered that Galan went to the plate 646 times without grounding into a double play.

Galan stood alone until his record was tied by Dick McAuliffe of the Tigers in 1968. But McAuliffe had 570 at bats, 76 fewer than Galan.

Augie made the All-Star squad in 1936 and contributed to the National League's first victory with a controversial home run. In the bottom of the fifth inning he smacked a line drive down the right field line at Braves Field. The ball struck the flagpole at the foul line and bounced into foul territory. After much deliberation, it was ruled a homer, the first by a Cub in an All-Star Game.

In 1937 Grimm took notice of Galan's shortcomings in throwing and switched him to left field. He again led the National League in stolen bases with 23. And on June 25, 1937, he switch-hit his way into the record books.

The Cubs whipped the Dodgers 11-2 at Wrigley Field. Galan, batting lefty, connected off Fat Freddie Fitzsimmons with Jurges aboard in the fourth inning. He homered batting righty against the legendary Ralph Birkofer in the eighth again with Jurges on base. There were no reports of Galan's feat on the nation's sports pages the following day.

Injuries continued to cut into Galan's playing time. He shattered his left knee after crashing into the concrete wall at Shibe Park in 1940. It took a draft physical for World War II to disclose the hidden elbow ailment.

The Cubs wanted to send him to the minor leagues in 1941, but Augie was positive he could help a big league club. He received permission to talk to general manager Larry MacPhail of the Brooklyn Dodgers, who paid a paltry $2,500 for Galan.

Galan bounced back as a .300 hitter during the war years, hitting .318, .307, and .310. He took to hitting left-handed exclusively to help alleviate the excruciating pain batting from the right side.

The Dodgers traded the 35-year-old Galan to Cincinnati in 1947. He responded with a .314 average. His final year was 1949 when he divided the season with the Giants and Athletics. In his 16-year career, Galan batted .287 with 1,706 hits and 100 homers.

Today's statisticians keep closer tabs on batting feats. Galan is officially credited with being the first to switch-hit homers in one game. But that's no mean feat. Another player came along a couple of decades later and did it 10 times—Mickey Mantle.

LARRY FRENCH

FRENCH, LAWRENCE
HERBERT
B. Nov. 1, 1907,
Visalia, Calif.
BB TL 6'1" 195 lb.

On D-Day, June 6, 1944, a V-mail letter arrived on the desk of National League president Ford Frick. It was from Lt. Cmdr. L. H. French.

"This is going to be a great show," said French in the letter. "It will be the largest of the kind the world has ever seen. And in years to come I will be proud to say that I was there in some capacity or other.

"Sorry that security stops me from telling you more. And when this is over, I'll go back and win the three games I need to fill out 200 wins for the Book."

Lawrence Herbert French never did return to pick up those three elusive victories. He served as landing craft material officer for the Normandy invasion at Omaha and Utah beaches and then went on to the Pacific theatre. From there, French became a career naval officer.

Larry French lacked the usual eccentric traits of a southpaw pitcher. He was born in Visalia, Calif., the same community that sent pitcher Orval Overall to Frank Chance's Chicago Cubs. As a member of the Phi Chi fraternity at the University of California, French had thoughts of entering medicine.

But in the summer of 1926 he pitched a no-hitter for Eugene, Ore., his fourth in semipro ball. That victory was witnessed by Roy Mack, Connie's son, who wanted to sign him to a Portland contract.

French was only 18, and his father signed with an agreement that he was to give baseball a short trial. If he didn't make good, he would return to Berkeley and take up medicine.

After one season at Ogden and two at Portland, French was in the major leagues. He made his debut for the Pittsburgh Pirates against the New York Giants at the Polo Grounds on May 5, 1929.

Andy Cohen was the first batter French faced. Cohen accorded the youngster with a rousing reception by hitting a homer. In the second inning, Chuck Fullis tagged French for another homer. Welcome to the big leagues, Larry. But French bore down, didn't allow another run, and went on to win 3-2 in 10 innings. French finished with a 7-5 record in his rookie season.

In his first start in 1930, French had a perfect game against the Reds with two out in the eighth inning before Bob Meusel singled. In the ninth inning, Ethan Allen homered, but French won 7-1.

For the next five seasons, French didn't hurl a no-hitter nor win 20 games, but he was the workhorse of the Pirates staff with 17, 15, 18, 18, and 12 victories.

The Pirates, believing French had lost his stuff, traded him to the Cubs after the 1934 season with third baseman Fred Lindstrom for pitchers Guy Bush, Jim Weaver, and outfielder Babe Herman.

French was the left-handed pitcher the Cubs had lacked since Hippo Vaughn departed 14 years earlier. French helped the Cubs win the 1935 pennant, winning 17 games. He was a handy teammate in the clubhouse.

A go-getter type, French possessed good business acumen. He was the advisor of many of the Cubs in transactions of all kinds and served as an income tax consultant. Off the field he dabbled in real estate, owning several apartment houses and an auto loan business. In addition, he was the team badminton champion.

The amiable southpaw continued as a winner for the Cubs throughout the late 1930s, winning 18, 16, 10, 15, and 14. If Larry had one weakness it was Giants slugger Mel Ott who French-fried his offerings like a hot potato.

Then there was that elusive no-hitter. French came close again in June 1937 against his old Pirate mates. This time, Arky Vaughan doubled off the wall to nix French's bid in the eighth inning.

After hurting his thumb and slipping to 5-14 in 1941, French was sent packing to the Dodgers for the $7,500 waiver price. What a mistake. French bounced back with a knuckleball and a 15-4 record. He said farewell to baseball on Sept. 23, 1942, with a 6-0 shutout against the Phillies, allowing one hit and facing just 28 batters.

French joined the navy and vowed he'd return. "I still need three winning games to paste 200 in my scrapbook. I want them and I won't be satisfied with my career until I get them."

French, however, became a career officer in the navy. He was awarded the Legion of Merit for "exceptional service and resourcefulness as a commanding officer." He retired in 1969 after 27 years.

His overall record was 197 victories and 171 losses with 199 complete games and 40 shutouts. As a Cub, French had 95 wins and 74 losses and tossed 21 shutouts.

FREDDIE LINDSTROM

Hall of Famer Freddie Lindstrom, briefly a Cub, is best remembered for a hard luck play that could not have occurred at a less opportune time. It was the seventh and deciding game of the 1924 World Series between the Giants and the Senators at Washington. Freddie, a rookie, was playing third base for New York in the bottom of the 12th inning when Earl McNeely's slow roller struck a pebble and bounced over Lindstrom's shoulder, allowing the winning run to cross the plate.

Manager John McGraw never blamed the mishap on Lindstrom,

LINDSTROM, FRED CHARLES

B Nov. 21, 1905, Chicago, Ill.

D. Oct. 4, 1981, Chicago, Ill.

BR TR 5'11" 170 lb.

157

who quickly became a star in spite of only two years of seasoning in the minors with Toledo of the American Association. He enjoyed six consecutive .300 plus seasons in the Big Apple, including a .358 mark in 1928 and a .379 log in '30.

Following two seasons at Pittsburgh, Lindstrom and Larry French were sent to the Cubs on Nov. 22, 1934, for Guy Bush, Babe Herman, and Jim Weaver. Although Lindy was thrilled to be playing in his home town, he started the 1935 season as a combination of part-time outfielder and back-up third baseman to Stan Hack. When he did get to play, however, Freddie made a hit with his practice of tossing the ball to the Wrigley Field fans whenever he made the final putout of the game.

Late in the season Chuck Klein, the Cubs' regular right fielder, was benched because of a prolonged batting slump.

That was when Lindstrom finally got his chance. Frank Demaree was moved from center to right while Freddie supplanted Demaree in center—and rose to the occasion. When the Cubs won 21 in a row during the stretch drive, Freddie's 18 RBI were second only to Augie Galan's 22. Freddie jacked his average up to .275 in 90 games. On the pennant clincher, Sept. 27, Lindy drove in four runs on three hits as the Cubs took the defending champion Cardinals 6-2 in game one of a twin bill. Unfortunately, he ran out of gas in the World Series, batting only .200 as the Tigers ate up the Cubs in six games.

Following one season with the Dodgers, Lindstrom retired in 1936, a .311 hitter with 1,747 hits and 103 home runs. Later he briefly managed in the minors, served as baseball coach for Northwestern University in the early 1950s, and finally served as Postmaster of Evanston, Ill. In 1976 Freddie joined the ranks of the hallowed when he entered the Hall of Fame.

CLAY BRYANT

BRYANT, CLAIBORNE HENRY
B. Nov. 16, 1911, Madison Heights, Va.
BR TR 6'2½" 195 lb.

Although he spent only six years in the majors (1935–40), Clay Bryant was a fixture in organized ball for nearly 45 seasons. Bryant made his debut with Chambersburg of the Blue Ridge League in 1930 and worked his way along the minor league trail to New Orleans, Springfield (Ill.), Burlington (Mo.), Zanesville, and Birmingham before being called up to the Cubs late in 1935. He began pitching on and off two years later, winning 9-of-12 decisions.

On Aug. 28, 1937, he gave Cub fans an unforgettable thrill by winning his own game with a grand-slam homer in the top of the 10th to beat the Braves 10-7 at Boston. Surprisingly, Cub starter Charlie Root had homered earlier in the game.

In 1938 Clay blossomed into a real "comer," winning 19 and losing 11 as his contribution to the Cubs' dramatic pennant drive. His 135 strikeouts were high in the league—as were his 125 walks. The future looked bright, but he was stricken with arm trouble the following year. By 1941 he was gone. Bryant left behind a 32-20 record and a .266 batting average—not bad for a pitcher.

After hobbling along in the minors for a couple of years, Clay began his second career. For the next 30 years he served as a coach, pitching instructor, and minor league manager, first with the Dodger organization and later with the Indians' system. As a manager, he won pennants for Zanesville in the Mid-Atlantic League in 1947, Asheville in the Tri-State League in '48, and Montreal in the International League in '58. He also had four second-place finishes.

N icknamed "Tex" for obvious reasons, James Carleton was a good journeyman pitcher whose contributions were generally overlooked and forgotten.

TEX CARLETON

CARLETON, JAMES OTTO
B. Aug. 19, 1906, Comanche, Tex.
D. Jan. 11, 1977, Ft. Worth, Tex.
BR TR 6'1½" 180 lb.

Tex got his start with Texarkana of the East Texas League in 1925, and later appeared in that league with Marshall and Austin. He pitched for Houston of the Texas League in 1927 and '28 before moving on to Rochester of the International League for two years. By 1931 Tex was back at Houston, where he toiled in the shadow of a promising 20-year-old named Dizzy Dean.

Dean won 26 games and Tex took 20. Their performances earned them a pair of berths on the Cardinals the following year. Although the brash, colorful Dean received most of the publicity, Carleton gave the Cardinals 43 wins over the next three seasons, including a 17-11 mark in 1933.

Following the 1934 season, Tex was traded to the Cubs for Lyle Tinning, Dick Ward, and cash. Upon coming to Chicago, he was doomed to be a background figure again, this time to aces Lon Warneke, Bill Lee, and Larry French.

Nevertheless, the long, tall Texan put in four productive years at Wrigley Field, posting records of 11-8, 14-10, 16-8, and 10-9. His four shutouts in 1936 were tied for the league leadership with six others, including Cub pitching mates Warneke, Lee, and French.

On June 25, 1937, Carleton was the winning pitcher when Cub outfielder Augie Galan made history by becoming the first player to hit home runs right-handed and left-handed in the same game, as the Cubs polished off Brooklyn 11-2. Tex's 3.15 ERA that season was tops on the Cub staff.

After spending 1939 with Milwaukee of the American Association, Tex had one final fling in the majors with the Dodgers. Although he won only six games, one of them was the best of his career—a 3-0 no-hitter over the Reds on April 30, 1940.

It was Brooklyn's ninth straight win, but Cincy took the pennant, 12 games ahead of the Bums.

Carleton, meanwhile, retired for keeps, a lifetime 100-76 hurler with a 3.91 ERA.

CARL REYNOLDS

REYNOLDS, CARL
NETTLES
B. Feb. 1, 1903,
La Rue, Tex.
D. May 29, 1978,
Houston, Tex.
BR TR 6' 194 lb.

Carl Reynolds was the only player—so far—to bat over .300 in a full season for both the Cubs and the White Sox. He hit .317 and .359 for the Sox in 1929 and '30 and .302 for the Cubs in '38. He was also famed for having had his jaw broken by Bill Dickey of the Yankees.

Reynolds came up to the Sox in 1927, spending five years with the Pale Hose before moving on to Washington in 1932. He then went to the Browns, Red Sox, and back to the Senators before coming to the Cubs in 1937.

Reynolds was a vital contributor to the Cubs' pennant drive in 1938, but went hitless in the World Series as the Yankees steamrolled the Cubs in four straight. After dropping to .246 the following year, he retired.

Lifetime, he was a .302 hitter with 1,357 hits.

RIPPER COLLINS

COLLINS, JAMES
ANTHONY
B. March 30, 1904,
Altoona, Pa.
D. April 16, 1970,
New Haven, Conn.
BB TL 5'9" 165 lb.

Jimmy Collins was a product of the coal mines near his native Altoona. He acquired the nickname "Ripper" during his semipro days when the cover of a ball he walloped was ripped off after it struck a nail in the fence.

Collins was always a right-handed batter until he noticed every park had a left field fence a mile away from home plate and a right field fence just back of first. He decided to switch-hit.

"I used to get into a vacant lot with a bunch of kids. Then I'd bat left-handed all afternoon," said Collins. Eventually he began to hit the ball harder left-handed than right.

The black-haired first baseman with the prominent schnozz continued to dig coal when a minor league scout refused to give him $5 to sign. Collins finally got a tryout with York of the New York-Penn League in 1923. He didn't advance to the St. Louis Cardinals until 1931, after hitting .376 at Rochester.

Although he stood only 5' 9" on his tippy-toes, Collins became the regular first baseman on the Cardinals' famed Gashouse Gang. He enjoyed his finest season in 1934 when the Cards won the pennant and beat the Detroit Tigers in a seven-game World Series.

Collins ripped the ball for a .333 average on 200 hits and a league-leading .615 slugging average. In addition, Collins tied Mel Ott of the Giants for the homer leadership with 35. He capped the season with a .367 series mark, collecting 11 base hits.

The Ripper lost his regular role to a slugger named Johnny Mize in 1936 and was traded with pitcher Tarzan Parmelee to the Cubs for pitcher Lon Warneke.

Cub fans were aghast at losing their favorite pitcher, but Collins soon won them over with his timely hitting and engaging personality. He was the finest juggler in baseball, played a bass drum, lugged a typewriter as a part-time sportswriter, and was a polished after dinner jokester. Collins also collected broken bats, shellacked them, and used them to build a picket fence around his house in Rochester, N. Y.

Ripper also had a flair for the unlikely. On June 29, 1937, Collins played the entire game without touching the ball—no putouts and no assists. It wasn't a low-hit game either. The Cubs beat the Cardinals 11–9.

"We'd throw the ball around every inning and I didn't realize I didn't have a total chance," said Collins. One of his teammates bet him that he'd just set a record. "So I lost $5 on the game."

Collins was leading the Cubs in homers with 16 on Aug. 9, 1937, when he slid home, got a "roll and a shove" from Pirates' catcher Al Todd, and snapped an ankle. He was out for the season and the Cubs, missing Collins's bat, finished second, three games behind the Giants.

Ripper bounced back in 1938 as the Cubs overtook the Pirates on Gabby Hartnett's famed homer. Lesser known is Collins's contribution down the stretch. On Sept. 23, he swiped a bat belonging to Mickey Weintraub of the Phillies and collected 15 hits, including six-for-nine against the Pirates. In addition, his 13 homers were high for the team.

But against the mighty Yankees in the World Series, the Ripper and his magic Mickey Weintraub warclub had only two singles in 15 trips for a .133 average. Needless to say, the Yankees swept the Cubs in four games.

The following spring Collins received a jolt. Cub owner P. K. Wrigley sold his contract to the Los Angeles Angels of the Pacific Coast League, stating the "Ripper was too old." The Cubs decided to go with youngsters Phil Cavarretta and another Ripper, Glenn Russell, at first base.

The shocker came on Collins's 35th birthday and stirred deep resentment among the players. They couldn't understand how Ripper could be waived out of the league.

Collins stood in front of his locker. There were tears in his eyes. Los Angeles was a long way from his home and "it ain't the major leagues." The Cubs' loss was LA's gain. Collins ripped the Coast League apart, batting .334 and leading with 28 homers and 134 RBI. Still there was no call from the big leagues.

He remained with the Angels in 1940, and hit .327 with 206 hits, 18 homers and 111 RBI. This time the Pirates buzzed, but Collins hit only .210 as a sub for Elbie Fletcher in 1941.

Collins left the big leagues and began a new career as a player-manager in Albany, N.Y., where he remained for five seasons and even won the Eastern League batting title with a .396 average.

He also managed at San Diego, Pawtucket, and Hartford before joining the Wilson Sporting Goods Co., in Chicago as director of baseball sales and promotions.

The Ripper left that job in 1961 to become a Cubs' coach in their "musical chairs" era, but never advanced to the hot seat. After a heart attack he worked in the public relations department. Ill health forced him out of the game, and he died of a heart attack at age 66 in New Haven, Conn.

Collins had a career batting average of .296 with 135 homers, 29 in a Cub uniform.

DIZZY DEAN

DEAN, JAY HANNA

B. Jan. 16, 1911, Lucas, Ark.

D. July 17, 1974, Reno, Nev.

BR TR 6'2" 182 lb.

The veins in Lena Blackburne's neck flared and protruded. "Don't let that Dizzy rookie fool ya," screamed the White Sox manager as he watched his hitters trudge back to the dugout, bat in hand.

It was only an exhibition game on a barnstorm through the bushes, but Blackburne's futile utterances gave birth to a name that stuck—Dizzy Dean. It was a popular name for the Cardinals' gangling country boy who set the Sox batsmen on their ears.

Dizzy Dean succeeded Babe Ruth as the game's most colorful character during the Depression era. Perhaps he was baseball's supreme pitcher during the 1930s, even topping Lefty Grove and King Carl Hubbell.

Dean's birthplace was in the Arkansas hills about three miles from the town of Lucas. The date was given as Jan. 16, 1911. At the height of his popularity Dean would give reporters different birthdays, birthplaces, and names, so they each would have their own scoops.

Holdenville, Okla., was sometimes listed as his birthplace, and the probable name of Jay Hanna sometimes gave way to Jerome Herman. But he was always Ol'Diz.

Dizzy was the middle of three brothers in a family that wandered through the Southwest during the cotton pickin' season. In his teens Dean ran away from home and joined the army. "That's where I got my first pair of shoes," boasted Dean.

His father discovered he was in the army at Ft. Sam Houston in San Antonio, Tex., and got the underaged youngster his release. "I didn't like the army even if they did give me shoes," added Dean.

Scout Don Curtis saw Dean pitch with the army team and signed him to a Cardinals' contract in 1930. He was sent to St. Joseph (Mo.) of the Western League where he was 17-8. Before the season was over, he was shipped to Houston of the Texas League and compiled an 8-2 record.

The Cardinals had already clinched the pennant by Sept. 28, so they decided to have a look at the lanky right-hander. Dean toyed with the Pirates in his debut, tossing a three-hitter and winning 3-1. Thus, in one season, Dean made the jump to the majors, compiling a 26-10 record in three leagues.

Surprisingly, Dean was sent back to Houston in 1931 for more seasoning. Ol' Diz set the Texas League upside down, winning 26, with 303 strikeouts and a 1.57 ERA. He even took himself a bride. He planned to be married at home plate, but she balked.

In 1932 Dean began his six exciting years with the Cardinals. As main fuel pump for the Gashouse Gang, Dean won 134 and lost 75. In one 1933 contest, Dean struck out a record 17 Cub batters.

His best season was 1934, when he won 30 and lost only 7. He was joined that season by younger brother Paul "Daffy" Dean, who won 19. They combined for two wins each in the 1934 World Series, defeating the Detroit Tigers in seven games.

On Sept. 21, 1934, Dizzy pitched a three-hit shutout in the first game of a doubleheader at Brooklyn's Ebbets Field, and Daffy had a no-hitter in the nightcap. "Gee, if I'd known Paul was going to do it, I'd a done it, too," boasted Dizzy.

In the 1937 All-Star Game, Dean suffered an injury that was to cut short his playing career. A smash off the bat of Cleveland's Earl Averill broke one of Dean's toes. He changed his pitching motion to avoid placing too much pressure on the injured toe.

Then his arm went bad because of the unnatural pitching motion and he never regained his form. Dean was damaged goods. However, on April 16, 1938, Cub owner P. K. Wrigley bought Dean for $185,000 and even tossed in pitchers Curt Davis and Clyde Shoun and outfielder Tuck Stainback.

Dean described his switch from the impoverished Cardinals to the wealthy Cubs as "going from hamburgers to steaks." He set out at age 27 to prove he wasn't washed up.

In a way the deal was a plus for the Cubs. Dean proved a drawing card and the Cubs won the 1938 pennant. Dizzy's contribution was a 7-1 record and only 75 innings pitched. But he did come up with a clutch performance against the Pittsburgh Pirates during the stretch drive.

Cub manager Gabby Hartnett twirled his cigar and selected Dean to face the Pirates, who were one and a half games up on the Cubs on Sept. 27. "I never had nothin' " confessed Dean. "I couldn't break a pane of glass and I knew it. But I pitched."

For eight innings Dean had shut out the Pirates. "They had to get me outta there in the ninth. I was leading 2-0, but there were a couple of runners on base." Bill Lee relieved Dean and tossed a wild pitch, scoring one run, but the Cubs held on to win 2-1.

The following day, Hartnett hit his famed "Homer In The Gloamin'," and the Cubs zoomed into the World Series against the mighty Yankees. New York swept the series in four games, but guess who was the lone Cub to grasp some glory? The lame-armed Dean.

The second game on Oct. 6 was a classic matchup of colorful characters—Dizzy Dean against Goofy Gomez. Dean's lone asset was his "nothing ball." With it he held off the Bronx Bombers for seven innings.

He went into the eighth inning with a 3-2 lead on guts and heart and 42,108 Wrigley Field partisans cheering him on. Then, disaster struck. Frank Crosetti hit a two-run homer in the eighth and Joe DiMaggio reached him for another two-run homer in the ninth. The Yankees prevailed 6-3.

After two mediocre seasons (6-4 in 1939 and 3-3 in '40) the Cubs optioned Dean to Tulsa in 1941. Dizzy instead opted to become a baseball announcer for the St. Louis Browns.

He threw grammatical curves on radio and made St. Louis schoolmarms see red by remarks like "sluddin" into base and "threwed" the ball. There were howls of protest about Ol' Diz's mangled English. Dean commented that "a lot of folks that ain't sayin', ain't, ain't eatin'." Class dismissed.

When TV entered the picture, Dean became a "commultator" on the "Game of the Week" and earned more money than he did as a pitcher. His life was portrayed by another DD (Dan Dailey) in the 1952 film "Pride of St. Louis."

He was later immortalized in 1953 with his election into baseball's Hall of Fame. After all, he was the National League's last 30-game winner; he had four straight 20-plus victory seasons; and his career winning percentage was 644 on 150 wins against only 83 losses. He was even a winner as a Cub, posting a 16-8 record.

The son of a cotton picker soon retired to his five-acre grapefruit ranch in Phoenix. He spent his leisure time playing golf. He died in Reno, Nev., on July 17, 1974, at age 63.

HANK LEIBER

LEIBER, HENRY EDWARD

B. Jan 17, 1911, Phoenix, Ariz.

BR TR 6'1½"

205 lb.

Like the story of Pete Reiser, the career of Hank Leiber was a sad example of a would-be immortal who was destroyed by injuries.

A husky blond with the build of a coal stoker, Leiber attended the University of Arizona for a time before breaking in with Winston-Salem of the Piedmont League in 1932, batting .362 in 134 games. The Giants gave him a brief trial early the next season, but decided he needed more experience.

After additional minor league stops at Memphis, Jersey City, and Nashville, Leiber was back in the Big Apple by late 1934. The following year he paid big dividends, batting .331 with 203 hits, 22 homers and 107 RBI. On Aug. 24, 1935, he smashed two homers in one inning.

Hank soon found that the walls of the Polo Grounds were getting in his way. Following a disappointing showing in 1936, he sustained a severe head injury the season after, limiting his play to only 51 contests.

When his batting average fell to .269 in 98 games in 1938, the Giants decided they had seen enough. That winter he, Gus Mancuso, and Dick Bartell were dispatched to the Cubs for Frank Demaree, Billy Jurges, and Ken O'Dea.

It turned out that the Giants had given up on Leiber too soon. As the Cubs' regular center fielder in 1939, Hank started off slowly because of a variety of ailments. Finally, on Independence Day, he began to regain his former potency by stroking three home runs in a 6-4 loss to the Cardinals.

In September, he really hit his stride, socking 10 homers that month, including a grand slammer off Bill Posedel of the Braves on Sept. 10.

For the season, Hank batted .310 with 24 homers and 88 runs

driven in, his best totals in four years. The fact that he came to bat only 365 times made his home run and RBI totals all the more impressive.

Once the regular season was over, Hank's bat remained hot. On Oct. 7, the Cubs had two on with two out in the bottom of the ninth during the fourth game of the City Series. One more out and the White Sox would have a 3-2 victory. But the blond Giant-turned-Cub would have none of it.

Instead, he belted one over the left field wall at Wrigley Field for a sudden death 5-3 Cub win, giving the North Siders a 3-1 game edge in the series.

Unfortunately, Leiber's dramatic blast became obscured after the Sox won the next three games to capture the city title, in a finish that brought Cub fans to the brink of jumping off the Wrigley Building.

After Hank followed up in 1940 with a .302 average, 17 homers and 86 RBI, it looked as if he were back on the road to superstardom.

Then the jinx struck again. Suffering a brain concussion, he dropped to .216 in 1941, appearing in only 53 games. The following year, he was back in a Giant uniform. After an equally poor showing he turned in his uniform at the premature age of 31.

During his decade in the majors, Leiber entered a .288 lifetime batting average with 101 homers among his 808 hits. One can only speculate on the accomplishments that might have been.

Rowdy Richard Bartell was a pepperpot at shortstop. He enjoyed 17 seasons in the majors and one miserable one with the Cubs. His lifetime average was .284 and he collected 2,165 base hits.

DICK BARTELL

BARTELL, RICHARD WILLIAM
B. Nov. 22, 1907, Chicago, Ill.
BR TR 5'9" 160 lb.

But the only thing he drew in Chicago was the ire of the fans, who chanted "Error, Bartell" during the 1939 season. Bartell had replaced Billy Jurges, a Cub favorite at shortstop, and the team slipped to fourth place after a pennant-winning season.

Actually, Bartell came to the Cubs in a six-player deal with the New York Giants, but he was the focus of attention. Perhaps his fate was sealed during spring training at Catalina Island.

Bartell saw Cub traveling secretary Bob Lewis and a baseball writer stroll by. Both were of considerable girth. Bartell shouted "When do the blimps go up?" within earshot of the two.

The writer, who often served as official scorer, wasn't too lenient on ground balls hit to Bartell. Soon, Bartell started fumbling balls and making errant throws. "Error, Bartell" became a watchword.

He made 34 errors and his batting average dipped to .238, the lowest of his career. On Dec. 6, 1939, the Cubs quietly shipped Bartell to the Detroit Tigers for shortstop Billy Rogell. It was the end of an error, err, era.

Wrigley Field,
Chicago—1938
World Series

Next come the glory years — from 1941-45, when the Cubs
won the pennant, continuing on through the 1985 season
when, we hope, the Cubs will do it again. All the rosters and
details appear in a companion book called
The New Era Cubs 1941-1985.

Inquire at your bookstore or write:

Bonus Books, Inc., 160 East Illinois St., Chicago, IL 60611

Cubs All-Time Roster

A

Abbey, Albert	1893-95
Abernathy, Ted	1965-66, 1969-70
Aberson, Clifford	1947-49
Adair, James	1931
Adams, Bobby	1957-59
Adams, Bobby	1976-77
Adams, Charles ("Red")	1946
Adams, Earl ("Sparky")	1922-27
Adams, Karl	1915
Addis, Robert	1952-53
Addy, Robert	1876
Adkins, Dewey	1949
Aguirre, Henry	1969-70
Aker, Jack	1972-73
Alderson, Dale	1943-44
Aldridge, Vic	1917-18, 1922-24
Alexander, Grover	1918-26
Alexander, Matt	1973-74
Allen, Artemus ("Nick")	1916
Allen, Ethan	1936
Allison, Milo	1913-14
Altamirano, Porfirio	1984
Altman, George	1959-62, 1965-67
Amalfitano, Joseph	1964-67
Amor, Vincente	1955
Anderson, Bob	1957-62
Andre, John	1955
Andrews, James	1890
Andrus, Fred	1876, 1884
Angley, Thomas	1929
Anson, Adrian ("Cap")	1876-97
Arcia, Jose	1968
Archer, James	1909-17
Asbell, James	1938
Ashburn, Richie	1960-61
Aspromonte, Kenneth	1963
Atwell, Maurice ("Toby")	1952-53
Averill, Earl	1959-60

B

Baczewski, Fred	1953
Baecht, Edward	1931-32
Bailey, Abraham ("Sweetbreads")	1919-21
Bailey, Edgar	1965
Baker, Gene	1953-57
Baker, Thomas	1963
Baldwin, Mark	1887-88
Balsamo, Anthony	1962
Banks, Ernie	1953-71
Barber, Turner	1917-22
Barber, Stephen	1970
Barnes, Ross	1876-77
Barragan, Facundo ("Cuno")	1961-63
Barrett, Robert	1923-25
Barrett, Tracy	1943
Barry, John	1904-05

Bartell, Richard	1939
Barton, Vincent	1931-32
Bastian, Charles	1889
Bates, John	1914
Bauers, Russell	1946
Baumann, Frank	1965
Baumholtz, Frank	1949, 1951-55
Beals, Thomas	1880
Beaumont, Clarence	1910
Beck, Clyde	1926-30
Becker, Heinz	1943, 1945-46
Beckert, Glenn	1965-73
Beebe, Frederick	1906
Bell, Lester	1930-31
Benton, Al	1982
Berry, Joe	1942
Bertell, Dick	1960-65, 1967
Bielaski, Oscar	1876
Biittner, Larry	1976-80
Bilko, Stephen	1954
Bird, Doug	1981-82
Bishop, William	1889
Bithorn, Hiram	1942-43, 1946
Blackburn, Earl	1917
Blackwell, Tim	1978-81
Bladt, Richard	1969
Blair, Clarence ("Footsie")	1929-31
Blake, John ("Sheriff")	1924-31
Block, Seymour ("Cy")	1942, 1945-46
Bobb, Randy	1968-69
Boccabella, John	1963-68
Bolger, Jim	1955, 1957-58
Bonds, Bobby	1981
Bonetti, Julio	1940
Bonham, Bill	1971-77
Bonura, Henry ("Zeke")	1940
Borchers, George	1888
Bordi, Rich	1983-84
Borkowski, Robert	1950-51
Boros, Stephen	1963
Borowy, Henry	1945-48
Bosley, Thad	1983-84
Bottarini, John	1937
Bouchee, Edward	1960-61
Bourque, Pat	1971-73
Bowa, Larry	1982-84
Bowman, Bill	1891
Bowman, Robert	1942
Bradley, Bill	1899-1900
Bradley, George	1877
Bransfield, William ("Kitty")	1911
Breeden, Danny	1971
Breeden, Harold	1971
Bresnahan, Roger	1900, 1913-15
Brett, Herb	1924-25
Brewer, James	1960-63
Brewster, Charles	1944

Bridwell, Albert	1913	Carlson, Harold	1927-30
Briggs, Herbert ("Buttons")	1896-98, 1904-05	Carney, William	1904
		Cardwell, Don	1960-62
Briggs, Johnny	1956-58	Carpenter, Robert	1947
Bright, Harry	1965	Carroll, John	1892
Brillheart, John	1927	Carroll, Samuel ("Cliff")	1890-91
Brinkopf, Leon	1952	Carson, Alexander	1910
Broberg, Pete	1977	Carter, Joe	1983
Brock, Lou	1961-64	Carter, Paul	1916-20
Broglio, Ernest	1964-66	Carty, Rico	1973
Bronkie, Herman	1914	Caruthers, Robert	1893
Brooks, Jonathan ("Mandy")	1925-26	Casey, Hugh	1935
Brosnan, James	1954-58	Casey, James ("Doc")	1903-05
Brown, Joseph	1884	Cassidy, John	1878
Brown, Jophery	1968	Caudill, Bill	1979-81
Brown, Lewis	1879	Cavarretta, Phil	1934-35
Brown, Mordecai ("Three-Finger")		Ceccarelli, Arthur	1959-60
	1904-12, 1916	Cey, Ron	1983-84
Brown, Ray	1909	Chambers, Clifford	1948
Brown, Tommy	1952-53	Chance, Frank	1898-1912
Brown, Walter ("Jumbo")	1925	Chapman, Harry	1912
Browne, Byron	1965-67	Cheeves, Virgil	1920-23
Browne, George	1909	Cheney, Lawrence	1911-15
Brusstar, Warren	1983-84	Childs, Clarence	1900-01
Bryan, Charles	1888	Childs, George ("Pete")	1901
Bryant, Claiborne	1935-40	Chipman, Robert	1944-49
Bryant, Don	1966	Chiti, Harry	1950-56
Buckner, Bill	1977-84	Christopher, Lloyd	1945
Bues, Arthur	1914	Church, Emory	1953-55
Buhl, Bob	1962-66	Church, Leonard	1966
Burdette, Freddie	1962-64	Churry, John	1924-27
Burdette, Lew	1964-65	Clark, Frederick	1902
Burgess, Forrest ("Smoky")	1949, 1951	Clarke, Henry	1898
Burke, Leo	1963-65	Clarke, Sumpter	1920
Burns, Thomas	1880-91	Clarke, Tommy	1918
Burris, Ray	1973-75	Clarkson, John	1884-87
Burrows, John	1943-44	Clausen, Frederick	1893-94
Burton, Ellis	1963-65	Clemens, Clement	1916
Burwell, Richard	1960-61	Clemens, Douglas	1964-65
Bush, Guy	1923-34	Cline, Ty	1966
Butler, Johnny	1928	Clingman, William	1900
Buzhardt, John	1958-59	Clymer, Otis	1913
		Coakley, Andrew	1908-09
		Cogan, Richard	1899

C

Callaghan, Martin	1922-23	Coggins, Frank	1972
Callahan, James ("Nixey")	1897-1900	Cohen, Hyman	1955
Callison, Johnny	1969-71	Colborn, James	1969-71
Calmus, Richard	1967	Cole, David	1954
Camilli, Adolph	1933-34	Cole, Leonard	1909-12
Camp, Llewellyn	1893-94	Coleman, Joe	1976
Camp, Winfield	1894	Collins, James	1937-38
Campbell, Arthur ("Vin")	1908	Collins, Philip	1923
Campbell, Bill	1982-83	Collins, Robert	1940
Campbell, Gilly	1933	Collins, William	1911
Campbell, Joseph	1967	Collum, Jack	1957
Campbell, Ronald	1964-66	Comellas, Jorge	1945
Canava, James	1892	Compton, Clint	1972
Cannizzaro, Chris	1971	Congalton, William	1902
Capilla, Doug	1979-81	Connally, Fritz	1983
Cardenal, Jose	1972-77	Connor, James	1892, 1897-99
Carleton, James ("Tex")	1935-38	Connors, Bill	1966
Carlsen, Donald	1948	Connors, Kevin ("Chuck")	1951

168

Cook, James	1903
Cooney, James	1890-1892
Cooney, James	1926-27
Cooper, Wilbur ("Arlie")	1925-26
Cooper, Mort	1949
Cooper, Walker	1954-55
Corcoran, Lawrence	1880-85
Corcoran, Mike	1884
Corriden, John	1913-15
Corridon, Frank	1904
Cosman, James	1970
Cotter, Harvey	1922, 1924
Cotter, Richard	1912
Cotto, Henry	1984
Cottrell, Ensign	1912
Coughlin, Roscoe ("William")	1890
Covington, Wes	1966
Cowan, Billy	1963-64
Cox, Larry	1978, 1982
Croft, Henry	1901
Crosby, George	1884
Crosby, Ken	1975-76
Cross, Joffre	1948
Cruz, Hector	1978, 1981-82
Culler, Richard	1948
Culp, Ray	1967
Cunningham, Bert	1900-01
Curley, Walter ("Doc")	1899
Currie, Clarence	1903
Curtis, Jack	1961-62
Cusick, John	1951
Cuyler, Hazen ("Kiki")	1928-35
Cvengros, Louis	1929

D

Dahlen, William	1891-98
Dahlgren, Ellsworth ("Babe")	1941-42
Daily, Cornelius	1896
Dallessandro, Dominic	1940-44, 1946-47
Dalrymple, Abner	1879-86
Daly, Thomas	1887-88
Daly, Thomas	1918-21
Dark, Alvin	1958-59
Darling, Conrad	1887-89
Darwin, Bobby	1977
Davidson, William	1909
Davis, Bryshear	1970-71
Davis, Curt	1936-37
Davis, James	1954-56
Davis, Jody	1981-84
Davis, Thomas	1970, 972
Day, Charles	1970
Deal, Charles	1916-21
Dean, Jerome ("Dizzy")	1938-41
Dean, Wayland	1927
Decker, George	1892-97
Decker, George ("Joe")	1969-72
DeJesus, Ivan	1977-81
Delahanty, James	1901
Del Greco, Robert	1957
Demaree, Albert	1917
Demaree, Frank	1932-33, 1935-38

Demarris, Frederick	1890
DeMontreville, Eugene	1899
Denzer, Roger	1897
Dernier, Bobby	1984
Derrick, Claud	1914
Derringer, Paul	1943-45
Dettore, Tom	1974-76
Dexter, Charles	1900-02
Diaz, Mike	1983
Dillard, Steve	1979-81
Dillhoefer, William	1917
Dilone, Miguel	1979
Distaso, Alec	1969
Dobbs, John	1902-03
Dobernic, Jess	1948-49
Dolan, John	1895
Dolan, Patrick	1900-01
Dolan, Thomas	1897
Donahue, Timothy	1895-1900
Donnelly, Edward	1959
Donnelly, Frank	1893
Doolan, Mike	1916
Doscher, John	1903
Doscher, Herm	1879
Douglas, Phillip	1915, 1917-19
Douthit, Taylor	1933
Dowling, Dave	1966
Downey, Thomas	1912
Downs, Jerome	1912
Doyle, James	1911
Doyle, John	1901
Doyle, Lawrence	1916-17
Drabowsky, Moe	1956-60
Drake, Samuel	1960-61
Drake, Solomon	1956
Driscoll, John ("Paddy")	1917
Drott, Dick	1957-61
Dubiel, Walter	1949-52
Duffy, Hugh	1888-89
Dumovich, Nicholas	1923
Dunegan, James	1970
Dungan, Sam	1892-94, 1900
Dunn, Ron	1974-75
Durbin, Blaine	1907-08
Durham, Leon	1981-84
Dwyer, John	1888-89

E

Eaddy, Donald	1959
Egan, William	1893
Earl, Howard	1890
Early, Arnie	1966
Eason, Malcolm	1900-02
Easterwood, Roy	1944
Eastwick, Rawly	1981
Eaves, Vallie	1941-42
Eckersley, Dennis	1984
Eden, Charles	1877
Edwards, Bruce	1951-52, 1954
Edwards, Henry	1949-50
Eggler, David	1877
Eiteljorg, Edward	1890

Elia, Lee	1968	Frey, Linus	1937, 1947
Elko, Peter	1943-44	Friberg, Bernard	1919-20, 1922-25
Elliott, Allen	1923-24	Friend, Daniel	1895-98
Elliott, Carter	1921	Friend, Owen	1955-56
Elliott, Harold	1916-18	Fryman, Woody	1978
Ellis, James	1967	Fuhr, Oscar	1921
Ellsworth, Dick	1958, 1960-66	Fussell, Frederick	1922-23
Elston, Don	1953, 1957-64		
English, Elwood	1927-36	**G**	
Epperly, Albert	1938	Gabler, William	1958
Erickson, Paul	1941-48	Gabrielson, Leonard	1964-65
Ernaga, Frank	1957-58	Gagliano, Philip	1970
Errickson, Richard	1942	Galan, August	1934-41
Estrada, Chuck	1966	Gamble, Oscar	1969
Eubanks, Uel	1922	Gannon, William	1901
Everett, William	1895-1900	Ganzel, John	1900
Evers, Johnny	1902-13	Garagiola, Joseph	1953-54
		Garbark, Robert	1937-39
F		Gardner, Richard	1967
Fanning, William	1954-57	Gardner, James	1902
Fanzone, Carmen	1971-74	Garman, Mike	1976
Farrell, Charles	1888-89	Garrett, Adrian	1970, 1973-75
Farrell, Edward	1930	Garriott, Cecil	1946
Fast, Darcy	1968	Garvin, Virgil ("Ned")	1899-1900
Faul, Bill	1965-66	Gassaway, Charles	1944
Fear, Luvern	1952	Gastfield, Edward	1885
Felderman, Marvin	1942	Gaw, George	1920
Felske, John	1968	Geisel, Dave	1978-79, 1981
Ferguson, Bob	1878	Geiss, Emil	1887
Ferguson, Charles	1901	George, Charles	1941
Fernandez, Frank	1971-72	Gerard, David	1962
Figueroa, Jesus	1980	Gerberman, George	1962
Filer, Tom	1982	Gernert, Richard	1960
Fischer, William	1916	Gessler, Harry	1906
Fisher, Robert	1914-15	Gibson, Bob	1890
Fisher, William	1877	Gigon, Norman	1967
Fitzgerald, Howard	1922-24	Gilbert, Charles	1941-43, 1946
Flack, Max	1916-22	Gill, Johnny	1935-36
Flavin, John	1964	Gillespie, Paul	1942, 1944-45
Fleming, Leslie ("Bill")	1942-44, 1946	Giusti, Dave	1977
Fletcher, Scott	1981-82	Glade, Frederick	1902
Flint, Frank	1879-89	Gleeson, James	1939-40
Flores, Jesse	1942	Glenalvin, Robert	1890, 1893
Fluhrer, John	1915	Glenn, Edward	1902
Flynn, George	1896	Glenn, John	1876-77
Flynn, John	1886-87	Glossop, Al	1946
Fodge, Gene	1958	Goetz, John	1960
Fondy, Dee	1951-57	Goldsmith, Frederick	1880-84
Foote, Barry	1979-81	Golvin, Walter	1922
Foster, Elmer	1890-91	Gonzales, Miguel ("Mike")	1925-29
Foxen, William	1910-11	Good, Wilbur	1911-15
Foxx, James	1942, 1944	Goodman, Ival	1943-44
Frailing, Ken	1974-76	Gordon, Mike	1977-79
France, Ossie	1890	Gore, George	1879-86
Fraser, Charles	1907-09	Gornicki, Henry	1941
Frazier, George	1984	Goryl, Johnny	1957-59
Freeman, Alexander	1921-22	Grabarkewitz, Bill	1974
Freeman, Hershell	1958	Grace, Earl	1929, 1931
Freeman, Mark	1960	Graham, George	1903, 1911
Freese, George	1961	Grammas, Alex	1962-63
Freigau, Howard	1925-27	Grampp, Henry	1927, 1929
French, Lawrence	1935-41	Grant, Tom	1983

Grantham, George	1922-24	Hebner, Richie	1984
Graves, Joseph	1926	Hechinger, Michael	1912-13
Green, Edward ("Danny")	1898-1901	Hegan, James	1960
Gregory, Leroy	1964	Heist, Alfred	1960-61
Griffin, John ("Hank")	1911	Hemsley, Ralston	1931-32
Griffin, Mike	1981	Hendley, Robert	1965-67
Griffith, Clark	1893-1900	Henderson, Ken	1979-80
Griffith, Edward	1892	Henderson, Steve	1981-82
Griffith, Thomas	1925	Hendrick, Harvey	1933
Grigsby, Denver	1923-25	Hendricks, Elrod	1972
Grimes, Burleigh	1932-33	Hendricks, John	1902
Grimes, Oscar ("Ray")	1921-24	Hendrix, Claude	1916-20
Grimm, Charles	1925-36	Hennessey, George	1945
Groth, Edward	1904	Henry, William	1958-59
Gudat, Marv	1932	Henshaw, Roy	1933, 1935-36
Gumbert, Addison	1888-89, 1891-92	Herman, Floyd ("Babe")	1933-34
Gura, Larry	1970-73	Herman, William	1931-41
Gustine, Frank	1949	Hermann, LeRoy	1932-33
Guth, Emil ("Charlie")	1880	Hermanski, Eugene	1951-52
		Hernandez, Ramon	1968, 1976-77

H

		Hernandez, Salvador ("Chico")	1942-43
Haas, Eddie	1957	Hernon, Thomas	1897
Hack, Stan	1932-47	Herrnstein, John	1966
Hacker, Warren	1948-57	Herzog, Charles	1919-20
Hagerman, Kurt ("Casey")	1914	Hiatt, Jack	1970
Hagerman, Zeriah	1909	Hibbard, John	1884
Hairston, Johnny	1969	Hickey, Mike	1901
Hall, Jimmie	1969-70	Hickman, Jim	1968-73
Hall, Mel	1981-84	Higbe, Kirby	1937-39
Hallinan, James	1877-78	Higginbotham, Irving	1909
Hamner, Ralph	1947, 1949	Hildebrand, R. E.	1902
Hands, Bill	1966-72	Hiller, Frank	1950-51
Haney, Frederick	1927	Hillman, Dave	1955-59
Hankinson, Frank	1878-79	Hines, Paul	1876-77
Hamilton, Steve	1972	Hiser, Gene	1971-75
Hanlon, William	1903	Hoak, Donald	1956
Hanson, Earl	1921	Hobbie, Glen	1957-64
Hanyzewski, Edward	1942-46	Hoeft, Billy	1965-66
Harbidge, William	1878-79	Hoffman, Lawrence	1901
Hardie, Lewis	1886	Hofman, Arthur ("Solly")	1904-12, 1916
Hardin, William	1952	Hogg, Brad	1915
Hardy, Alex	1902-03	Holley, Edward	1928
Hardy, John	1907	Hollison, John	1892
Hargesheimer, Alan	1983	Hollocher, Charles	1918-24
Hargrave, Eugene	1913-15	Holm, Billy	1943-44
Harley, Richard	1903	Holmes, Frederick	1904
Harper, Charles	1906	Holtzman, Ken	1965-71, 78-79
Harrell, Raymond	1939	Honan, Martin	1890-91
Harris, Vic	1974-75	Hooton, Burt	1971-75
Hartenstein, Charles	1965-68	Horne, Berlyn	1929
Hartnett, Leo ("Gabby")	1922-40	Hornsby, Rogers	1929-32
Hartsel, Tullos	1902	Hosley, Tim	1975-76
Harvey, Erwin	1900	Houseman, John	1894
Hassey, Ron	1984	Howard, George	1907-09
Hatcher, Billy	1984	Howe, Calvin	1952
Hatten, Joseph	1951-52	Howell, Jay	1981
Hatton, Grady	1960	Hubbs, Ken	1961-63
Hayden, John	1908	Hudson, Johnny	1941
Hayes, Bill	1980-81	Hughes, Edward	1902
Healy, John	1889	Hughes, James	1956
Heath, William	1969	Hughes, Roy	1944-45
Heathcote, Clifton	1922-30	Hughes, Terry	1970

Hughes, Thomas	1900-01	Katoll, John	1898-99
Hughey, James	1893	Kaufman, Anthony	1921-27
Humphreys, Robert	1965	Kearns, Edward ("Ted")	1924-25
Humphries, Bert	1913-15	Keating, Walter	1913-15
Hundley, Randy	1966-73, 76-77	Keen, Howard	1921-25
Hunter, Herbert	1916-17	Kelleher, John	1921-23
Huntzinger, Walter	1926	Kelleher, Mick	1976-80
Hurst, Don	1934	Kellert, Frank	1956
Hutchinson, Edward	1890	Kelly, George	1930
Hutchison, William	1889-95	Kelly, Joseph	1916
Hutson, Herb	1974	Kelly, Joseph	1926, 1928
		Kelly, Michael	1880-86

I

		Kelly, Robert	1951-53
Irvin, Monford	1956	Kennedy, Junior	1982-83
Irwin, Charles	1893-95	Kennedy, Sherman	1902
Isbell, Frank	1898	Kennedy, Theodore	1885
		Kenzie, Walter	1884

J

		Keough, Marty	1966
Jackson, Larry	1963-66	Kerr, John ("Mel")	1925
Jackson, Louis	1958-59	Kessinger, Don	1964-75
Jackson, Ransom	1950-55, 1959	Kilduff, Peter	1917-19
Jacobs, Tony	1948	Killefer, William	1918-21
Jacobs, Elmer	1924-25	Killen, Frank	1900
Jacobs, Morris	1902	Kilroy, Matthew	1898
Jacobs, Raymond	1928	Kimball, Newell	1937-38
Jacobson, Merwin	1916	Kimm, Bruce	1979
Jaeckel, Paul	1964	Kindall, Gerald	1956-58, 1960-61
Jaegar, Joseph	1920	Kiner, Ralph	1953-54
Jahn, Arthur	1925	King, Charles	1958-59
James, Cleo	1970-71, 1973	King, James	1955-56
James, Richard	1967	Kingman, Dave	1978-80
Jeffcoat, Harold	1948-55	Kirby, James	1949
Jelincich, Frank	1941	Kitsos, Christopher	1954
Jenkins, Ferguson	1966-73, 1982-83	Kittredge, Malachi	1890-97
Jestadt, Gary	1971	Klein, Charles	1934-36
Jimenez, Manuel	1969	Kling, John	1900-08, 1910-11
Johnson, Abraham	1893	Klippstein, John	1950-54
Johnson, Benjamin	1959-60	Klugman, Joseph	1921-22
Johnson, Bill	1984	Knabe, Franz ("Otto")	1916
Johnson, Cliff	1980	Knisely, Peter	1913-15
Johnson, Dave	1978	Knowles, Darold	1975-76
Johnson, Donald	1943-48	Koenig, Mark	1932-33
Johnson, Kenneth	1969	Koestner, Elmer	1914
Johnson, Louis	1960, 1968	Koonce, Calvin	1962-67
Johnson, Richard	1958	Korwan, James	1897
Johnson, James	1914	Kowalik, Fabian	1935-36
Johnstone, Jay	1982-84	Kravec, Ken	1981-82
Joiner, Roy	1934-35	Kreevich, Michael	1931
Jones, Charles	1877	Kremmel, Jim	1974
Jones, Clarence	1967-68	Krietner, Albert ("Mickey")	1943-44
Jones, Davey	1902-04	Krieg, William	1885
Jones, Percy	1920-22, 1925-28	Krock, August	1888-89
Jones, Samuel	1955-56	Kroh, Floyd	1908-10
Jones, Sheldon	1953	Krug, Chris	1965-66
Jonnard, Claude	1929	Krug, Martin	1922
Jurges, William	1931-38, 1946-47	Krukow, Mike	1976-81
		Kuenn, Harvey	1965-66

K

		Kush, Emil	1941-42, 1946-49
Kahoe, Michael	1901-02, 1907		
Kaiser, Al	1911		

L

Kaiser, Donald	1955-57		
Kane, John	1909-10	LaCock, Peter	1972-75
		Lade, Doyle	1946-50

Lake, Steve	1983-84	
Lamabe, John	1968	
Lamar, Pete	1902	
Lamp, Dennis	1976-80	
Landrith, Hobert	1956	
Landrun, Don	1962-65	
Lanfranconi, Walter	1941	
Lange, William	1893-99	
Larkin, Frank ("Terry")	1878-79	
LaRoche, David	1973-74	
LaRose, Victor	1968	
Larsen, Donald	1967	
Larson, Dan	1982	
LaRussa, Tony	1973	
Lary, Al	1954-55, 1962	
Laver, John ("Chuck")	1890	
Lavender, James	1912-16	
Lazzeri, Anthony	1938	
Leach, Thomas	1912-14	
Lear, Frederick	1918-19	
Leathers, Harold	1920	
Lee, Don	1966	
Lee, Thomas	1884	
Lee, William	1934-43, 1947	
Lefferts, Craig	1983	
Leiber, Henry	1939-41	
Leifield, Albert	1912-13	
LeMay, Richard	1963	
Lemonds, David	1969	
Lennon, Robert	1957	
Lennox, Ed	1912	
Leonard, Emil	1949-53	
Leslie, Roy	1917	
Lezcano, Carlos	1980-81	
Lillard, Robert ("Gene")	1936, 1939	
Lindstrom, Fred	1935	
Littlefield, Dick	1957	
Littrell, Jack	1957	
Livingston, Thompson	1943, 1945-47	
Lobert, John ("Hans")	1905	
Locker, Robert	1973-75	
Logan, Robert	1937-38	
Long, Dale	1957-59	
Lopes, Davey	1984	
Loviglio, John	1983	
Lowdermilk, Grover	1912	
Lowe, Robert	1902-03	
Lown, Omar ("Turk")	1951-54, 1956-58	
Lowrey, Harry ("Peanuts")	1942-43, 1945-49	
Luby, John ("Pat")	1890-92	
Luderus, Frederick	1909-10	
Lum, Mike	1981	
Lundgren, Carl	1902-09	
Lundstedt, Thomas	1973-74	
Lynch, Henry	1893	
Lynch, Matt	1948	
Lynch, Michael	1902	
Lynn, Japhet	1944	
Lytle, Edward	1890	

M

Mack, Raymond	1947
Mack, William	1908
Macko, Steve	1979-80
Madden, Leonard	1912
Maddern, Clarence	1946, 1948-49
Madlock, Bill	1974-76
Madrid, Salvador	1947
Magee, Lee	1919
Magoon, George	1899
Maguire, Fred	1928
Mains, Willard	1888
Maisel, George	1921-22
Malarkey, John	1899
Malone, Pat	1928-34
Maloney, Billy	1905
Mancuso, August	1939
Manders, Harold	1946
Mann, Ben	1944
Mann, Leslie	1916-19
Manville, Richard	1952
Maranville, Walter ("Rabbit")	1925
Maroney, James	1912
Marquez, Gonzalo	1973-74
Marquez, Louis	1954
Marriott, William	1917, 1920-21
Marshall, James	1958-59
Marshall, William	1908
Martin, Elwood	1918-22
Martin, Frank	1898
Martin, J. C.	1970-72
Martin, Jerry	1979-80
Martin, Morris	1959
Martin, Stuart	1943
Martinez, Carmelo	1983
Marty, Joseph	1937-39
Martz, Randy	1980-81
Massa, Gordon	1957-58
Mathews, Nelson	1960-63
Matthews, Gary	1984
Mattick, Robert	1938-40
Mauch, Gene	1948-49
Mauck, Harold	1893
Mauro, Carmen	1948, 1950-51
May, Frank	1931-32
Mayer, Edward	1957-58
McAfee, William	1930
McAnany, James	1961-62
McAuley, James ("Ike")	1925
McBride, Algernon	1896
McCabe, William	1918-20
McCall, Robert	1948
McCarthy, Alexander	1915-16
McCarthy, John	1900, 1903-05
McCauley, Jim	1885
McChesney, Harry	1904
McClellan, William	1878
McConnell, George	1914, 1916
McCormick, James	1885-86
McCormick, Barry	1896-1901
McCullough, Clyde	1940-43, 1946-48, 1953-56

McDaniel, Lyndall	1963-65	Morehead, Seth	1959-60
McDonald, Edward	1913	Moreland, Keith	1982-84
McFarland, LaMont	1895-96	Morgan, Robert	1957-58
McGill, William	1893-94	Morgan, Vernon	1954-55
McGinn, Dan	1972	Morhardt, Meredith ("Moe")	1961-62
McGinnis, August	1893	Moriarity, George	1903-04
McGlothen, Lynn	1979-81	Morris, Ed	1922
McIntire, Harry	1910-12	Morrissey, Deacon	1902
McKnight, James	1960, 1962	Moryn, Walter	1956-60
McLarry, Polly	1915	Moskau, Paul	1983
McLean, John ("Larry")	1903	Mosolf, James	1933
McLish, Calvin	1949, 1951	Moss, Mal	1930
McMath, Jimmy	1968	Mudrock, Phil	1977-79
McMillan, Norman	1928-29	Mulligan, Edward	1915-16
McVey, Calvin	1876-77	Muncrief, Robert	1949
Meakim, George	1892	Munson, Joseph	1925-26
Meers, Russell	1941, 1946-47	Murcer, Bobby	1977-79
Mejias, Sam	1979	Murphy, Daniel	1960-62
Menefee, John	1900-03	Murray, Anthony	1923
Meoli, Rudy	1978	Murray, James	1902
Meridith, Ron	1984	Murray, John	1915
Merkle, Fred	1917, 1920	Myers, Richard	1956
Merriman, Lloyd	1955	Myers, William	1941
Merritt, William	1891		
Mertes, Samuel	1898-1900		

N

Merullo, Leonard	1941-47	Nagle, Thomas	1890-91
Mesner, Stephen	1938-39	Napier, Buddy	1918
Metkovich, George	1953	Needham, Thomas	1909-14
Metzger, Roger	1970	Neeman, Cal	1957-60
Metzler, Alexander	1925	Nehf, Arthur	1927-29
Meyer, Lambert	1937	Nelson, Lynn	1930, 1933-34
Meyer, Russell	1946-48, 1956	Nen, Richard	1968
Michaels, Ralph	1924-26	Newkirk, Joel	1912, 1920
Mickelson, Ed	1957	Newman, Charles	1892
Mikkelsen, Peter	1967-68	Newman, Ray	1971
Miklos, John	1944	Newsom, Bobo	1932
Miksis, Edward	1951-56	Nichols, Art	1898-1900
Miller, Dakin	1902	Nichols, Dolan	1958
Miller, Henry	1892	Nicholson, William	1939-48
Miller, John	1947	Nicol, George	1891
Miller, Lawrence ("Hack")	1922-25	Nicol, Hugh	1881-82
Miller, Robert	1970-71	Niekro, Joe	1967-69
Miller, Roy	1910	Noles, Dickie	1982-84
Miller, Ward	1912-13	Noonan, Peter	1906
Milstead, George	1924, 1926	Nordhagen, Wayne	1983
Minner, Paul	1950-56	Noren, Irving	1959-60
Mitchell, Michael	1913	Norman, Fred	1964, 1966-67
Mitterwald, George	1974-75	North, Bill	1971-72
Moisan, William	1953	Northey, Ronald	1950, 1952
Molinaro, Bobby	1982	Nottebart, Donald	1969
Mollwitz, Frederick	1913-14, 1916	Novikoff, Louis	1941-44
Monday, Rick	1972-75	Novotney, Ralph	1949
Montreuil, Al	1972	Nye, Richard	1966-69
Moolic, George	1886		
Moore, Charles	1912		

O

Moore, Donnie	1975, 1977-79	O'Berry, Mike	1980
Moore, Earl	1913	O'Brien, John	1893
Moore, Johnny	1928-29, 1931-32, 1945	O'Brien, Peter	1890
Mooty, Jacob	1940-43	O'Connor, John	1916
Morales, Jerry	1974-77, 1981-83	O'Dea, Ken	1935-38
Moran, Patrick	1906-09	O'Farrell, Robert	1915-25, 1934
Moran, William	1895	O'Hagan, Harold	1902

Oliver, Gene	1968-69
Oliver, Nate	1969
Oliver, Richard	1943
Olsen, Bernard	1941
Olsen, Vernon	1939-42, 1946
O'Neill, Emmet	1946
O'Neill, John	1904-05
Ontiveros, Steve	1977-80
Oritz, Jose	1971
Osborn, Bob	1925-27, 1929-30
Osborne, Ernest	1922-24
Ostrowski, John	1943-46
Otero, Regino	1945
Ott, William	1962, 1964
Overall, Orval	1906-10, 1913
Ovitz, Ernest	1911
Owen, Arnold ("Mickey")	1949-51
Owen, Dave	1983-84

P

Packard, Gene	1916-17
Pafko, Andrew	1943-51
Page, Vance	1938-41
Pagel, Karl	1978-79
Pappas, Milt	1970-73
Parker, Harley	1893, 1895-96
Parmelee, Roy	1937
Parrott, Thomas	1893
Parrott, Walter	1892-95
Paskert, George	1918-20
Passeau, Claude	1939-47
Patterson, Reggie	1983-84
Paul, Mike	1973-74
Pawelek, Ted	1946
Pearce, George	1912-16
Pechous, Charles	1916-17
Pedroes, Charles	1902
Pena, Roberto	1965-66
Penner, Kenneth	1929
Pepitone, Joe	1970-73
Perkowski, Harry	1955
Perry, Scott	1916
Peters, Johnny	1876-77, 1879
Pettit, Robert	1887-88
Petty, Jesse	1930
Pfeffer, Francis	1905, 1910
Pfeffer, Fred	1883-89, 1891, 1896-97
Pfiester, John	1906-11
Phelan, Art	1913-15
Phelps, Gordon	1933-34
Phillips, Adolfo	1966-69
Phillips, Taylor	1958-59
Phoebus, Tom	1972
Phyle, William	1898-99
Pick, Charles	1918-19
Pick, Edward	1927
Pierce, Raymond	1924
Piercy, Andrew	1881
Piercy, William	1926
Piktuzis, George	1956
Pina, Horacio	1974
Pittenger, Clark	1925

Pizarro, Juan	1970-73
Platt, Mizell	1942-43
Plummer, William	1968
Poholsky, Thomas	1957
Pollet, Howard	1953-55
Ponder, Elmer	1921
Poorman, Thomas	1880
Popovich, Paul	1964, 1966-67, 1969-73
Porterfield, Bob	1959
Powell, William	1912
Powers, Philip	1878
Prall, Willie	1975
Pramesa, Johnny	1952
Prendergast, Mike	1916-17
Pressnell, Forest	1941-42
Prim, Raymond	1943, 1945-46
Prince, Donald	1962
Pyecha, John	1954
Pyle, Harry	1887

Q

Qualls, Jimy	1969
Quest, Joseph	1879-82
Quinn, Frank	1899
Quinn, Joseph	1877
Quinn, Wellington	1941

R

Radatz, Richard	1967
Rader, Dave	1978
Raffensberger, Ken	1940-41
Ragan, Pat	1909
Rainey, Chuck	1983-84
Ramazzotti, Robert	1949-53
Ramsdell, Willie	1952
Randall, Newt	1907
Randle, Lennie	1980
Ranew, Merritt	1963-64
Raub, Tommy	1903
Raudman, Robert	1966-67
Raymer, Frederick	1901
Reberger, Frank	1968
Regan, Phil	1968-72
Reich, Herman	1949
Reilly, Harold	1919
Reilly, Josh	1896
Reis, Laurie	1877-78
Reitz, Ken	1981
Remsen, John	1878-79
Renko, Steve	1976-77
Reulbach, Edward	1905-13
Reuschel, Paul	1975-78
Reuschel, Rick	1972-81, 1983-84
Reynolds, Archie	1968-70
Reynolds, Carl	1937-39
Rhoades, Robert	1902
Rice, Del	1960
Rice, Harold	1954
Rice, Leonard	1945
Richards, Fred	1951
Richbourg, Lance	1932
Richie, Lewis	1910-13

Richmond, Beryl	1933	Schultz, Joseph	1915
Richter, Emil	1911	Schultz, Robert	1951-53
Rickert, Marvin	1942, 1946-47	Schulze, Don	1983-84
Riley, George	1979-80	Schurr, Wayne	1964
Ripley, Allen	1982	Schuster, William	1943-45
Roach, Melvin	1961	Schwenck, Rudolph	1909
Roach, Skel	1899	Scott, Floyd	1926-27
Roat, Frederick	1892	Scott, Milton	1882
Roberts, Dave	1977-78	Scott, Richard	1964
Roberts, Robin	1966	Scott, Rodney	1978
Robertson, Daryl	1962	Seaone, Manny	1978
Robertson, Davis	1912-21	Seaton, Thomas	1916-17
Robertson, Donald	1954	Secory, Frank	1944-46
Rodgers, Andre	1961-64	Segelke, Herman	1982
Rodriguez, Fernando	1958	Selma, Dick	1969
Rodriguez, Roberto	1970	Sember, Mike	1977-78
Rogell, Billy	1940	Serena, William	1949-54
Rohn, Dan	1983-84	Sewell, Thomas	1927
Root, Charles	1926-41	Shaffer, George	1879
Rosello, David	1972-77	Shamsky, Art	1972
Ross, Gary	1968-69	Shannon, Maurice	1926
Rowan, John	1911	Shantz, Robert	1964
Rowe, David	1877	Shaw, Robert	1967
Roy, Luther	1927	Shaw, Samuel	1893
Roznovsky, Victor	1964-65	Shay, Marty	1916
Rudolph, John	1904	Shealy, Albert	1930
Rudolph, Ken	1969-73	Shean, David	1911
Ruether, Walter	1917	Sheckard, Jimmy	1906-12
Rush, Robert	1948-57	Shoun, Clyde	1935-37
Russell, Glen	1939-42	Sicking, Edward	1916
Russell, Jack	1938-39	Signer, Walter	1943, 1945
Ruthven, Dick	1983-84	Silvera, Charles	1957
Ryan, James	1885-89, 1891-1900	Simmons, Curtis	1966-67
		Simpson, Thomas	1953

S

		Singleton, Elmer	1957-59
Saier, Victor	1911-17	Sizemore, Ted	1979
Sandberg, Ryne	1982-84	Skidmore, Roe	1970
Sanderson, Scott	1984	Slagle, James	1902-08
Santo, Ron	1960-73	Slapnicka, Cyril	1911
Sauer, Edward	1943-45	Slaughter, Sterling	1964
Sauer, Hank	1949-55	Sloat, Dwain	1949
Savage, Ted	1967-68	Smalley, Roy	1948-53
Sawatski, Carl	1948, 1950, 1953	Smith, Alexander	1904
Schaefer, Herman	1901-02	Smith, Bobby Gene	1962
Schaffer, Jimmie	1963-64	Smith, Charles	1911-14
Schaffernoth, Joseph	1959-61	Smith, Charles	1969
Scheffing, Robert	1941-42, 1946-50	Smith, Earl	1916
Schenz, Henry	1946-49	Smith, Harry	1877
Schick, Maurice	1917	Smith, Lee	1980-82
Schlafy, Larry	1902	Smith, Louis	1906
Schmidt, Fred	1947	Smith, Paul	1958
Schmitz, John	1941-42, 1946-51	Smith, Robert	1931-32
Schorr, Edward	1915	Smith, Robert W.	1959
Schramka, Paul	1953	Smith, Willie	1968-70
Schreiber, Henry	1926	Solis, Marcelino	1958
Schriver, William	1891-94	Solomon, Eddie	1975
Schroll, Albert	1960	Somers, Rudolph	1912
Schult, Arthur	1959-60	Sommers, Pete	1889
Schulte, John	1929	Spalding, Albert	1876-78
Schulte, Frank	1904-16	Spangler, Al	1967-71
Schultz, Barney	1961-63	Speake, Bob	1955, 1957
Schultz, Buddy	1975	Sperring, Rob	1974-75

Sponsberg, Carl	1908	Taylor, Daniel	1929-32
Sprague, Charles	1887	Taylor, Harry	1932
Spring, Jack	1964	Taylor, John	1898-1903, 1906-07
Stack, Eddie	1913-14	Taylor, Sammy	1958-62
Stainback, George	1934-37	Taylor, Tony	1958-60
Staley, Gale	1925	Taylor, Zack	1929-33
Standridge, Pete	1915	Teachout, Arthur	1930-31
Stanky, Edward	1943-44	Tebeau, Oliver	1887
Stanley, Joseph	1909	Tener, John	1888-89
Stanton, Harry	1904	Terry, William A.	1894-97
Starr, Raymond	1945	Terry, Zebulon	1920-22
Start, Joseph	1878	Terwilliger, Wayne	1949-51
Statz, Arnold	1922-25	Thacker, Morris	1958, 1960-62
Stauffer, Charles ("Ed")	1923	Thomas, Frank	1960-61, 1966
Stedronske,	1879	Thomas, LeRoy	1966-67
Steevens, Morris	1962	Thomas, Robert	1921
Stein, Bill	1982	Thompson, Scot	1976-83
Stein, Edward	1890-91	Thomson, Robert	1958-59
Steinfeldt, Harry	1906-10	Thornton, Andre	1973-76
Stelmaszek, Dick	1974	Thornton, Walter	1895-98
Stenzel, Jacob	1890	Thorpe, Robert	1955
Stephenson, Chester	1971	Tidrow, Dick	1979-82
Stephenson, Joseph	1944	Tiefenauer, Bobby	1968
Stephenson, John	1967-68	Tincup, Benjamin	1928
Stephenson, Riggs	1926-34	Tinker, Joseph	1902-12, 1916
Stephenson, Walter	1935-36	Tinning, Lyle	1932-34
Stewart, Asa	1895	Todd, Alfred	1940-41, 1943
Stewart, Charles	1913-14	Todd, Jim	1974
Stewart, James	1963-67	Tolson, Chester	1926-27, 1930
Stewart, William	1944-45	Tompkins, Ron	1971
Stoddard, Tim	1984	Toney, Frederick	1911-13
Stone, Steve	1974-75	Torres, Hector	1971
Stoneman, Bill	1967-68	Toth, Paul	1962-64
Strain, Joe	1981	Tracy, Jim	1980
Strang, Samuel	1900	Traffley, William	1878
Stratton, Scott	1894-95	Tremel, William	1954-56
Stringer, Louis	1941-42, 1946	Trillo, Manny	1975-78
Stueland, George	1921-23, 1925	Triplett, Coacker	1938
Sturgeon, Robert	1940-42, 1946-47	Trout, Steve	1983-84
St. Vrain, James	1902	Truby, Harry	1895-96
Sullivan, John	1921	Turgeon, Gene ("Pete")	1923
Sullivan, Martin	1887-88	Turner, Theodore	1920
Sullivan, Michael	1890	Twombly, Clarence	1920-21
Sullivan, William	1878	Tyler, George	1918-21
Summers, John	1975-76	Tyree, Earl	1914
Sunday, William	1883-87	Tyrone, James	1972, 1974-75
Sutcliffe, Edward	1884-85	Tyrone, Wayne	1976
Sutcliffe, Rick	1984	Tyson, Mike	1980-81
Sutter, Bruce	1976-80		
Sweeney, William	1907, 1914	**U**	
Sweetland, Lester	1931	Upham, John	1967-68
Swisher, Steve	1974-77	Usher, Robert	1952

T

V

Tabb, Jerry	1976	Vail, Mike	1978-80
Tabler, Pat	1981-82	Valentinetti, Vito	1956-57
Talbot, Dale	1953-54	Vandenberg, Harold	1944-45
Tanner, Chuck	1957-58	Vander Meer, John	1950
Tappe, Elvin	1954-56, 1958, 1960, 1962	Van Haltren, George	1887-89
Tappe, Theodore	1955	Van Zandt, Charles	1904
Tate, Harry ("Bennie")	1934	Varga, Andrew	1950-51
Taylor, Charles	1925	Vaughn, James	1913-21

Verban, Emil	1948-50
Vernon, Joseph	1912
Veryzer, Tom	1983-84
Vickery, Thomas	1891
Vogel, Otto	1923-24
Voiselle, William	1950

W

Waddell, George ("Rube")	1901
Wade, Benjamin	1948
Wade, Gale	1955-56
Waitkus, Edward	1941, 1946-48
Waitt, Charles	1877
Walker, Albert	1948-51
Walker, Harry	1949
Walker, Roy	1917-18
Wallace, Jack	1915
Waller, Tye	1981-82
Wallis, Joe	1975-78
Walls, Lee	1957-59
Walsh, Thomas	1906
Ward, Chris	1972, 1974
Ward, Preston	1950, 1953
Ward, Richard	1934
Warneke, Lon	1930-36, 1942-43, 1945
Warner, George	1921
Warner, Jack	1962-65
Warstler, Harold ("Rabbit")	1940
Warwick, Carl	1966
Watson, Charles	1913
Watt, Eddie	1975
Weaver, Harry	1917-19
Weaver, James	1934
Weaver, Orville	1910-11
Webb, Earl	1927-28
Webster, Ramon	1971
Weimer, Jacob	1903-05
Weinert, Philip ("Lefty")	1927-28
Weis, Arthur	1922-25
Welch, Johnny	1926-28, 1931
Wheeler, Floyd	1923-24
Whisenant, Peter	1956
White, Elder	1962
White, James ("Deacon")	1876
White, Jerry	1978
Whitehill, Earl	1939
Wicker, Robert	1903-06
Wiedemeyer, Charlie	1934
Wilcox, Milt	1975
Wilhelm, Hoyt	1970

Wilke, Harry	1927
Will, Bob	1957-58, 1960-63
Williams, Arthur	1902
Williams, Billy	1959-74
Williams, Dewey	1944-47
Williams, Frederick ("Cy")	1912-17
Williams, Otto	1903-04
Williams, Walter	1902-03
Williams, Washington	1885
Williamson, Edward ("Ned")	1879-89
Wills, Bump	1982
Willis, James	1953-54
Wilmot, Walter	1890-95
Wilson, Arthur	1916-17
Wilson, Lewis ("Hack")	1926-31
Winceniak, Edward	1956-57
Wirts, Elwood	1921-23
Wise, Casey	1957
Wolfe, Harry	1917
Wolter, Harry	1917
Wolverton, Harry	1898-1900
Woods, Gary	1982-84
Woods, Jim	1957
Woods, Walter	1898
Wortman, William	1916-18
Wright, David	1897
Wright, Melvin	1960-61
Wright, Patrick	1890
Wright, Robert	1915
Wyse, Henry	1942-47

Y

Yantz, George	1912
Yerkes, Charles	1932-33
Yerkes, Stephen	1916
York, Anthony	1944
York, James	1921
Yost, Gus	1893
Yoter, Elmer	1927-28
Young, Don	1965, 1969

Z

Zabel, George	1913-15
Zahn, Geoff	1975-76
Zamora, Oscar	1974-76
Zeider, Rollie	1916-18
Zick, Robert	1954
Zimmer, Donald	1960-61
Zimmerman, Henry	1907-16
Zwilling, Edward	1916

Index